Crisis in the Eurozone

C. Lapavitsas, A. Kaltenbrunner, G. Labrinidis, D. Lindo,
J. Meadway, J. Michell, J.P. Painceira, E. Pires, J. Powell,
A. Stenfors, N. Teles, L. Vatikiotis

Introduction by Stathis Kouvelakis

VERSO

London • New York

First published by Verso 2012
The collection © Verso 2012
The contributions © The contributors 2012

'This book is a revised version of three reports on the eurozone crisis published online by Research on Money and Finance, namely *Eurozone Crisis: Beggar Thyself and Thy Neighbour*, March 2010; *The Eurozone Between Austerity and Default*, September 2010; and *Breaking Up? A Route Out of the Eurozone Crisis*, November 2011. The first RMF report also appeared as an article in the *Journal of Balkan and Near Eastern Studies*, vol. 12, issue 4. The authors would like to thank the journal for permission to republish this material.

3 5 7 9 10 8 6 4

Verso

UK: 6 Meard Street, London W1F 0EG
US: 20 Jay Street, Suite 1010, Brooklyn, NY 11201
www.versobooks.com

Verso is the imprint of New Left Books

ISBN-13: 978-1-84467-969-0

British Library Cataloguing in Publication Data
A catalogue record for this book is available from the British Library

Library of Congress Cataloging-in-Publication Data
A catalog record for this book is available from the Library of Congress

Typeset in Minion Pro by Bibliosynergatiki, Greece
Printed and bound by CPI Group (UK) Ltd, Croydon, CR0 4YY

CONTENTS

PREFACE

The storm buffeting the common currency of Europe is an integral part of the great crisis that commenced in 2007. Barely five years after bank speculation in the US real estate market had caused international money markets to freeze, three peripheral countries of the eurozone were in receipt of bailout programmes, Greece was on the brink of exiting the monetary union, and the mechanisms of the euro faced breaking pressure.

The causal chain linking US financial market turmoil to European Monetary Union instability has been analysed by several economists, including those authoring the present book. Summarily put, the collapse of Lehman Brothers in 2008 led to a major financial crisis that ushered in a global recession; the result was rising fiscal deficits for several leading countries of the world economy. For countries in the eurozone periphery, already deeply indebted after years of weakening competitiveness relative to the eurozone core, fiscal deficits led to restricted access to international bond markets. Peripheral states were threatened with insolvency, posing a risk to the European banks that were among the major lenders to the periphery. To rescue the banks, the eurozone had to bail out peripheral states. But bailouts were accompanied by austerity that induced deep recessions and rendered it hard to remain in the monetary union, particularly for Greece.

The threat to the euro would perhaps have been understood earlier had more attention been paid to history. In 1929 speculation in the New York Stock Exchange induced a crash that led to global recession; by 1932 it had become necessary to abandon the gold standard that had only been reintroduced in 1926. The recessionary forces in the world economy had grown vast in part because states had been trying to protect gold reserves and associated fixed exchange rates. It became impossible to cling on to the rigid system of metallic world money.

The European Monetary Union, needless to say, is quite different from the gold standard. It is a system of managed money that is free from the blind and automatic functioning of gold in the world market. At the very least, member states do not need large reserves of euros, in contrast to the pressure to hold gold reserves under the gold standard. But it is similar to the gold standard inasmuch as it fixes exchange rates, demands fiscal conservatism, and requires flexibility in labour markets. And, insofar as it imposes a common monetary policy across all member states, it is even more rigid.

The ruling strata of Europe have been determined to create a form of money capable of competing against the dollar in the world market, and thereby furthering the interests of large European banks and enterprises. Governments have not desisted even when the mechanisms of the euro have grossly magnified the recessionary forces present in the European economy. The burden has been passed onto the working people of Europe in the form of reduced wages and pensions, higher unemployment, unravelling of the welfare state, deregulation and privatisation.

To force the costs of defending the common currency onto working people, leading European governments have spared no warning of the dire consequences that would follow the dismantling of monetary union. In this endeavour, they have received support from the research departments of banks as well as from academics willing to paint apocalyptic pictures of life after the euro. In this regard too, the European Monetary Union is similar to the gold standard. Public discourse in the late nineteenth and early twentieth century recoiled in horror at the suggestion of its abandonment.

The gold standard was, of course, abandoned without the world coming to an end. International monetary unions, moreover, tend to have a limited life span, even when constructed with the most solemn pledges. Regardless of what politicians and journalists may say, the European Monetary Union is untenable in its current form. As the inherent tensions come to a head, the countries of Europe will be forced to devise new monetary arrangements for their domestic and international transactions.

The inculcation of fear has been made easier by the domination of Europeanism among the intellectual and political forces that could have offered an alternative narrative. For more than two decades, the notion that the euro is the epitome of European unity has grown in influence among the politicians and the opinion makers of Europe. Even more strikingly, a form of money that aims at serving the interests of big banks and big business has been presented as an inherently social-democratic project.

The belief that the monetary union represents social progress that could truly benefit working people through judicious institutional intervention has commanded support in unexpected quarters. Thus, vocal supporters of the euro have come from the Keynesian tradition, even though the latter has historically rejected rigid international monetary arrangements. Astoundingly, support for the euro has also come from sections of the European Left, including its furthest reaches. Who would have imagined that putative heirs of Karl Marx would be transmogrified into defenders of a variant of the gold standard?

Support for the monetary union from the European Left has decisively affected the political fallout from the crisis. Many have spoken volubly about the iniquities of capitalism, the disastrous nature of neoliberalism, the absurdity of austerity, the poison of inequality, and so on, and so forth. But whenever the discussion has turned to the euro, which has, after all, been the focal point of the crisis, much of the Left has sought simply to change the subject. Or it has put forth proposals with impeccable mainstream credentials, including issuing eurobonds and lending by the European Central Bank to member states. In the face of the deepest crisis of European capitalism since the Second World War, the left alternative has often appeared as a reworking of Bagehot's advice to the British ruling class at the end of the nineteenth century, namely to lend freely and ask questions later. It is no wonder that the Left has been marginal to the politics of the crisis so far.

Analysis in this book treats the euro as integral to the crisis facing the European Union. The theoretical framework is based on the tradition of Marxist political economy, particularly the theory of world money, while drawing extensively on mainstream economics. The aim has been to identify the social and economic causes of the storm that has engulfed the eurozone since late 2009. The most distinctive feature of the work, however, and fully in line with its intellectual underpinnings, is its readiness to discuss abandoning the EMU. Europe currently needs radical ideas to shake it out of the intellectual torpor of neoliberalism as well as to determine a path that would be beneficial to working people. But a radicalism that is not prepared to contemplate quitting the common currency has little to contribute either to public debate, or to political struggle currently taking place in Europe.

The book is a collective effort by members of Research on Money and

Finance at the School of Oriental and African Studies in London. Parts of it began to appear in March 2010, taking the form of RMF reports that have been widely read. In two distinctive ways the work could only have been produced at SOAS. First, it draws on the School's vibrant tradition of Marxist political economy which has always been fully familiar with the methods and arguments of the mainstream as well as open to ideas from heterodox economics. Second, it draws on the School's even longer tradition of development economics and expertise in analysing IMF interventions in developing countries facing debt and currency crises. For us at SOAS, the likely outcomes of the 'rescue' programmes imposed on peripheral Europe were painfully apparent at the outset.

Europe is currently on the cusp of a profound transformation. If the conservative response to the crisis finally prevails, the future looks grim. Financial and industrial interests will impose a settlement condemning working people to stagnant incomes, high unemployment, and weakened welfare provision. Democratic rights will be in doubt and the continent will head toward even faster decline. If, on the other hand, radical forces prevail, the balance could be tilted against capital and in favour of labour. European societies could be rejuvenated economically, ideologically and politically. Soon we shall know.

Costas Lapavitsas
London
March 2012

ACKNOWLEDGEMENTS

The analysis of the eurozone crisis in this book has drawn on continuous debate within RMF. Particular thanks are due to J. Arriola, A. Callinicos, A. Cibils, R. Desai, P. Dos Santos, G. Dymski, I. Levina, T. Marois, O. Onaran, J. Rodrigues, S. Skaperdas, E. Stockhammer, A. Storey, D. Tavasci, J. Toporowski, and J. Weeks.

All responsibility for errors lies with the authors.

INTRODUCTION: THE END OF EUROPEANISM

The history of capitalism is the history of its crises. Each time it had to confront an outburst of its own contradiction, the mode of production had no solution but to reinvent itself, to push its own limits further back, thereby gaining new strength but always at a certain cost, recreating those limits at a larger but transformed scale. New contradictions thus appear, leading to further crises and reconfigurations within the same fundamental structural coordinates. This is, at least, the pattern of all the major crises of the system – those which have affected its historical core since the nineteenth century.

The crisis of 1870s and 1880s led to the end of the classical liberal era and the passage to monopolies, another wave of imperial expansion and the first attempts to rationalise the economy and regulate the class antagonism by the means of state intervention. This first 'great transformation' of the mode of production led in its turn to World War One – or rather, to the new thirty years' war of the 'short twentieth century', out of which emerged a socialist bloc as system of states, the dismantling of the colonial empires, new forms of imperialist domination and, last but not least, the welfare state. This domesticated form of capitalism was restricted to the core Western countries, but it combined unprecedented economic growth with conditions of parliamentary democracy and political stability, setting new standards of legitimacy for the mode of production.

With hindsight, it became clear that this configuration was the product of exceptional circumstances – the impact of two world wars and the weight of a victorious socialist revolution over one sixth of the globe – very unlikely to be reiterated in the future. In any case, its impetus was exhausted after three decades, and a new era started: neoliberalism, an era during which – thanks to the crisis, followed by the collapse of the 'socialist camp' – the mode of production succeeded in rolling back most of the concessions previously made to the working classes. A new world emerged, built on the ruins of the socialist experiments, including their attenuated welfare-statist versions – the world of global finance–oriented capitalism.

It is too early to say whether the current crisis, which started as a real estate crisis in the US, morphed into a crisis of the banking system and then crystallised in a sovereign debt crisis, will mark the end of the neoliberal era. In a way, the tectonic plates have only started moving and the balance of forces is still uncertain, although the strategic advantage achieved by the dominant classes during the period of high neoliberalism still operates fully. What looks certain however is that this crisis will leave behind at least one casualty: the so-called 'European project', or 'European integration', embodied in the institutions of the European Union with, at their core, the Economic and Monetary Union. If we think that this project has been the only one of any real importance consciously designed by the dominant classes of the Old Continent, it becomes clear that we are witnessing a turning point of world historical importance, comparable in some senses to the victory of the West in the Cold War. The importance of the project undertaken by Costas Lapavitsas and his collaborators of the SOAS-based Research on Money and Finance group lies in their pathbreaking contribution to explaining the causes of this major upheaval.

Of course, concerning the EU, we knew that the coordination and diffusion of neoliberal policies have consistently been at the core of the project, especially after its relaunching in 1986 with the Single European Act. It is also well known, thanks especially to the powerful argumentation of Perry Anderson,[1] that insulation from any form of popular control and accountability is the founding logic of all the complex nexus of technocratic and expert-staffed agencies which form the backbone of the EU institutions. What has been euphemised as the 'democratic deficit', actually a denial of democracy, legitimised in various ways by the apologists of the European project, has become especially obvious since the 2005 French and Dutch referenda on the proposed constitution of the EU, several years before the start of the current turmoil. The missing element from the picture back then was however the political economy of the edifice. It seems that the coming of the crisis acted, as it usually happens in these cases,

---

1 Anderson, P. (2009) *The New Old World*, London: Verso.

as a detonator, bringing to the surface pre-existing contradictions and making it possible to reflect theoretically upon them.

Ever since the 1992 Maastricht Treaty, it became clear that the whole EU project, not only in its economic and political dimensions but also as the fundamental theme of Europeanist ideology, was increasingly dependant on the realisation of the EMU. It was indeed the first time in history that a currency common to more than 300 million people living in seventeen different countries was created from scratch, without a unified state behind it. In highlighting the rationale of this enterprise – its sources of strength but also its intrinsic limitations and contradictions – the analysis proposed by Lapavitsas and his RMF colleagues in the following chapters is crucial.

Let us note first that it is no coincidence if this analysis is initiated by one of the rare Marxist economists who has been working for a long time on issues of monetary theory and contemporary finance. Indeed the euro can only be understood in the context of an increasingly financialised capitalism, both as an expression of this now dominant trend and as a powerful tool leading to its further expansion. The euro is a project of world currency, functioning both as a reserve currency and as a means of circulation and payment, designed to compete with the US dollar. And this imperial type of ambition could not have been carried by any national currency within the EU, including that of the most powerful economy, Germany. But neither could it have been accomplished by the currency of a unified European super-state, because European capitalism does not exist except as a convergence of national economies, of nationally defined spaces for the accumulation of capital, or to put it another way, of national social formations, each of which is shaped by its specific configuration and balance of class forces.

The solution to the 'neither ... nor' oscillation, which epitomises the nature of the European project as a whole, lies in the famous stability pacts, generalising in the entire eurozone the founding principles of what Habermas at his best had very aptly called 'Deutsche-mark nationalism': an independent central bank, absolute priority given to fighting inflation, strict budgetary discipline and a whole culture of procedural approaches neutralising political choices under the cover of sound and virtuous technocratic management. What is at stake here is much more than some particular tradition whether cultural (supposedly 'Protestant') or political (that of the Federal Republic emerging from the ashes of an irrevocably defeated project of imperial expression), or even the simple expression of the leading economic role of Germany within the EU. These conditions, which inscribe neoliberalism into the genetic code of the EMU, are actually necessary prerequisites of the project of a world currency in the highly particular, indeed unique, circumstances mentioned above. This is why they provided the terrain for a voluntary strategic convergence of the dominant classes of Europe while at the same time giving to Germany a properly hegemonic role – although never politically explicit – 'always-already', as if it were wrapped up in some 'post-national' and generally 'European' form of legitimation.

The consequences of this are far-reaching. One of the most essential achievements of the demonstration of Lapavitsas and his collaborators lies in their analysis of the way in which a polarisation between a 'core' and a 'periphery' emerges out of the very structure of the EMU. The general idea, and the terms themselves, are of course familiar to any reader of the rich Marxist and radical literature on combined and uneven development, the gap between the 'metropolis' and the 'periphery' and spatial inequalities of a systemic type. But now we have a systematic demonstration of the specific way this applies to the area of the most developed countries of European capitalism. The various reports included in this book show how the loss of competitiveness of the periphery (the now famous 'PIGS': Portugal, Ireland, Greece, Spain), as the result of higher inflationary levels and rise in nominal labour costs, was just the flip side of the export prowess of Germany and other core countries, with the deficits of the first group mirroring the increasing surpluses of the second. This whole mechanism has been hugely amplified by the sheer existence of the common currency, resulting in cheap credit, both for private agents and for states, and by securing high credibility for this public and private debt bonds in the international markets. Who could dare to think that there was the slightest risk of default from a country part of such a strong and successful world-currency zone as the eurozone?

The success lasted a few years, boosting the overall financialisation of economies internationally, 'bubbles' of all kinds in the periphery (especially in real estate, banking and credit-fuelled private consumption), accompanied by export performances and gigantic lending flows from the core. Rising social inequalities, environmental destruction, weakening of the productive capacities of the 'losers' – this unpleasant downside remained backstage, obliterated by the success story of the new single currency bringing prosperity and stability to all. It was the moment of the triumph of the Europeanist ideology: a Greek or a Portuguese pensioner, with a few hundred euros as a monthly income, felt part of the club of the rich and mighty, on an equal footing with her Northern European counterparts. 'Europe', at last, meant something more concrete, and symbolically binding, than remote bureaucratised institutions, deprived of any popular legitimacy. As Marx famously wrote, quoting Shakespeare, money is 'the radical leveller that ... does away with all distinctions'. [2]

With the start of the 2007–8 downturn, repressed reality took its revenge, dissolving the fetishism of the single currency and euro-euphoria. It would be foolish, of course, to blame the euro as such for the crisis, which is of international proportions and has deep roots in the contradictions of the existing mode of production itself. But the euro, and more generally the entire mechanism of the EU, is of paramount importance in explaining the specific form the crisis took in this area of the world, and in the strategies adopted by the dominant groups to confront it. To put it differently, the pre-existing divergence between the euro-periphery and the core started now looking like an abyss.

Despite its low growth rates in the early years of the new millennium, and the 2009 downturn, the German economy proved resilient, whereas the PIGS plunged into continuous recession, with Greece once again the 'weak link' of European capitalism, experiencing a 1930s-type Great Depression. But this pattern is not the outcome of the blind interplay of pure economic forces. Every step of this descent into the depths has been mediated by the entire set of EU institutions, with the IMF playing only a secondary, and relatively lenient, role. With the transformation of the banking crisis into a sovereign debt crisis, the nightmare took hold in the peripheral states. Every EU summit, every round of negotiation between debtors and creditors led to a long series of 'bailouts' accompanied by draconian 'memoranda', endless austerity packages and 'shock therapies' fully conforming to the standard IMF models previously applied to the South, with entire countries placed under regimes of 'limited sovereignty'. The crisis of the eurozone opened the way for 'disaster capitalism' moving now westwards, to the edges of the Old Continent which has become a laboratory of policies which will eventually be implemented, if only in a modified and possibly softer ways, elsewhere.

---

2 Marx, K. (1887), *Capital*, vol. 1, chapter 3, section 3A.

It is only now that the full power of that blend of hybrid supranational, but still interstate, authoritarianism and of institutionally embedded neoliberalism, which constitutes the DNA of the EU, can be fully apprehended and understood. And this process could not leave the ideological realm untouched. The dark side of Europeanism has now come to the surface: blaming the losers, the 'lazy' and 'profligate' southerners, has now become the conventional wisdom of the mainstream media and politicians. It is crucial however to stress here that the revival of these racist stereotypes should not be understood as a return to the past, even if it draws heavily from an old Orientalist stockpile. This intra-European neo-racism is rather the purest outcome of the newly polarised reality created by the internal logic of so-called 'European integration', the realities of which were already quite familiar to the inhabitants of the European *Mezzogiorno* constituted by the former Eastern Bloc countries.

The reader will find in the following pages a clinical step-by-step analysis of this process, fully confirming the scenarios presented in the first RMF report (March 2010) on the effects of the austerity policies. She will also find an uncompromising critique of the illusions created by all the supposedly 'left' variants of Europeanist ideology, which converge in their disregard of the real mechanisms operating within the EMU and its institutional framework. On paper, of course, it is perfectly possible to show that a single unified European entity, undertaking full fiscal and monetary responsibilities, could easily tackle issues such as the Greek sovereign debt. A European Central Bank with the backing of a proper state apparatus could rescue the European banks and manage the losses. But this amounts to pretending that, by virtue of some *fiat*, the existing reality could be changed magically into its very opposite. In other words it amounts to the type of wishful thinking which has paralysed the entire European Left, even those currents which refused to compromise with neoliberalism and fought, sometimes with success (like in the 2005 French referendum), against certain aspects of the European project. Such an outlook has prevented the Left from realising that the more 'European' each 'solution' or 'strategy' was, the more it was synonymous with radicalised neoliberalism and anti-democratic regression.

Apart from leading to political impotence, this perspective has also proved to be a kind of 'epistemological obstacle' to the analysis of the recent crisis, and more specifically to an understanding of the manner in which the general systemic trends (such as the instability created by financialisation, the issues of profitability and the pressures on labour) are mediated by political actors, by states or alliances between groups of states of uneven economic and political weight acting within a hybrid supranational framework such as the EU. In this sense, the euro should be understood not only as a ferocious class mechanism for disciplining labour costs – starting with the wages of German workers, which remained flat during the whole first decade of the new century – but also as a means through which the hegemony of German capital is forged and imposed on the European and, more broadly, the international stage. This is why every political agenda which claims to be serious in its objective of breaking with neoliberalism, even within an overall 'reformist' or 'gradualist' perspective, must pose the question of breaking with the euro and confronting the EU as such.

This brings us to the final but probably also most crucial point of the material collected in this volume: not satisfied with providing a pioneering analysis of the specificities of the capitalist crisis within the eurozone, Lapavitsas and his RMF collaborators went one step further, providing us with the outline of an alternative strategy. This outline starts with the proposal of default on the sovereign debt – a matter of sheer survival for the countries of the periphery, starting of course with Greece – and extends to exiting unilaterally from the euro for the countries which need to default, allowing them to regain control of a part of their national sovereignty and to escape from the cataclysm of internal devaluation imposed by EU-designed shock therapies. These measures, of course, need to be supplemented by a set of others, such as the nationalisation under genuine public control of the banking system, the control of capital flows and income redistribution, including a reform of the tax system which would counter years of neoliberal tax-alleviation in favour of the wealthy and corporate power. This proposal for an alternative path immediately sparked controversy, starting in Greece, but gradually shaped the entire agenda of the debate within the Left but also beyond it.

Some found these ideas absurdly radical, others saw them as too modest and moderate. They were criticised for being 'nationalist' or 'utopian', 'reformist' or 'adventurist'. One needs, at the very least, to acknowledge that they mark a sharp break with the entirety of the aforementioned deeply rooted tradition of Europeanist wishful thinking, with its belief that this meticulously built neoliberal authoritarian fortress could be amended and transformed from within. Let us note that the method followed here by Lapavitsas and his colleagues is faithful to what a certain tradition of the workers' movement has called 'transitional demands'.

What is meant by this? Neither the 'maximum' nor the 'minimum' programme, neither the cry for utopian 'impossibility' nor the management of the existing order of things, but a cohesive set of concrete demands strategically designed to hit the adversary in the heart, where the contradictions of the situation tend to concentrate, in order to create the necessary lever to change the overall balance of forces. Questions such as the default on sovereign debt, the dismantlement of the EMU and confrontation with the authoritarian *fuite en avant* of the EU are the contemporary equivalent of the demands of peace, bread, land and popular self-government on which depended the outcome of the first assault on Heaven of the twentieth century. Urgently posed as issues of immediate relevance where the current crisis has hit the hardest – that is, in the europeriphery and more particularly in Greece – they are central to the strategic debate of the Left in the Old Continent as a whole.

At a time where any type of strategic thinking has become increasingly rare, and even more so on the Left, and where the crisis of capitalism seems to inspire perplexity and embarrassment amongst what remains of its organised adversaries rather than new energy to wage further battles, the work undertaken in the volume at hand needs to be recognised in its proper measure: a major intellectual achievement combining rigorous and innovative scholarship with lucid but also radical political commitment.

Stathis Kouvelakis

GLOSSARY

BIS: Bank of International Settlements
BoG: Bank of Greece
CAC: Collective Action Clauses
CB: Central Bank
CDO: Collateralised Debt Obligation
EBA: European Bank Authority
ECB: European Central Bank
EFSF: European Financial Stability Facility
ELA: Emergency Liquidity Assistance
ELG: Eligible Liabilities Guarantee
EMU: Economic and Monetary Union of the European Union
ESCB: European System of Central Banks
ESM: European Stability Mechanism
GDP: Gross Domestic Product
IMF: International Monetary Fund
MFI: Monetary Financial Institution
MRO: Main Refinancing Operation
NCB: National Central Banks
NPV: Net Present Value
OMO: Open Market Operation
SME: Small and Medium Enterprises
SMP: Securities Market Programme
SPV: Special Purpose Vehicle
TAF: Term Auction Facility
TARGET: Trans-European Automated Real-time Gross Settlement Express Transfer System
VAT: Value Added Tax

Part 1 BEGGAR THYSELF AND THY NEIGHBOUR

C. Lapavitsas, A. Kaltenbrunner, D. Lindo, J. Michell,
J.P. Painceira, E. Pires, J. Powell, A. Stenfors, N. Teles
March 2010

1. SEVERAL DIMENSIONS OF A PUBLIC DEBT CRISIS

A crisis with deep roots

The sovereign debt crisis that broke out in Greece at the end of 2009 is fundamentally due to the precarious integration of peripheral countries in the eurozone. Its immediate causes, however, lie with the crisis of 2007–9. Speculative mortgage lending by US financial institutions, and trading of resultant derivative securities by international banks created a vast bubble in 2001–7, leading to crisis and recession. State provision of liquidity and capital in 2008–9 rescued the banks, while state expenditure prevented a worsening of the recession. The result in the eurozone was a sovereign debt crisis, exacerbated by the structural weaknesses of monetary union.

The crisis of public debt, thus, represents Stage Two of an upheaval that started in 2007 and can be called a crisis of financialisation.[1] Mature economies have become 'financialised' during the last three decades resulting in growing weight of finance relative to production. Large corporations have come to rely less on banks, while becoming more engaged in financial markets. Households have become heavily involved in the financial system through assets (pension

---

1 Financialisation has been extensively discussed by political economists. A useful, but not complete, survey can be found in van Treeck, T. (2009), 'The political economy debate on "financialization" – a macroeconomic perspective', *Review of International Political Economy*, 16:5, 907–944. The theoretical views underpinning this report can be found in Lapavitsas, C. (2009), 'Financialised capitalism: crisis and financial expropriation', *Historical Materialism*, 17:2, 114–148 and Dos Santos, P. (2009), 'On the content of banking in contemporary capitalism', *Historical Materialism*, 17:2, 180–213.

and insurance) and liabilities (mortgage and unsecured debt). Banks have been transformed, seeking profits through fees, commissions and trading, rebalancing their activities toward households rather than corporations. Financial profit has emerged as a large part of total profit.[2]

But financialisation has unfolded in different ways across mature countries, including those within the European Union. Germany has avoided the explosion of household debt that recently took place in other mature countries and peripheral eurozone countries. The performance of the German economy has been mediocre for many years, while great pressure has been applied on German workers' pay and conditions. The main source of growth for Germany has been its current account surplus inside the eurozone, resulting from pressure on pay and conditions rather than on superior productivity growth. This surplus has been recycled through foreign direct investment and German bank lending to peripheral countries and beyond.

The implications for the eurozone have been severe. Financialisation in the periphery has proceeded within the framework of the monetary union and under the dominant shadow of Germany. Peripheral economies have acquired entrenched current account deficits. Growth has come from expansion of consumption financed by expanding household debt, or from investment bubbles characterised by real estate speculation. There has been a general rise of indebtedness, whether of households or corporations. Meanwhile, pressure has been applied to workers' pay and conditions across the periphery, but not as persistently as in Germany. The integration of peripheral countries in the eurozone, then, has been precarious, leaving them vulnerable to the crisis of 2007–9 and eventually leading to the sovereign debt crisis.

Institutional bias and malfunction in the eurozone

The institutional mechanisms surrounding the euro have been an integral part of the crisis. To be more specific, European Monetary Union is supported by a host of treaties and multilateral agreements, including the Maastricht Treaty, the Stability and Growth Pact and the Lisbon Strategy. It is also supported by

---

2 See, for example: Krippner, G. (2005) 'The financialization of the American economy', *Socio-Economic Review*, 3, 173–208; and Dumenil, G. & Levy, D. (2004), 'The real and financial components of profitability', *Review of Radical Political Economics*, 36, 82–110.

the European Central Bank, in charge of monetary policy across the eurozone. The combination of these institutions has produced a mix of monetary, fiscal, and labour market policies with powerful social implications.

A single monetary policy has been applied across the eurozone. The ECB has targeted inflation and focused exclusively on the domestic value of money. To attain this target the ECB has taken cognisance of conditions primarily in core countries rather than assigning equal weight to all. In practice this has meant low interest rates across the eurozone. Further, the ECB has operated deficiently since it has not been allowed to acquire and manage state debt. And nor has it actively opposed financial speculation against member states. As a result, the ECB has emerged as protector of financial interests and guarantor of financialisation in the eurozone.

Fiscal policy has been placed under the tight constraints of the Stability and Growth Pact, though considerable residual sovereignty has remained with member states. Fiscal discipline has been vital to the acceptability of the euro as international reserve, allowing the euro to act as world money.[3] Since it lacks a unitary state and polity, the eurozone has not had either an integrated tax system or fiscal transfers between areas. In practice, fiscal rules have been applied with some laxity in core countries and elsewhere. Peripheral countries have attempted to disguise budget deficits in a variety of ways. Nonetheless, fiscal stringency has prevailed during this period.

Given these constraints, national competitiveness within the eurozone has depended on the conditions of work and the performance of labour markets, and in this regard EU policy has been unambiguous. The European Employment Strategy has encouraged greater flexibility of employment as well as more part-time and temporary work. There has been considerable pressure on pay and conditions resulting in a race to the bottom across the eurozone. The actual application of this policy has, however, varied considerably, depending on welfare systems, trade union organisation, and social and political history.

It is apparent that the institutions of the eurozone are more than plain technical arrangements to support the euro as domestic common currency

---

3 The concept of world money and its significance for the analysis of the eurozone crisis are considered in some detail in Part 3 of this book. The same Part offers further discussion of the institutional mechanisms of the eurozone.

as well as world money. Rather, they have had profound social and political implications. They have protected the interests of financial capital by lowering inflation, fostering liberalisation, and ensuring rescue operations in times of crisis. They have also worsened the position of labour compared to capital. And not least, they have facilitated the domination of the eurozone by Germany at the expense of peripheral countries.

Peripheral countries in the shadow of Germany

Peripheral countries joined the euro at generally high rates of exchange – ostensibly to control inflation – thereby signing away some competitiveness at the outset. Since monetary policy has been set by the ECB and fiscal policy has been constrained by the Stability and Growth Pact, peripheral countries have been encouraged to improve competitiveness primarily by applying pressure on their workers. But they have faced two major problems in this regard. First, real wages and welfare states are generally worse in the periphery than in the core of the eurozone. The scope for gains in competitiveness through pressure on workers is correspondingly less. Second, Germany has been unrelenting in squeezing its own workers throughout this period. During the last two decades, the most powerful economy of the eurozone has produced the lowest increases in nominal labour costs, while its workers have systematically lost share of output. EMU has been an ordeal for German workers.

German competitiveness has thus risen further within the eurozone. The result has been a structural current account surplus for Germany, mirrored by current account deficits for peripheral countries. This surplus has been the only source of dynamism for the German economy throughout the 2000s. In terms of output, employment, productivity, investment, consumption, and so on, German performance has been mediocre. At the core of the eurozone lies an economy that delivers growth through current account surpluses deriving in large part from the arrangements of the euro. German surpluses, meanwhile, have been translated into capital exports – primarily bank lending and foreign direct investment – the main recipient of which has been the eurozone, including the periphery.

This is not to imply that workers in peripheral countries have avoided pressures on pay and conditions. Indeed, the share of labour in output has declined across the periphery. It is true that the remuneration of labour has increased in nominal and real terms in the periphery, but productivity has risen by more – and generally faster than in Germany. But conditions within the eurozone have not encouraged rapid and sustained productivity growth in peripheral countries – partly due to middling levels of technology – with the exception of Ireland. Peripheral countries have thus lost competitiveness as the nominal compensation of German workers has remained practically stagnant throughout the period.

Confronted with a sluggish but competitive Germany, peripheral countries have opted for growth strategies that have reflected their own history, politics and social structure. Greece and Portugal have sustained high levels of consumption, while Ireland and Spain have had investment booms that involved real estate speculation. Across the periphery, household debt has risen as interest rates fell. The financial system has expanded its weight and presence across the economy. But in 2009–10 it became apparent that these strategies were incapable of producing positive long-term growth results.

The integration of peripheral countries in the eurozone has been precarious as well as rebounding in favour of Germany. The sovereign debt crisis has its roots in this underlying reality rather than in public profligacy in peripheral countries. When the crisis of 2007–9 hit the eurozone, the structural weaknesses of monetary union emerged violently, taking the form of a public debt crisis for Greece, and potentially for other peripheral countries.

The impact of the crisis of 2007–9 and the role of finance

The immediate causes of the crisis of 2007–9 lay in the US mortgage bubble which became global due to securitisation of subprime assets. European banks began to face liquidity problems after August 2007, and German banks in particular found that they were heavily exposed to problematic, subprime-related securities. During the first phase of the crisis, core eurozone banks continued to lend heavily to peripheral borrowers in the mistaken belief that peripheral countries were a safe outlet. Net exposure rose substantially in 2008.

But reality gradually changed for banks as liquidity became increasingly scarce in 2008, particularly after the 'rescue' of Bear Stearns in early 2008 and the collapse of Lehman Brothers six months later. To rescue banks, the ECB has engaged in extensive liquidity provision, accepting many and debatable types of paper as collateral for secure debt. ECB actions have allowed banks to begin to adjust their balance sheet, thus engaging in deleveraging. By late 2008 banks were already reducing their lending, including to the periphery. Banks also stopped buying long-term securities preferring to hold short-term instruments – backed by the ECB – with a view to improving liquidity. The result was credit shortage and accelerated recession across the eurozone, including the periphery.

These were the conditions under which states – both core and periphery of the eurozone but also the UK and other states – began to seek additional loanable funds in financial markets. A major cause of rising state borrowing was the decline of public revenue as recession lowered the tax intake. State expenditure also rose in several countries after 2007 as the rescuing of banks proved expensive, and to a lesser extent as states attempted to support aggregate demand. Accelerated public borrowing in 2009 was induced by the crisis, and hence by the earlier speculations of the financial system. In this respect, the Greek state was typical of several others, including the USA and the UK.

In the conditions of financial markets in 2009, with the banks reluctant to lend, the rising supply of state paper put upward pressure on yields. Speculators found this environment conducive to their activities. In the past, similar pressures in financial markets would have led to speculative attacks on currencies and collapsing exchange rates for the heavy borrowers. But this was obviously impossible within the eurozone, and hence speculative pressures appeared as falling prices of sovereign debt.

Speculators focused on Greek public debt on account of the country's large and entrenched current account deficit as well as because of the small size of the market in Greek public bonds. Credibility was also lost by the Greek government because of systematic fiddling of national statistics to reduce the size of budget deficits. But the broader significance of the Greek crisis was not due to the inherent importance of the country. Rather, Greece represented potentially the start of speculative attacks on other peripheral countries – and even on countries beyond the eurozone, such as the UK – that faced expanding public debt.

The Greek crisis, therefore, is symptomatic of a wider malaise. It is notable that the institutions of the eurozone, above all the central bank, have performed badly in this context. For the ECB private banks were obviously 'too big to fail' in 2007–9, meriting extraordinary provision of liquidity. But there was no similar sensitivity toward peripheral countries that found themselves in dire straits. It made little difference that the problems of public debt were largely caused by the crisis as well as by the very actions of the ECB in providing banks with liquidity.

To be sure the ECB has been hamstrung by its statutes which prevent it from directly acquiring public debt. But this is yet more evidence of the ill-conceived and biased nature of European Monetary Union. A well-functioning central bank would not have simply sat and watched while speculators played destabilising games in financial markets. At the very least, it would have deployed some of its ingenuity to constrain speculation, and the ECB has demonstrated considerably ingenuity in generously supplying private banks with liquidity in 2007–9. Not least, a well-functioning central bank would not have decided what types of paper to accept as collateral on the basis of ratings provided by the discredited private organisations that were instrumental to the bubble of 2001–7.

Policy options for peripheral countries

The crisis is so severe that there are neither soft options, nor easy compromises for peripheral countries. The choices are stark, similar to those of developing countries confronted with repeated crises during the last three decades.

The first alternative is to adopt austerity by cutting wages, reducing public spending and raising taxes, in the hope of reducing public borrowing requirements. Austerity would probably have to be accompanied by bridging loans, or guarantees by core countries to bring down commercial borrowing rates. It is likely that there would also be 'structural reform', including further labour market flexibility, tougher pension conditions, privatisation of remaining public enterprises, privatisation of education, and so on. The aim of such liberalisation would presumably be to raise the productivity of labour, thus improving competitiveness.

This is the preferred alternative of ruling elites across peripheral and core countries, since it shifts the burden of adjustment onto working people. But there are several imponderables. The first is the opposition of workers to austerity, leading to political unrest. Further, the eurozone lacks established mechanisms both to provide bridging loans and to enforce austerity on peripheral members. There is also strong political opposition within core countries to rescuing others within the eurozone. On the other hand, the option of forcing a peripheral country to seek recourse to the IMF would be damaging for the eurozone as a whole.[4]

Yet, despite legal constraints, it is not beyond the EU to find ways of advancing bridging loans while at the same time enforcing austerity through political pressure. The real problem with this option is not the institutional machinery of the eurozone. It is, rather, that the policy is likely to lead to aggravated recession in peripheral countries making it even more difficult to meet public borrowing targets. Poverty, inequality and social division will increase substantially. Even worse, it is unlikely that there will be long-term increases in productivity through a strategy of liberalisation. Productivity increases require investment and new technologies, neither of which will be provided spontaneously by liberalised markets.

Peripheral countries would probably find themselves lodged in an unequal competitive struggle against Germany, whose workers would continue to be severely squeezed. Attempting to remain within the eurozone by adopting austerity and liberalisation would lead to sustained falls in real wages in the vain hope of reversing current account deficits against Germany. The eurozone as a whole, meanwhile, would continue to be faced with a weaker world economy due to the crisis of 2007–9. It is a grim prospect for working people in the periphery, and far from a bed of roses for German workers.

The second alternative is to reform the eurozone. There is almost universal agreement that unitary monetary policy and fragmented fiscal policy have been a dysfunctional mix. There is also widespread criticism of the ECB for the way it has provided abundant liquidity to banks, while keeping aloof of borrowing states, even to the extent of ignoring speculative attacks. A range of reforms that would not challenge the fundamentals of the Maastricht Treaty, the Stability and Growth Pact, and the Lisbon agenda might well be possible. The aim would be to produce smoother interaction of monetary and fiscal forces, while maintaining the underlying conservatism of the eurozone.

---

4 These lines were written well before the institutional changes that have taken place in 2010–11 to deal with precisely the problems identified here, and thus to allow the EU to pursue austerity. The most important of these changes are discussed in Parts 2 and 3. In editing this book, however, it was decided to leave the text unchanged because it captures the spirit of the time (March 2010) and it has proved prescient.

There is very little in such reforms that would be attractive to working people, or that could indeed deal with the structural imbalances within the eurozone. Hence there have been calls for more radical reforms, including abolition of the Stability and Growth Pact and altering the statutes of the ECB to allow it regularly to lend to member states. The aim of such reform would be to retain monetary union, while creating a 'good euro' that would be beneficial to working people. The 'good euro' strategy would involve significantly expanding the European budget to deliver fiscal transfers from rich to poor countries. There would be an active European investment strategy to support new areas of economic activity. There would also be a minimum wage policy, reducing differentials in competitiveness, and lowering inequality across the eurozone.

The 'good euro' strategy, appealing as it sounds, would face two major problems. The first is that the eurozone lacks either a unitary or a federal state, and there is no prospect of acquiring one in the near future, certainly not with the required progressive disposition. The current machinery of the eurozone is entirely unsuited to this task. The strategy would face a continuous conflict between, on the one hand, its ambitious pan-European aims and, on the other, the absence of state mechanisms that could begin to turn these aims into reality.

At a deeper level, the 'good euro' strategy would clash with the putative role of the euro as world money. If fiscal discipline was relaxed among member states, there would be a risk that the value of the euro would collapse in international markets. Were that to happen, at the very least, the international operations of European banks would become extremely difficult. The international role of the euro, which has been vital to the project from the beginning, would come under heavy pressure. It is not clear, then, that the 'good euro' strategy would be compatible with monetary union. In this light, a 'good euro' might end up as 'no euro'. Those who advocate this strategy ought to be aware of its likely implications, i.e., leading to the end of monetary union; their institutional, political and social demands have to be tailored accordingly.

The third alternative is to exit from the eurozone. Even here, however, there are choices. There is 'conservative exit', which is increasingly discussed in the Anglo-Saxon press, and would aim at devaluation. Some of the pressure of adjustment would be passed onto the international sphere, and exports would revive. But there would also be losses for those servicing debt abroad, including banks. Workers would face wage declines as the price of tradable goods would rise. Devaluation would probably be accompanied by austerity and liberalisation, compounding the pressure on workers.

Long-term improvements in productivity would, however, occur only if market forces began spontaneously to develop new capacity in the tradable goods sector. This is extremely difficult for peripheral eurozone countries, with middling technology and middling real wages. It is notable that the ruling elites of peripheral countries are aware of these difficulties, as well as of their own lack of capacity to deal with them. They have implicitly admitted that they possess neither the means nor the will to pursue an independent path. Consequently, conservative exit might lead to stagnation with repeated devaluations and decline in incomes.

There is, finally, 'progressive exit' from the eurozone, which would require a shift of economic and social power toward labour in peripheral countries. There would be devaluation accompanied by cessation of payments and restructuring of public debt. To prevent collapse of the financial system there would have to be widespread nationalisation of banking, creating a system of public banks. Controls would also have to be imposed on the capital account to prevent outflows of capital. To protect output and employment, finally, it would be necessary to expand public ownership over key areas of the economy, including public utilities, transport and energy.

On this basis, it would be possible to develop industrial policy that could combine public resources with public credit. There are broad areas of the national economy in peripheral countries that call for public investment, including infrastructure. Opportunities exist to develop new fields of activity in the 'green' economy. Investment growth would provide a basis on which to improve productivity, ever the Achilles heel of peripheral economies. Financialisation could then begin to be reversed by lessening the relative weight of finance.

A radical policy shift of this type would require transforming the state by establishing mechanisms of transparency and accountability. The tax and transfer payments of the state would then take a different shape. The tax base would be broadened by limiting tax evasion by the rich as well as by capital. Public provision for health and education would be gradually improved, as would redistribution policies to alleviate high inequality in peripheral countries.

A policy of progressive exit for peripheral countries would come with evident costs and risks. The broad political alliances necessary to support such a shift do not exist at present. This absence, incidentally, is not necessarily due to lack of popular support for radical change. More important is that no credible political force in Europe has had the boldness to oppose austerity hitherto. Beyond political difficulties, a major problem for progressive exit would be to avoid turning into national autarky. Peripheral countries are often small and need to maintain access to international trade and investment, particularly within Europe; they also need technology transfer.

International alliances and support would be necessary in order to sustain flows of trade, skills and investment. These would be far from easy to secure if the rest of the EU remained under the spell of monetary union. But note that progressive exit by the periphery would also offer fresh prospects to core eurozone countries, particularly to labour which has suffered throughout this period. If the eurozone unravelled generally, economic relations between core and periphery could be put on a more cooperative basis.

The order of analysis in Part 1

Part 1 focuses on the peripheral countries of the eurozone, above all, Greece, Portugal, Spain and Ireland. When appropriate, Italian data and performance have also been considered, though Italy cannot easily be considered a peripheral country to the EU. The core of the eurozone is taken to comprise Germany, France, Belgium and the Netherlands.[5] Comparisons are usually made with Germany, the leading country of the core and the EU as a whole. The introduction of the euro in 1999 – and 2001 for Greece – provides a natural point of reference for all comparisons. Each country has had its own distinctive institutional, social and historical trajectory, and therefore some pretty brutal generalisations are deployed below. But there are also evident commonalities

---

5 Needless to say the EU also has a Central and Eastern European periphery, including the Czech Republic, Poland, the Baltic countries, Hungary, and so on. This is an important part of the EU economy, particularly as production is increasingly relocated from the core, above all, Germany. But these countries are not members of the eurozone, and hence they have been left out of the analysis. Still, the crisis of 2007–9 hit the central and eastern periphery first, forcing several countries to adopt IMF programmes that enforced severe austerity. The trigger was rising indebtedness associated with free capital flows. In this respect, there are similarities with the public debt crises in the periphery of the eurozone.

which derive in large part from worldwide patterns of economic development in recent years, as well as from the nature of the EU and the eurozone.

Thus, chapter 2 discusses macroeconomic performance of peripheral countries compared to Germany. Chapter 3 moves to labour markets, the remuneration of labour and the patterns of productivity growth. Chapter 4 then turns to international transactions particularly within the eurozone. On this basis, chapter 5 considers the evolution of public finance and the expansion of public indebtedness after 2007. Chapter 6 places the growth of public debt in the context of the operations and performance of the financial sector following the crisis of 2007–9. Chapter 7 concludes by considering the alternatives available to peripheral countries.

2. MACROECONOMIC PERFORMANCE: STAGNATION IN GERMANY, BUBBLES IN THE PERIPHERY

Growth, unemployment and inflation

Growth rates among the countries in the sample were generally lower in the 2000s than in the 1990s (fig. 1). This fits the pattern of steadily declining growth rates across developed countries since the late 1970s. But there is also significant variation. Ireland registered very high rates of growth in the 1990s, driven by investment by US multinational corporations that were given tax breaks. Profit repatriation has been substantial, creating a large disparity between Irish GDP and GNP. Much of Irish growth has been due to transfer pricing within multinationals, thus also inflating productivity growth. Greek growth also accelerated in the early 2000s, bolstered by expenditure for the Olympic Games. Spanish growth, finally, has been reasonably high throughout the period.

However German growth rates have remained anaemic throughout, with the exception of a minor burst in the second half of the 2000s. Exports have

FIG. 1 GDP Growth Rates

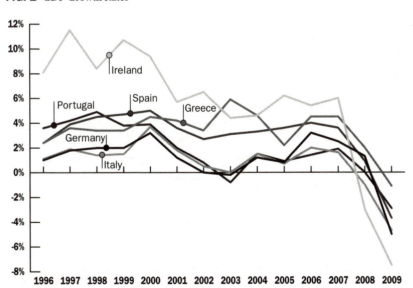

Source: *Eurostat*

played a significant role in causing this uptick of growth, a development of the first importance for the evolution of the eurozone. Portuguese and Italian growth has barely diverged from German growth rates since the introduction of the euro.

Unemployment rates are consistent with growth rates (fig. 2), showing convergence toward lower levels in the 2000s compared to the 1990s. This is mostly because Spanish and Irish unemployment rates declined rapidly at the end of the 1990s. Spanish unemployment, however, remained at the high end of the spectrum throughout, and has risen faster than in other countries once the crisis of 2007–9 materialised. Unemployment seems to expand rapidly in Spain at the first sign of economic difficulty. The Greek labour market is probably not very different, bearing in mind that official statistics tend to underestimate unemployment. Greek unemployment rose rapidly in 2009, once the crisis had hit hard. Equally striking, however, have been the high rates of German unemployment throughout this period, if anything exhibiting an upward trend. The same holds for Portugal, which has followed Germany in this respect too.

FIG.2 Unemployment Rates

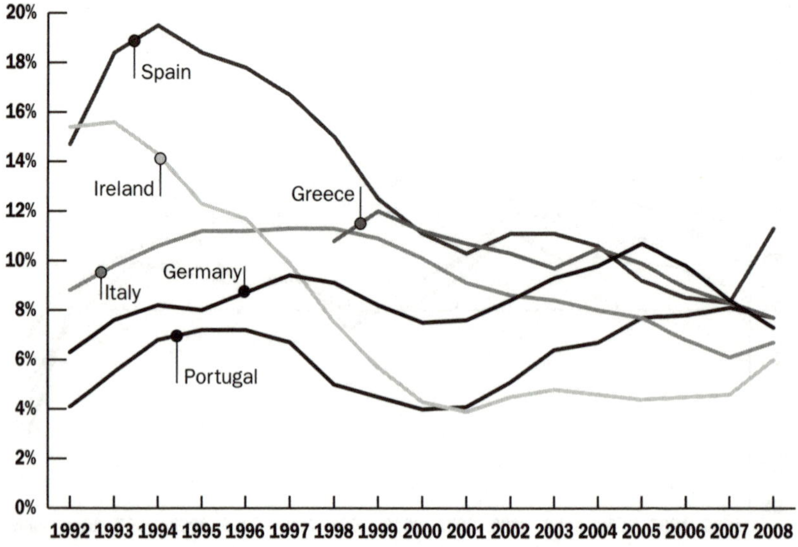

Source: *Eurostat*

Inflation rates, on the other hand, present a more complex pattern (fig. 3). Rates converged to a fairly narrow range of 2–4 percent in 2001, at the time of the introduction of the euro. However, in the following three years rates diverged, only to converge again in 2004, this time to a narrower range of 2–3 percent. Inflation targeting by the ECB and the application of a common monetary policy took some time to produce the desired effect. The picture is at most a qualified success for the ECB as inflation rates accelerated again in 2007–8. The most important element of figure 3, however, is that German inflation rates have remained consistently below the rest throughout the period, rarely exceeding 2 percent. This performance lies at the heart of the problems of the eurozone.

In short, the German economy has produced a characteristic macroeconomic performance throughout the period, marked by mediocre growth, high unemployment and low inflation. German performance has set the tone for the eurozone and placed its stamp on the operation of the euro. The sovereign debt crisis has its roots as much in the performance of Germany, as it does in the actions of peripheral countries.

FIG. 3 Inflation Rates (Harmonised Index of Consumer Prices)

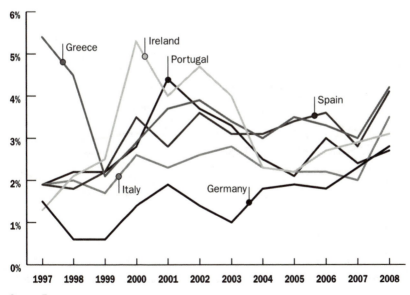

Source: *Eurostat*

Investment and consumption

A closer look at the components of aggregate demand gives further insight into macroeconomic performance. Before looking at investment and consumption, however, note that the economies in the sample are generally service-based. The secondary sector contributes slightly less than 30 percent of GDP in Germany, Italy, Spain and Portugal. It amounts to roughly 45 percent of GDP in Ireland, but that is largely due to the presence of multinationals. Greece is also an exception, the secondary sector standing at about 20 percent of GDP – an aspect of persistent de-industrialisation since the 1980s. Agriculture makes a minor contribution to output in all eurozone countries.

Investment performance has been poor, with the exception of Spain and Ireland (fig. 4), both of which even underwent investment booms in the late 2000s. But Irish investment in the 1990s was in large part due to US multinational activities. Generally, there has not been a strong wave of investment in the eurozone.

A better picture of underlying trends is given by investment net of housing (fig. 5). It then becomes clear that the investment boom in Ireland in the 2000s

FIG. 4 Gross Fixed Capital Formation (percent of GDP)

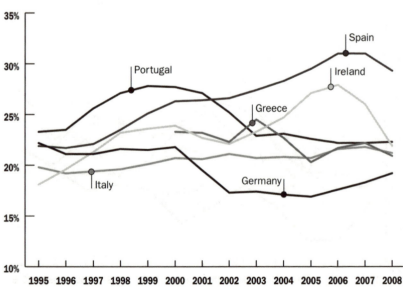

Source: *Eurostat*

FIG. 5 Gross Fixed Capital Formation Net of Housing (percent of GDP)

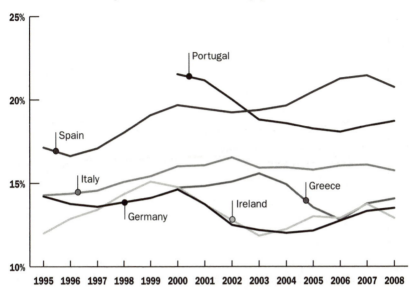

Source: *Eurostat*

was primarily due to a real estate bubble. The Spanish investment boom was also heavily based on real estate. Investment in the productive sector has been generally weak in all the countries considered.

Consumption, on the other hand, has remained pretty flat relative to GDP, with the exception of Portugal where it rose significantly after the introduction of the euro (fig. 6). The striking aspect of consumption, however, is the exceptionally high level of Greece, rapidly approached by Portugal in the second half of the 2000s. High household consumption has been the mode of integration for both countries in the eurozone. This is a significant difference with Spain and Italy, and has important implications for indebtedness, as is shown below. The other exception is Ireland, where private consumption has been a very low proportion of GDP.

The patterns of consumption are broadly reflected in saving (fig. 7). For both Greece and Portugal saving as a percentage of GDP became negative in the second half of the 2000s. Thus, high and rising consumption has been supported by rising household debt. However, saving has also declined in Spain,

FIG. 6 Household Consumption (percent of GDP)

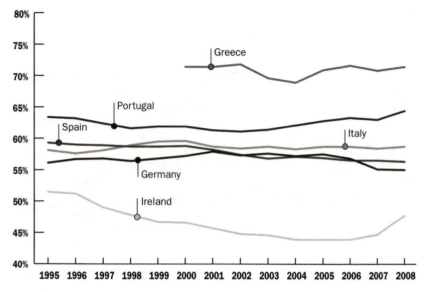

Source: *Eurostat*

FIG. 7 Saving (percent of GDP)

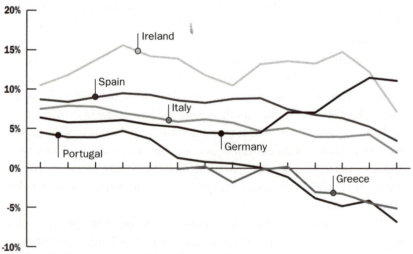

Source: *Eurostat*

Italy, and even in Ireland in the 2000s. Households across the periphery have found it difficult to sustain consumption on current income. The exception is Germany, where saving rose in the second half of the 2000s, in line with weak consumption. German growth, such it has been in the 2000s, has come neither from investment nor from consumption, but from exports. Persistent pressures of stagnation, and even contraction, in the domestic German economy have been fundamental to the evolution of the euro, directly contributing to the sovereign debt crisis.

Debt

Household debt has risen consistently across peripheral countries in the sample. Financialisation of individual worker incomes has proceeded apace among peripheral countries of the eurozone throughout the last two decades. Growth of debt has been driven by consumption but also by rising prices of real estate. Low interest rates in the 2000s, as the ECB applied the same monetary policy across the eurozone, allowed workers to increase indebtedness. In particular,

FIG. 8 Household Liabilities (percent of GDP)

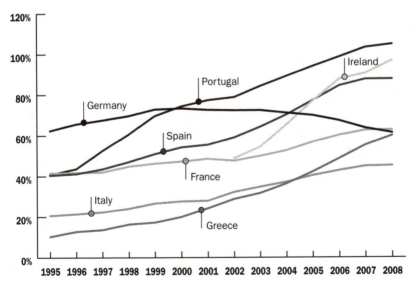

Source: *Eurostat, CB and FSA of Ireland*

Portugal, Spain and Ireland have approached ratios of household debt to GDP of around 100 percent (fig. 8). These are very high levels of debt that will be difficult to support if unemployment and interest rates rise in the near future.

The vital exception is again Germany, where household indebtedness has declined, in line with weak consumption and the absence of a housing bubble. While households in peripheral countries have been accumulating debt as part of the integration of these countries in the eurozone, German households have been reducing the relative burden of their debt. This contrast is an integral part of the differential response of eurozone countries to the shock of the crisis of 2007–9, contributing to the sovereign debt crisis.

Corporate debt, meanwhile, has not shown a tendency to rise significantly across the sample in the years following the introduction of the euro, with the exception of Spain and Ireland, the only countries in which investment also rose significantly during the period (fig. 9).

Recapping, macroeconomic performance of peripheral countries relative to Germany has demonstrated considerable variation but also common patterns.

FIG. 9 Non-financial Corporation Liabilities (percent of GDP)

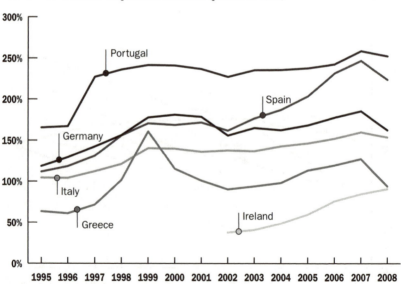

Source: *Eurostat*, *CB* and *FSA of Ireland*

At the core of the eurozone, Germany has been marked by low growth, flat investment, stagnant consumption, rising saving, and falling household debt. Germany has not been a dynamic capitalist economy on any score. The only source of dynamism has been exports, for reasons that will become clear below.

Confronted with the stagnant and export-oriented performance of the dominant country of the eurozone, peripheral countries have adopted a variety of approaches. Thus, Spain and Ireland have had investment booms that were based heavily on real estate speculation and bubbles. Greece and Portugal, meanwhile, have relied on high consumption, driven by household debt. Indeed, household debt has risen substantially across peripheral countries. Italy, finally, has been lodged in what could only be described as stagnation throughout this period.

Integration of peripheral countries into the eurozone, in other words, has been precarious. This is apparent in their export performance, which is the mirror image of German performance, as is shown below. It is also apparent in the patterns of household financialisation, which have moved in the opposite direction to Germany. These structural contrasts lie at the root of the current crisis. The evidence also shows that it is fallacious to interpret the crisis as the result of inefficient peripheral economies being unable to deal with the efficient German economy. It is the size of the German economy and its export performance – which has very specific causes attached to the euro – that have allowed it to dominate the eurozone. Efficiency has had little to do with it. Consider now the labour market in order fully to establish this point.

3. LABOUR REMUNERATION AND PRODUCTIVITY: A GENERAL SQUEEZE, BUT MORE EFFECTIVE IN GERMANY

A race to the bottom

The EU has systematically promoted labour market reform aimed at reinforcing the process of monetary integration. Starting with the Maastricht Treaty (1992), social provisions began to be included in European treaties apparently to reinforce economic coordination. Labour market policies have been considered national initiatives; however, the Luxembourg European Council (1997) launched the first European Employment Strategy, followed by the Lisbon Strategy in 2000. The Lisbon Strategy stated the need for more flexibility in labour markets. The apparent aims were to achieve full employment, to create a knowledge intensive labour market, and to raise employment rates.

During the 2000s the Lisbon agenda was repeatedly reinforced, including by "Guidelines for Growth and Jobs", "National Reform Programmes" and "Recommendations" from the European Council. Particularly after the de Kok report (2004), policy toward labour markets has stressed the need for flexibility, contract standardisation, promotion of temporary and part-time work, and creation of (tax) incentives to encourage labour force participation.[6] It is also true that improving the quality of employment was emphasised by the Council meetings of Nice (2000) and Barcelona (2002). In practice, however, the pressure of reform has led to a race to the bottom for workers' pay and conditions. Several European legislative initiatives have met with strong resistance in recent years, for instance, reform of the internal market in services (Bolkenstein directive), or the new Working Time directive that would potentially increase the working week to sixty-five hours. Partly as a response, the European Commission has recently promoted a general agenda of reform focused on the Danish model of "flexicurity" – weak legal protection of labour relations compensated by strong state support for the unemployed.

Given that a single monetary policy has applied across the eurozone, and given also the tough constraints on fiscal policy (through the Stability and Growth Pact) labour market policy has been one of the few levers available to different countries to improve external competitiveness. Therefore, the effects

---

6 http://ec.europa.eu/growthandjobs/pdf/kok_report_en.pdf

of labour market policies have varied profoundly among different eurozone countries. Core countries have been historically characterised by high real wages and strong social policies, while peripheral countries have typically had low real wages and weak welfare states. Political and trade union organisation has also differed substantially among eurozone countries. All eurozone countries have joined the race to impose labour market flexibility and compress labour costs, but from very different starting points and with different mechanisms.

Of fundamental importance in this connection has been labour market policy in Germany. Put in a nutshell, Germany has been more successful than peripheral countries at squeezing workers' pay and conditions. The German economy might have performed poorly, but Germany has led the way in imposing flexibility and restraining real wages. Characteristic of the trend have been the labour market reforms of 2003 introduced by the Social Democratic Party and known as Agenda 2010. New labour contracts have reduced social contributions and unemployment benefits. Since the early 1990s, furthermore, it has been possible for German capital to take full advantage of cheaper labour in Eastern Europe. The combined effect of these factors has been to put downward pressure on German wages, thus improving the competitiveness of the German economy.[7]

Peripheral countries with weak welfare states, lower real wages, and well-organised labour movements, such as Greece, Portugal, Italy and Spain, have been unable to squeeze workers equally hard. Ireland, on the other hand, has been at the forefront of imposing more liberal conditions on its workers. Unfortunately for the Irish elite, this did not spare the country from the severe impact of the crisis of 2007–9.

The determinants of German competitive success

The difference in outlook between Germany and the peripheral countries can

---

7 Germany has a long history of competitive real devaluation of the Deutschmark, to which labour unions have often been complicit. Nonetheless, union power has been significantly reduced under the social-democratic government of Schroeder. Equally, German unification has had a major impact on German labour relations weakening collective bargaining and creating large union-free zones in the east that are slowly spreading to parts of the west.

FIG. 10 Nominal Unit Labour Costs (1995 = 100)

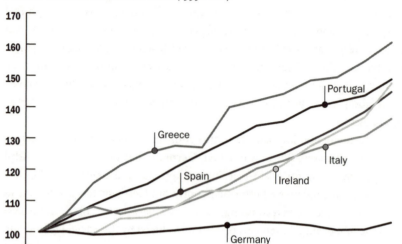

Source: *AMECO*

be demonstrated by considering the behaviour of nominal labour unit costs, that is, nominal labour remuneration divided by real output. Nominal unit costs can be disaggregated into nominal cost per hour of labour divided by labour productivity. This is a standard measure used to compare competitiveness internationally.[8] The trajectory of nominal unit costs, therefore, gives

---

8 Take W to be the nominal remuneration of labour, which is more than wages and includes other labour costs for employers. Take Y to be nominal output and P the price level. The nominal unit cost of labour would then be $W/(Y/P)$, a standard measure of international competitiveness. This could obviously be disaggregated into $(W/L)/(Y/PL)$. It would then show nominal remuneration per hour of labour divided by labour productivity, which is the variable traced in figure 10, allowing for comparisons in underlying trends. Note that real remuneration of labour is simply W/P, the variable captured in figure 11. If real remuneration was rendered per unit of real output, i.e., as $(W/P)/(Y/P)$, it would show the share of labour in real output, traced in figure 13.

FIG. 11 Real Compensation of Labour (1995 = 100)

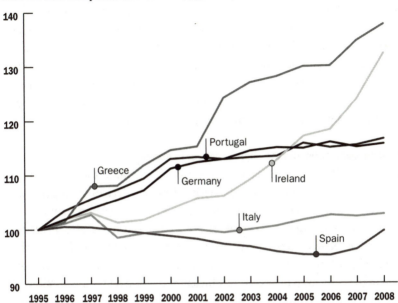

Source: *AMECO*

insight into the variation of nominal cost of labour relative to labour productivity. This trajectory is shown in figure 10 for all the countries in the sample
with 1995 as base year. Note that data on productivity is notoriously unreliable,
thus the evidence should be used with considerable caution.

The most striking aspect of this data is the flatness of nominal unit labour
costs in Germany. It appears that the opening of Eastern Europe to German
capital together with sustained pressure on pay and conditions has forced
nominal labour costs to move at an almost identical pace to productivity. However, in peripheral countries things have been different. Unit labour costs have
increased significantly as nominal labour costs have risen faster than productivity, with Greece in the lead. In short, peripheral countries have been losing
competitiveness relative to Germany in the internal eurozone market.

The more rapid rise in nominal labour costs was accompanied by generally higher inflation in the periphery compared to Germany, as was previously
shown in relation to figure 3. Nevertheless, nominal labour costs rose generally

faster than inflation, thus leading to increasing real compensation of labour in the periphery, as is shown in figure 11 (definition in footnote 8). Extra care is required here as real compensation is not the same thing as real wages, and moreover it hides a broad range of payments to managers and others in the form of wages and bonuses. Furthermore, the aggregate conceals considerable inequality in real wages among different groups of workers. Still, figure 11 shows that the real compensation of labour has risen faster in peripheral countries compared to Germany, with the exception of Spain.

Real compensation and the share of labour in output

It is no wonder, therefore, that conservative commentators in the press have remarked that the sovereign debt crisis ultimately derives from peripheral country workers receiving higher increases in compensation than German workers, leading to a loss of competitiveness.[9] This is true, but also misleading. The real problem has not been excessive compensation for peripheral workers but negligible increases for German workers, particularly after the introduction of the euro. Even in Greece, in which nominal and real compensation have increased the most, the rise in real compensation has been only of the order of 20 percent during the period of 2000–8, and that from a low base compared to Germany.

The modesty of labour remuneration in the periphery becomes clear when put in the context of productivity growth (fig. 12).

There has been weaker productivity growth in Germany compared to the rest during this period, with the exception of Spain which has been extremely weak. This is more evidence of the lack of dynamism of the German economy: Irish, Greek and Portuguese productivity rose faster, even if from a lower base (Irish productivity is probably exaggerated for reasons to do with multinational transfer pricing). Peripheral countries have generally improved productivity, and certainly done better than Germany, which has been a laggard. But the

---

9 See, for example: Roubini, N. and Parisi-Capone, E. (2010), 'An IMF rescue for Greece?', Forbes.com, 18 Feb. http://www.forbes.com/2010/02/17/greek-financial-crisis-imf-ecb-opinions-columnists-nouriel-roubini-elisa-parisi-capone.html. Also: Roubini, N. (2010), 'Teaching PIIGS to fly', Project Syndicate, 15 Feb. http://www.project-syndicate.org/commentary/roubini22/English

FIG. 12 Labour Productivity (1995 = 100)

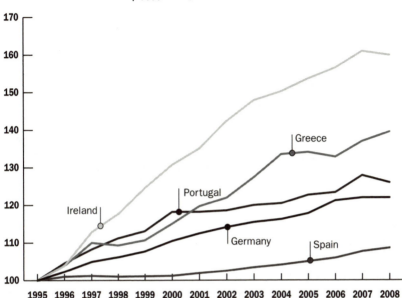

Source: *OECD*

Lisbon Strategy has not succeeded in putting peripheral countries on a strongly rising path of productivity. There has been no true catching up with the more advanced economies of the eurozone, with the partial exception of Ireland. Productivity increases have been respectable compared to Germany, but that is because Germany has performed badly.

Nonetheless, productivity growth has still been faster than the rise in real remuneration of labour. Consequently, labour has lost share in output more or less across the sample, as is shown in figure 13 (definition in footnote 6). The only sustained increase after the introduction of the euro has been in Ireland, but even there workers barely made good the losses sustained in the 1990s. Workers have generally lost relative to capital across the sample, German workers faring poorly compared to the others.

To sum up, labour market policies at national and EU level have applied sustained pressure on workers across the eurozone. This pressure has played an important role in determining competitiveness, given the rigidity of monetary

FIG. 13 Labour share in GDP (1995 = 100)

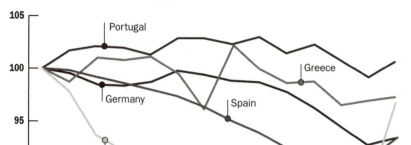

Source: *AMECO*

and fiscal policies. The result has been loss of output share by workers across the eurozone. In peripheral countries real compensation has increased in some countries, though productivity has increased even faster. Nonetheless, productivity did not rise fast enough to ensure catching up with the more advanced economies of the core.

In Germany, on the other hand, productivity, real compensation, and nominal unit labour costs have increased very slowly. It cannot be overstressed that gains in German competitiveness have nothing to do with investment, technology, and efficiency. The competitive advantage of German exporters has derived from the high exchange rates at which peripheral countries entered the eurozone and, more significantly, from the harsh squeeze on German workers. Hence Germany has been able to dominate trade and capital flows within the eurozone. This has contributed directly to the current crisis.

4. INTERNATIONAL TRANSACTIONS: TRADE AND CAPITAL FLOWS IN THE SHADOW OF GERMANY

Current account: Surplus for Germany, deficits for periphery

The international transactions of eurozone countries have been shaped in large measure by the policies adopted to support the euro. The euro has been devised as a common measure of value and means of payment within the eurozone; the intention was that it should also become means of payment and reserve outside the eurozone, thus competing directly with the US dollar as a form of world money in the world market. Monetary and fiscal policies of eurozone countries have had to be consistent with this aim, thus imposing a common monetary policy and tight constraints on fiscal policy for each state. The institutional and policy framework of the eurozone have not arisen merely due to ideological dominance of neo-liberal thinking within the EU. They have also been dictated by the need to sustain the euro in its role as world money within and outside the eurozone.

The pattern of international transactions that has emerged for eurozone countries is consistent with the putative role of the euro. In the first instance, peripheral countries were obliged to join the euro at generally high exchange rates. Core countries, above all Germany, insisted upon this policy with the ostensible purpose of ensuring low inflation. High inflation in individual countries would have undermined the ability of the euro to compete internationally against the dollar. The implication was to reduce at a stroke the competitiveness of peripheral countries in the internal market. To this poor start was added sustained loss of competitiveness, discussed in the previous section. The result, shown in figure 14, was inevitable: emergence of entrenched current account deficits for peripheral countries, matched by an equally entrenched current account surplus for Germany.

Care is obviously necessary in interpreting this picture. Greece, Portugal and Spain have run substantial balance of trade deficits, but they have also had significant surpluses on services. Ireland has followed the opposite path, again reflecting its own mode of integration into the eurozone based on higher investment, much of it directed to housing, and intensified labour flexibility. For all, inability to restrain nominal labour unit costs at German levels and, more fundamentally, inability to set productivity growth on a strongly rising path, resulted in current account deficits mirrored by sur-

FIG. 14 Current account balance (percent GDP)

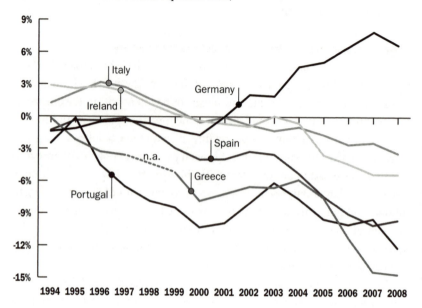

Source: *IMF BOP*

pluses for Germany. Note that two thirds of German trade is with the eurozone. Note also that the trade of the eurozone with the rest of the world is roughly in balance.

The euro and its attendant policy framework have become mechanisms ensuring German current account surpluses that derive mostly from the eurozone. Peripheral countries joined a monetary system that purported to create a new form of world money, thus signing away some of their competitiveness, while adopting policies that exacerbated the competitiveness gap. The beneficiary of this process has been Germany, because it has a larger economy with higher levels of productivity, and because it has been able to squeeze its own workers harder than others. Structural current account surpluses have been the only source of growth for the German economy during the last two decades. The euro is a 'beggar-thy-neighbour' policy for Germany, on condition that it beggars its own workers first.

FIG. 15 Capital and financial account (Net, $ bn)

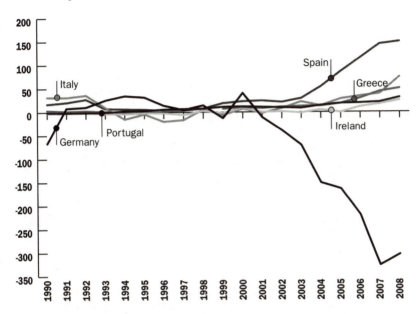

Source: *IMF BOP*

Financial account: German FDI and bank lending to the periphery

Inevitably, the picture appears in reverse on the capital and financial account (fig. 15). Germany has exported capital on a large scale, while peripheral countries have been importing capital.

The financial account comprises fundamentally foreign direct investment (FDI), portfolio flows, and 'other' flows that are heavily driven by banks. The direction of aggregate flows between Germany and the periphery of the eurozone can be gauged from the composition of the German financial account (fig. 16).

The driving forces behind sustained capital exports by Germany since the introduction of the euro have been 'other' and FDI flows. Portfolio flows have been weaker, even turning inward for much of the 2000s. Put summarily, Germany has been recycling its current account surpluses as FDI and bank lending abroad. Bank lending peaked in 2007–8 and, as is shown below, this has been a vital element of the current sovereign debt crisis.

FIG. 16 Composition of German financial account (euro, bn)

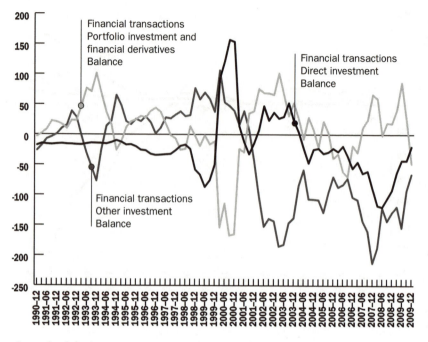

Source: *Bundesbank*

The geographical direction of the recycling of surpluses is clear, once again, from the composition of German capital exports. The eurozone has been the main recipient of German FDI (fig. 17), while also competing with the non-euro part of the EU for German bank lending in the 2000s (fig. 18). Once the crisis of 2007–9 broke out, German banks restricted their lending to non-euro EU countries but continued to lend significantly to eurozone countries.

To recap, international transactions of eurozone countries have been driven by the requirements and implications of monetary union. Peripheral countries have lost competitiveness relative to Germany because of initially high exchange rates as well as because of the ability of German employers to squeeze workers harder. The result has been a structural current account surplus for Germany, mirrored by structural current account deficits for peripheral countries. Consequently, German FDI and bank lending to the eurozone

FIG. 17 German outward FDI by region (euro, bn)

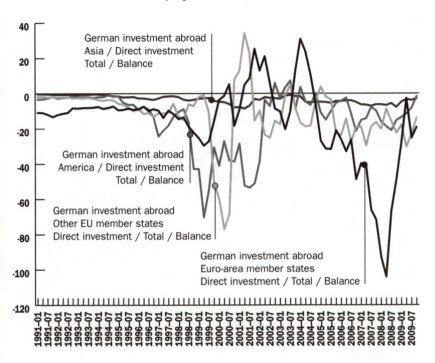

Source: *Bundesbank*

have increased significantly. 'Other' flows to peripheral countries rose rapidly in 2007–8 as the crisis unfolded, but then declined equally rapidly. That was the time when peripheral states were forced to appear in credit markets seeking funds.

FIG. 18 German 'other' outward flows by region (euro, bn)

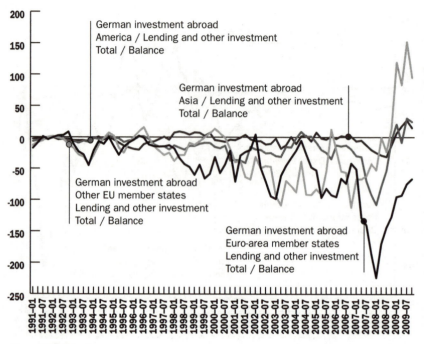

Source: *Bundesbank*

5. RISING PUBLIC SECTOR BORROWING: DEALING WITH FAILED BANKS AND WORSENING RECESSION

The straitjacket on fiscal policy

The public sector of peripheral countries, and above all Greece, has been at the epicentre of the current turmoil. The reasons for this, however, are only partially related to the intrinsic weaknesses of the public sector in peripheral countries. The current crisis is due to the nature of monetary union, to the mode of integration of peripheral countries in the eurozone, and to the impact of the crisis of 2007–9. Public sector debt has become a focus for the tensions that have emanated from these sources for reasons discussed below.

It is apparent that the sovereign debt crisis has not been chiefly caused by state incompetence, inefficiency and the like. Eurozone states have been operating within the framework of the Stability and Growth Pact, the main components of which emerged already in the early 1990s with the Maastricht Treaty. The underlying logic has been that, if the euro was going to become a world reserve currency and means of payment, there had to be coherence of fiscal policy to match the single monetary policy. Rising public deficits and accumulating state debt would have reduced the international value of the euro. The Stability and Growth Pact is important to making the euro a competitor to the dollar.

In this respect, the EU has faced an inherent contradiction because it is an alliance of sovereign states. Sovereignty means little without power and ability to tax, always reflecting the social composition of particular countries. Therefore, a compromise was reached, in large measure imposed by the core countries. The Growth and Stability Pact has imposed the arbitrary limit of 60 percent national debt relative to GDP and an almost equally arbitrary limit of 3 percent for budget deficits that would hopefully prevent the level of public debt from rising. Fiscal policy was placed in a straitjacket that has tormented eurozone states for nearly two decades.

The Stability and Growth Pact represents a loss of sovereignty for eurozone states. However, not all states within the eurozone were created equal. The loss of sovereignty has been more severe for peripheral states, as has been repeatedly demonstrated when France or Italy have exceeded the presumed limits on deficits and debt. It is no surprise, therefore, that peripheral states have resorted to the weapons of the weak, that is, subterfuge and guile. Some of the techniques used to hide public debt have been ruinous to public accounts in the long run. Greece has led the way with persistent manipulation of national statistics throughout the 2000s as well as by striking barely legal deals with Goldman Sachs that presented public borrowing as a derivative transaction. Public–private transactions have also been widely deployed in the periphery to postpone expenditure into the future, typically at a loss to the public.

But fiscal policy has continued to be the province of each individual state, and has remained fragmented compared to unified monetary policy. Furthermore, the Stability and Growth Pact has made no provision for fiscal transfers across the eurozone, as would have happened within a unitary or federal state. There are no centralised fiscal means of relieving the pressures of differential competitiveness and variable integration into the eurozone. The European budget is currently very small, at just over 1 percent of the aggregate GDP of all EU states, which is a small fraction of the German, French, and UK budgets. Moreover, it is not allowed to go into deficit.

This structural weakness of the eurozone has been much discussed in recent years, including during the course of the current crisis.[10] What is less discussed, however, is that it also has implications for the ECB. A key function of a central bank is to manage the debt of its state, handling the state's access to financial markets and ensuring the smooth absorption of fresh issues. A central bank is also able to acquire state debt directly, facilitating the financing of fiscal deficits for longer or shorter periods of time. But the ECB has no obligation to manage the debt of eurozone member states, and is expressly forbidden to buy state debt. On both scores, the ECB does not behave as a normal central bank. The inherent weakness of the ECB is part of the dysfunctional co-ordination of monetary and fiscal policy within the eurozone, which has been made apparent in the course of the sovereign debt crisis.

---

10 See Thomas Palley in *FT*, 10 Feb 2010, http://blogs.ft.com/economistsforum/2010/02/ euroland-is-being-crucified-upon-its-cross-of-gold. On the structural weaknesses of the eurozone see Arestis, P. and Sawyer, M. (2006), 'Macroeconomic policy and the European Constitution', in *Alternative Perspectives on Economic Policies in the European Union*, P. Arestis and M. Sawyer (eds.), Palgrave Macmillan, pp. 1–33. On the specific response of the EU to the crisis, see EuroMemorandum Group. (2009), 'Europe in crisis: a critique of the EU's failure to respond', available at http://criticalpoliticaleconomy.blogspot. com/2009/11/euromemorandum-20092010.html

Rising public deficits and debt due to the crisis

Turning to the actual path of public finances, it is important to note that public finance reflects the historical, institutional, and social development of each country. There can be no generalisation in this regard as welfare systems are variable, tax regimes reflect past compromises, the ability to collect tax depends on the efficiency of the state machine, and so on. Nonetheless, the Stability and Growth Pact has imposed certain common trends upon eurozone states.

Public expenditure declined steadily in the 1990s, with the exception of Greece, where it remained fairly flat (fig. 19). In the 2000s, expenditure stayed more or less flat, except for Germany, where it continued to fall steadily, and Portugal, where it rose gently. Once again, Germany has had considerable success in imposing fiscal austerity on itself, but also on other countries in the sample. Public expenditure turned upward after 2007 as the crisis hit and states attempted to rescue financial systems while also supporting aggregate demand. Once again, Germany is the exception as expenditure did not pick up.

FIG. 19 Government expenditure (percent GDP)

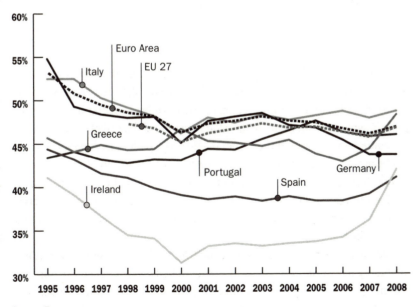

Source: *Eurostat*

FIG. 20 Government revenue (percent GDP)

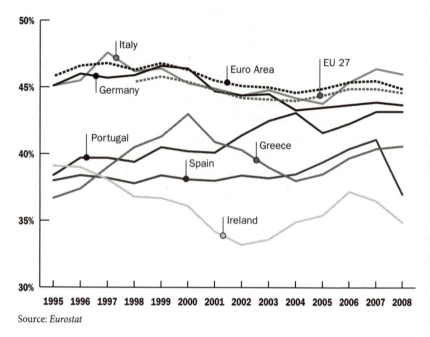

Source: *Eurostat*

Public revenue showed equal complexity, reflecting the particular conditions of each country (fig. 20). Greek public revenue slumped in the middle of the 2000s as taxation was lowered on the rich, while the operations of the tax-collecting mechanism were disrupted. It rose toward the end of the decade, but not enough to make good the earlier decline. The path of Irish public revenue has been the weakest, though an attempt was made to shore things up in the second half of the 2000s. Spain and Portugal maintained reasonable revenue intake throughout. Public revenue declined across the sample once the crisis of 2007–9 began to bite. Recession and falling aggregate demand were at the heart of the fall.

Declining revenue and rising expenditure, both caused by the crisis, inevitably led to rapid increase in public deficits. With deficits rising, several peripheral and other even out eurozone states arrived in the financial markets in 2009 seeking to borrow large volumes of funds. The pressure to

FIG. 21 Government primary balance (percent GDP)

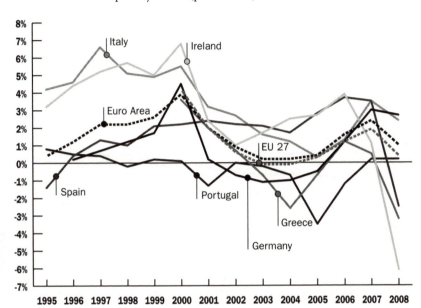

Source: *Eurostat*

borrow appears to have been particularly strong in Greece, Spain and Ireland, less so in Portugal.

Consequently, and inevitably, national debt also began to rise relative to GDP after 2007 (fig. 22). Note that there are significant differences in the volume of public debt among eurozone countries, again reflecting each country's respective economic and social trajectory.[11] But Greek debt, which has attracted enormous attention since the start of the crisis, was not the highest in the group, and nor has it been rising in the 2000s. On the contrary, Greek national debt declined gently as a proportion of GDP in the second half of the 2000s. Only in Germany and Portugal did national debt rise throughout this period,

---

11 The trajectory and components of private and public debt in eurozone countries are examined in detail in Part 2 of this book.

FIG. 22 General government gross debt (percent of GDP)

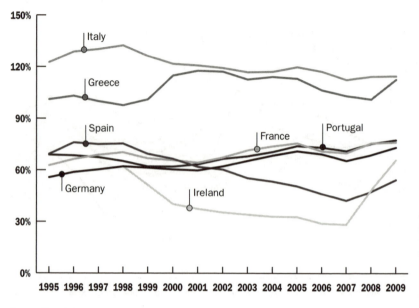

Source: *Eurostat*

though gently and from a fairly low base. The sudden rise of public debt across the eurozone in the last couple of years has been purely the result of the crisis of 2007–9.

Public sector performance in the eurozone can thus be easily summed up. The Stability and Growth Pact has imposed a straitjacket on member states, but its effect has been conditioned by residual sovereignty in each state. The fragmentation of fiscal policy has contrasted sharply with the unification of monetary policy. Nevertheless, eurozone states have generally restrained public expenditure, while maintaining a variable outlook on revenue collection. The decisive moment arrived with the crisis of 2007–9, which pushed peripheral states toward deficits. At that point the underlying weaknesses of integration in the eurozone emerged for each peripheral state, including current account deficits and rising capital imports from the core.

There are no structural reasons why the tensions of debt should have concentrated so heavily on Greece. No doubt the country has a relatively large public debt and therefore faces a heavy need for refinancing, particularly as the budget swung violently into deficit in 2009. But Italian public debt is also high. It is also true that Greek governments have been persistently manipulating data, and that the country faces a large current account deficit. But these pressures could have been handled reasonably smoothly if it was not for speculation in the financial markets. Even speculation could have been confronted decisively, if the eurozone authorities had shown any inclination to bring it to heel. To analyse the interplay of these factors it is now necessary to consider the financial sector, the part of the economy that is most heavily responsible for the crisis of 2007–9.

6. THE FINANCIAL SECTOR: HOW TO CREATE A GLOBAL CRISIS AND THEN BENEFIT FROM IT

An institutional framework that favours financial but also productive capital

The European Central Bank (ECB) and the national central banks constitute the European System of Central Banks (ESCB), which has price stability as its primary objective.[12] The ECB has normative power over the national central banks since decision-making on monetary (and financial) policy emanates from the ECB and then reaches national central banks. It can also make recommendations to national authorities relating to prudential supervision of credit institutions and the stability of the financial system.

The ECB is an unusual central bank. It has the exclusive right to authorise the issuing of banknotes in the EU, though notes are issued by individual central banks. It is also responsible for holding and managing official foreign reserves of member states. However, the ECB (and the national central banks) is prohibited from offering overdrafts or other credit facilities to member states, including the purchase of public debt instruments. The ECB is considered independent in the sense that no public institution or individual member state is authorised to influence its operations and decisions. But its substantial independence comes from the absence of a unitary European state with which it would have been obliged to interact.

The peculiar character of the ECB is also apparent in its own statutes. Subscription to ECB capital and the transfer of foreign reserve assets to the ECB, for instance, are proportionate to each member state's population and GDP. Furthermore, when the number of member states exceeds fifteen, participation in the decision-making process of the ECB is supposed to take place on the basis of GDP as well as on the aggregate balance sheet of the monetary financial institutions of each member state, again reflecting a hierarchy of state power.[13]

The ECB has supported financialisation in Europe mostly by protecting the interests of financial capital. European financial markets have been unified as

---

12 The institutional framework of the ECB and the Eurosystem is considered in detail in Part 3 of this book.

13 See the Consolidated Version of the Treaty on European Union and the Treaty on the Functioning of the European Union, in the *Official Journal of the European Union*, C115.

financial liberalisation has spread and become deeper. Restrictions on financial operations have been abolished among the member states. Monetary union and the establishment of the euro as world money have benefited European financial capital in competition with US and other global banks. The euro has also been marked by an appreciation bias, rising from around 0.95 to the dollar at its launch to reach a peak of 1.58 in July 2008. The euro has retreated since then, particularly following the sovereign debt crisis, and currently stands at around 1.35 to the dollar (March 2010). Without necessarily being deliberate, the appreciation bias has served the interests of financial capital since it has helped to induce global wealth holders to change the currency composition of their portfolios in favour of the euro.

It appears that the appreciation bias of the euro has not damaged the interests of the European productive sector, because it has forced productive capital to lower costs in order to be able to compete globally. This has meant steady pressure on workers' pay and conditions. German structural adjustment in the 2000s, in particular, has been based on squeezing workers, as was shown above. Productive capital has further benefited from reductions in uncertainty surrounding exchange rates as well as from differences in financial environment. Finally, a strong and rising euro has also supported European capital in undertaking mergers and acquisitions (M&A) in other parts of the world. In short, the euro as world money has served the international interests of both financial and productive capital in Europe.

For European banks in particular, the euro has provided liquidity facilities regulated by the ECB that have been able to support banking expansion across the world. The European banking system (above all, German and Dutch banks) steadily increased its net long US-dollar positions until the middle of 2007 (roughly $400 bn), with the ECB effectively acting as one of the main funding counterparties.[14] Note also that, in contrast to other central banks of mature countries, the ECB has always accepted private securities as collateral in its operations. Normal procedure for central banks is to accept only government securities. The Federal Reserve, for instance, started to accept private securities in 2008 only as an extraordinary response to the crisis.

---

14 Bank for International Settlements (2009), 'The US dollar shortage in global banking and the international policy response', Working Paper 291.

There is no doubt that the institutional arrangements of the euro have been beneficial to European finance. However, after the outbreak of the global crisis and as global banks faced trouble, the significance of the absence of coordination between the monetary and the fiscal spheres became apparent. In contrast to the USA and the UK, monetary union has revealed an underlying weakness, namely the absence of a unitary or federal state in Europe.

Given the absence of political union, the Stability and Growth Pact has acted as anchor for the euro in the world market. Contrary to the USA, which has been able to relax fiscal policy, the euro has required fiscal tightening as the crisis has unfolded. The implication has been to push member states toward policies that further squeeze workers in peripheral countries, while defending the interests of the European financial system. Thus, monetary union has meant an asymmetric adjustment between banks and states in the financial sphere after the crisis: banks have been protected, while the onus of adjustment has fallen on weaker peripheral states.

Banking in the eurozone: The core becomes exposed to the periphery

Financialisation has developed in both core and peripheral countries of the eurozone, as is clear from the rising volume of financial institution assets relative to GDP (See table 1).

There are no apparent differences between core and peripheral countries with respect to the underlying trend of financialisation; there is, however, considerable variety among them. Furthermore, there has been no dramatic increase in foreign bank ownership, unlike the trend toward growing foreign bank entry in several developing economies during the same period. Assets of foreign banks (both subsidiaries and branches) in the eurozone stand around 20–25 percent of total assets of credit institutions, the only exception being Ireland, with around 50 percent.[15]

The international investment position of European banks, however, presents several noteworthy features. Figure 23 shows that the aggregate cross-border claims of banks have been rising globally since the mid-1980s,

---

15 See tables 8, 15, 18, 21 and 24 in ECB: Structural analysis of the EU banking sector, 16/11/2002; tables 2, 11 and 13 in ECB: EU banking structures, 07/10/2005; tables 2, 11 and 13 in ECB: Structural indicators for the EU banking sector, 15/01/2010.

TABLE 1 Credit institutions, Total Assets/GDP

1997	1998	1999	2000	2001	2002	2003	2004	2005	2006	2007	2008	
107%	123%	142%	156%	155%	142%	124%	124%	142%	147%	167%	190%	Greece
262%	304%	240%	404%	461%	364%	413%	487%	583%	674%	715%	760%	Ireland
156%	143%	147%	152%	152%	161%	159%	164%	176%	189%	217%	231%	Italy
237%	286%	281%	274%	287%	263%	252%	240%	242%	255%	270%	290%	Portugal
170%	173%	178%	185%	193%	184%	192%	204%	237%	256%	281%	309%	Spain
227%	239%	247%	258%	272%	251%	263%	273%	295%	307%	329%	379%	Austria
306%	298%	304%	282%	303%	297%	302%	316%	349%	354%	392%	370%	Belgium
244%	239%	251%	247%	257%	247%	251%	266%	294%	317%	353%	371%	France
256%	275%	287%	299%	304%	297%	295%	298%	304%	307%	312%	316%	Germany
231%	255%	263%	286%	298%	292%	309%	342%	333%	351%	392%	376%	Netherlands

Source: *ECB (2010)*: Structural indicators for the European Union banking sector,
and *ECB (2005)*: European Union banking structures

and quite rapidly in the 2000s.[16] But the aggregate of cross-border claims of European banks rose much faster in the 2000s. The data is presented in US dollars, and the appreciating euro to US dollar exchange rate is shown on the right hand scale. To a certain extent, the appreciating euro has probably inflated balance sheets denominated in euro compared to those denominated in dollars. Nevertheless the growth in the international claims of European

---

16 Source is the BIS Locational Banking Statistics, Table 8 (http://www.bis.org/statistics/bankstats.htm). 'Aggregate of Major European Nations' is calculated as the sum of the International Position of reporting banks from Austria, Belgium, Cyprus, Denmark, Finland, France, Germany, Greece, Guernsey, Ireland, Isle of Man, Italy, Jersey, Luxembourg, Netherlands, Norway, Spain, Sweden, United Kingdom, Europe. 'Aggregate of other nations' is calculated as the reported item 'All Countries' minus the 'Aggregate of Major European Nations'.

FIG. 23 International positions by nationality of ownership of reporting banks (USD, bn)

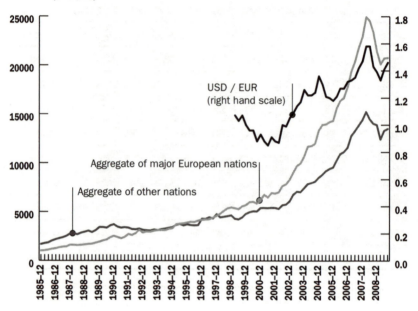

Source: *BIS Locational Banking Statistics*

banks appears also to reflect greater integration within the European Union, drawing on the beneficial effect of the single currency and single market for finance.

Turning to cross-border lending within the eurozone, it is useful to consider trends by splitting countries into core (Germany, France, Belgium and the Netherlands) and periphery, broadly understood (Greece, Ireland, Italy, Portugal, Spain). Lending has increased in both directions. As is shown in figure 24, gross exposure by banks grew from March 2005 until early 2008, after which it declined across the board as banks reined in their lending. It is important to stress, however, that even though there has been growth across the sample, flows from core to periphery have become more important in size than flows from core to core.

Furthermore, as figure 25 shows, net banking flows from core to periphery have been positive and increasing in the second half of the 2000s (starting

FIG. 24 Gross cross-border bank claims (euro, bn)

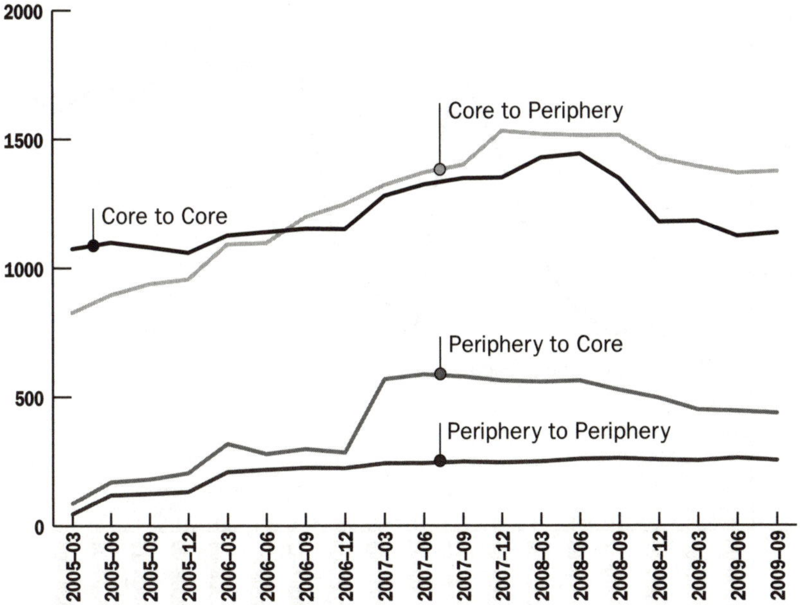

Source: *BIS Consolidated Bank Statistics*

March 2005, notwithstanding a statistical adjustment in March 2007)[17] peaking in September 2008. As gross flows in figure 24 indicate, this change has been driven mainly by lending from core to periphery, which rose throughout this period. It is also notable that claims by periphery to core began to fall earlier than those from core to periphery.

The evidence presented here shows that exposure of core banks to peripheral countries increased considerably after the first signs of the international financial crisis in 2007. There are several probable reasons for this

---

17 'Italian banks' foreign claims rose by $649 billion in March 2007, nearly twice the increase in the previous quarter, due to a change in reporting that led to a reclassification of a number of subsidiaries, particularly those located in Germany', *BIS Quarterly Review*, Sep. 2007, p.21.

FIG. 25 Net cross-border claims, core to periphery (euro, bn)

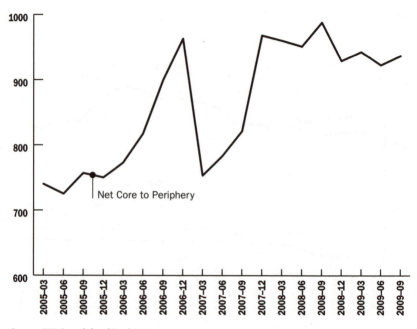

Source: *BIS Consolidated Bank Statistics*

phenomenon. Core banks had no concerns about the creditworthiness of peripheral states until 2009, indeed lending to governments seemed a reasonable course of action. ECB policy, furthermore, was to support all banks, thus increasing the creditworthiness of peripheral banks. Above all, money markets became very volatile after August 2007 and there were significant differences between individual inter-bank rates (LIBOR). Core banks found themselves holding surplus euro in 2007–8 and, given overall credit concerns, perceived peripheral banks to be safer than banks in other countries (especially the US and the UK). While the Anglo-Saxon financial systems had already been hit by the crisis, European countries appeared to be safer locations. This lack of concern about the state of the European periphery can also be inferred from the Credit Default Swap (CDS) spreads shown in figure 32, which were low and stable until mid September 2008 (when Lehman Brothers failed). Rising spreads in Greece and Portugal and a buoy-

FIG. 26 Core bank gross claims on periphery vs. capital & reserves (euro, bn)

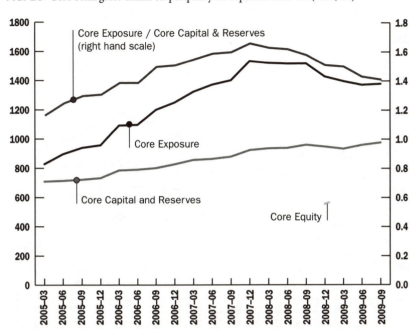

Source: *BIS Consolidated Banking Statistics; ECB Eurosystem Statistical Data Warehouse*

ant housing market in Spain appeared to offer high and reasonably secure returns to core banks.

Figure 26 above shows the gross exposure of the core countries compared to their Capital and Reserves. Additionally it shows the equity of the banking system at the end of 2008, which is the only date for which this type of data is available from the ECB or Eurosystem Central Banks. The graph shows that exposure of core banks to the periphery grew faster than their capital and reserves until early 2008. At that time banks began to rein in lending while continuing to strengthen their capital base. The main contributors to core lending to the periphery are France and Germany, whose trajectories are shown in figure 27.

The single point in figure 26 marks the equity of core banks in December 2008, allowing for visual assessment of exposure. At the end of 2008 the gross exposure of core banks to the periphery stood at around 1.4 trillion euros.

FIG. 27 French and German bank gross claims on periphery vs. capital & reserves (euro, bn)

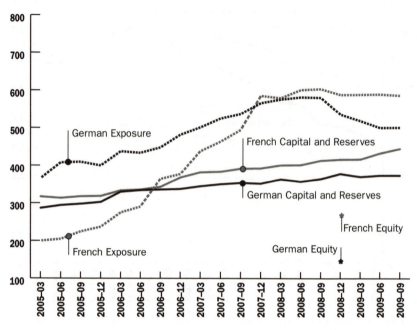

Source: *BIS Consolidated Banking Statistics; ECB Eurosystem Statistical Data Warehouse*

Meanwhile, total equity of the core banking system was 0.6 trillion euros, making the exposure to peripheral countries approximately 2.6 times equity. The two single points in figure 27 indicate the equity of French and German banks, respectively, in March 2009. On this basis, the exposure of German banks appears perhaps somewhat heavier than that of French banks.

Be that as it may, there is no doubt that core banks have become heavily exposed to peripheral countries. Yet, the assets are loans and therefore it is probable that they have not been entered on the balance sheet on a mark-to-market basis, reflecting current market prices. Consequently, provision against losses would presumably take place only when the possibility of default by borrowers became very high and the loans began to look impaired. Judging by Credit Default Swap (CDS) spreads (fig. 32), which capture risk premia, the risk to core banks did not look forbidding in March 2010.

However, things could change very rapidly, if peripheral countries took a turn for the worse.[18] A 10 percent drop in the value of banking assets would be serious for the core banking systems, but it may not necessarily be terminal. If, on the other hand, 50 percent of loans to the periphery defaulted with a 50 percent recovery ratio, resulting in a loss of 25 percent of total exposure; or equally, if an exit from the euro resulted in a 25 percent devaluation of domestic currencies, the outcome would be disastrous for the banking system of the core nations, given current levels of equity. German and French banks would be particularly vulnerable.

This was the hard reality behind the negotiations between core and periphery regarding a rescue plan for the weakest, in the first instance, Greece. If the periphery was not rescued and generalised default occurred, the banking system of the core would find itself in a very difficult position. Needless to say, banks were rescued by states once in 2007–9, and they would probably be rescued again, should this eventuality arise.

ECB operations allow banks to restrict their lending

When the financial crisis hit in 2007, many European banks found that their assets were worth less than estimated. In the preceding period European banks had attempted to keep in step with large US banks by borrowing to acquire speculative mortgage-backed and other asset-backed securities, thus raising their returns. When the interbank market froze in 2007–8, European banks struggled to find liquidity, thus coming under heavy pressure.

The most visible effect of this development in the money markets was the drastic widening of the LIBOR-OIS spreads. The LIBOR is a rate of interest closely linked to the interbank money market for maturities between 1 month and 1 year; the OIS (or EONIA in the eurozone) relates to the rate of interest for overnight cash. The result of the freeze was a sharp increase in money market rates, while overnight rates remained largely unchanged. The situation worsened after Lehman Brothers collapsed in September 2008. To confront the problem, the ECB decided to increase its long-term refinancing operations. The expectation was that this would re-establish confidence in the money markets, as well as induce banks to lend more freely beyond the interbank market.

---

18 This assessment was rapidly proven right as European banks faced emerging crisis conditions for most of 2010 and 2011.

FIG. 28 Securities and loans held by banks, cross-border positions (euro, bn)

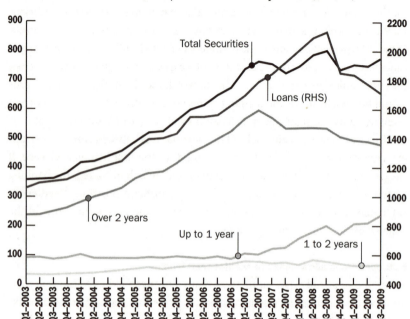

Source: *ECB (2010) Monetary, financial markets and balance of payments statistics*

Figure 28 shows that increased demand for liquidity by European banks resulted in a rising share of short-term assets on their balance sheets (represented here by securities up to 1 year).[19] At the same time, banks engaged in rapid restructuring of their balance sheets by reducing longer-term securities (securities of over 2 years) as well as loans. This is a characteristic feature of the general 'deleveraging' in which banks have engaged across the world following the crisis. In the eurozone this process has rested on increased liquidity provision (in euro) by the ECB, in exchange for long-term assets held by banks. Technically, short-term securities held by banks were increased as the ECB rapidly expanded its long-term refinancing operations (mostly securi-

---

19 Cross border positions are assumed to be a good proxy for the overall balance sheet of banks.

FIG. 29 Net central bank lending in the Eurosystem (main operations) (euro, bn)

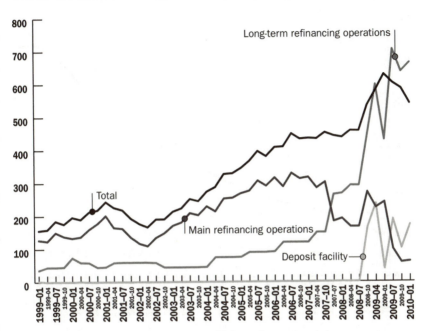

Source: *ECB (2010) Monetary, financial markets and balance of payments statistics*

ties with one year maturity, which is long for a central bank) as is shown in figure 29.

Intensified liquidity provision also took place by the national central banks of Spain, Portugal, Greece and Italy. Liquid short-term securities were supplied to the domestic banks in the wake of open market operations during the crisis. Figure 29 further shows a significant increase in bank deposits held at the central bank during this time. Banks have preferred to hold some of their reserves at the central bank instead of boosting their lending or acquiring securities. This development has, in turn, reinforced the process of banking deleverage, thus restricting the supply of credit to the economy, and worsening the recession.

Sovereign debt rises

Sovereign debt rose rapidly once the crisis had set in, as was discussed in chapter 5. The drop in output led to falling revenue, while expenditure rose chiefly

FIG. 30 Total outstanding debt, European markets (euro, bn)

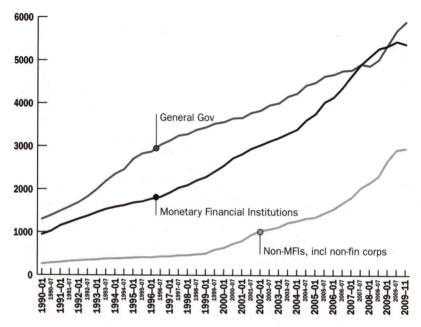

Source: *ECB (2010) Monetary, financial markets and balance of payments statistics*

to rescue the financial system. Figure 30 shows that sovereign debt rose slightly between September 2007 and September 2008; the outstanding amount climbing from 4.9 trillion to 5.1 trillion euro. But after September 2008, when the banking crisis turned into a global crisis that damaged all sectors in the economy, sovereign debt rose by almost 900 bn euro. The rise in public debt represents close to 60 percent of the entire increase in outstanding debt among all issuers in Europe, as is also shown in figure 30.

The immediate cause of the sovereign debt crisis is now clear: states have had to issue enormous amounts of debt at the 'worst time', thus facing increases in yield (as reflected in CDS spreads). Banks reduced their lending in 2009 and switched to holding short-term securities. They also avoided issuing bonds in 2009, fully aware of the rising pressure in financial markets, and opting to issue equities as figure 31 shows. The stock market revived in 2009 due to government support for the financial system, thus banks could obtain funds cheaply.

FIG. 31 Net issue of securities (euro, bn)

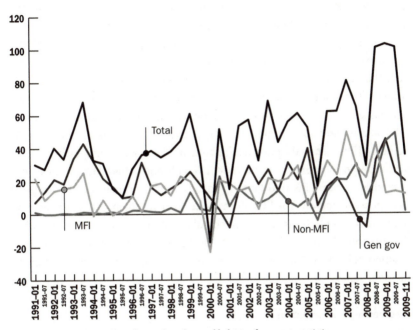

Source: *ECB (2010) Monetary, financial markets and balance of payments statistics*

Non-banks were able to issue fresh debt at yields similar to the previous period because they have more flexible term structure and timing of issuance. The brunt of the crisis has been shifted onto the public sector.

This outcome was facilitated by the ECB's response to the liquidity crunch which, as was shown above, was to flood the financial markets with liquidity in order to avert bank collapses. Co-ordinated action by the ECB allowed banks to start repairing their balance sheets. But ECB action helped to shift the problem onto the state, since the increase of ECB short-term securities made it more difficult for sovereigns to issue bonds, particularly as these have longer maturity. Furthermore, the ECB has extended the list of assets it accepts as collateral in liquidity operations by including further types of private securities. Currently government securities account for less than half of the nominal value of the securities on the list. Access to ECB liquidity facilities has thus been broadened for banks, negatively affecting demand for government securities.

States have been left struggling to raise funds, pushing up refinancing costs. In the absence of unified fiscal policy in the eurozone, each state has competed against the others, leading to higher yields for peripheral bonds.

The structural weaknesses of the EMU are apparent in this regard. All member states have the same access to the money markets; but they do not have the same access to credit, which is obtained at a different price by each country. The money market is unified in Europe as each domestic banking system has access to the ECB through national central banks, and faces the same interest rates and conditions; bank nationality does not matter for access to liquidity. However, in the government bond market each country faces particular conditions to refinance or issue debt. Supply and demand conditions – not to mention a country's credit rating – determine how much and at what price a country can borrow. The ECB does not act as government agent in managing public debt, highlighting the unique fiscal and monetary arrangement within the eurozone. In effect, the ECB does not act as a genuine central bank since it supports banks within the eurozone, but lacks power to extend support to member states.

A hothouse for speculation

The reaction of financial markets to the unfolding conditions was to foster speculation. Two related trends have prevailed in outburst of speculation: the weakening of the euro, and the widening of both government bond and CDS spreads of peripherals versus the core.

As national currencies no longer exist, it has not been possible for speculators to bet on a weakening of currencies due to public finances getting out of kilter. But selling the euro has been a win-win bet for speculators, and peripheral countries have been in the eye of the storm. From a speculator's perspective there were three main scenarios in early 2010. First, one or several peripheral countries could exit the eurozone, thus leaving the common currency in a much weaker position. Second, a bailout of peripheral countries could be agreed, even if it implied bending the rules of monetary union. This would in itself mean a loss of faith in the euro as a common currency. The third option, which might even lead to a strengthening of the euro, would be for peripheral countries to adjust their economies; but this would mean tremendous fiscal tightening and austerity imposed across peripheral countries.

In this context, the money markets have not provided a promising field for speculative activity. As was shown above, ECB policy has been to keep interest rates low and to continue with huge long-term refinancing operations. Thus, both the repo rate and the LIBOR-OIS spread have been at low levels since late 2009. Speculative attacks have focused on government bonds and CDS of peripheral countries versus the core. Greece was hit hardest, partly because of the lack of credibility as its public accounts have been fiddled repeatedly, partly because of its large current account deficit, and partly because the relatively small size of its bond market made it an easier target for speculation.

It is important to note that a considerable part of government bonds are held on an accrual basis. Consequently, despite its relatively small size, the CDS market has close similarities to the government bond market that is actively traded and marked-to-market. In addition, trading of sovereign CDS does not require a repo market or on-balance sheet reporting. As a result, CDSs have become another instrument for betting on a worsening of the crisis, or on outright default.

It is apparent from the preceding analysis that the crisis has not been caused by the CDS market on public debt. However, the CDS market has recently emerged as a benchmark for measuring, trading and speculating against the risk of a country defaulting. Sovereign borrowers are not only judged by rating agencies, but also receive a market judgement on the risk of default through CDS. Conceptually, the CDS benchmark resembles an independent index. Governments, central banks, rating agencies, and so on, have been forced to follow CDS spreads closely, making decisions accordingly. The CDS market might still be relatively small, but its impact is undoubtedly large.

The CDS spreads shown in figure 32 reveal how the perception of the euro has changed in light of the crisis. Bank and corporate CDS spreads were hit hard during the initial phase of the crisis. But the second phase, which began in 2009, has been marked mainly by widening sovereign CDS spreads. This cast an unforgiving light on the older arguments in favour of joining the euro, namely that it would not only reduce exchange rate volatility but also limit government funding costs. The assumption was that bond yields within the eurozone would converge, as indeed happened for a period. But the crisis has shown that this argument is seriously flawed. The structural weaknesses of monetary union and the impact of the crisis have raised the debt servicing

FIG. 32 CDS spreads (basis points), 5 years

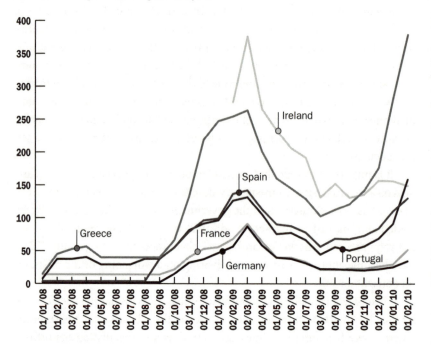

Source: *Bloomberg*

costs of peripheral countries. Speculators have acted as the trigger, and were able to profit from the difficulties of others as the ECB watched. The financial system was rescued by state intervention, only to turn and bite its rescuer.

7. POLITICAL ECONOMY OF ALTERNATIVE STRATEGIES TO DEAL WITH THE CRISIS[20]

EMU has been problematic for peripheral countries, above all, Greece, Portugal, Spain, and Ireland. It has been no less problematic for working people in the core countries, above all, in Germany. However, Germany has also benefited at the expense of peripheral countries, mostly through entrenched current account surpluses that have been translated into capital flows to the rest of the eurozone.

The sovereign debt crisis is the outcome of, first, precarious integration of peripheral countries in the eurozone and, second, the crisis of 2007–9. The public sector in peripheral countries has confronted an increased need of borrowing because it has rescued finance while attempting to forestall deep recession. The weaknesses of integration subsequently provided a field for speculative attacks by financial capital. The ECB has had neither the means nor the inclination to confront speculators.

The question now is: what strategies are available for peripheral countries? This is a huge topic that would merit separate study. However, on the basis of the preceding analysis, it is possible to sketch the broad outlines of alternatives. These could be split into three: first, imposing austerity on peripheral countries; second, seeking to alter the institutional structure of the eurozone; and third, exiting from the eurozone.

Austerity, or imposing the costs on workers in peripheral countries

The imposition of austerity has been the prevalent policy in Greece and elsewhere. It is, after all, in line with the standard response to financial crises during the last three decades, typically overseen by the IMF. The normal terms of intervention by the IMF include the advance of a rescue loan to stabilise financial and foreign exchange markets, accompanied by 'conditionality'. The content of conditionality has changed over the years, and there is evidence that the IMF is even beginning to countenance some relaxation of its rules.[21] But

---

20 This part of the work also reflects the time it was written (March 2010). But the analysis has been proven valid in all essentials and has required negligible editing.

21 Blanchard, O., Della Ariccia, G. and Mauro, P. (2010), 'Rethinking Macroeconomic Policy', *IMF Staff Position Note*, 12 Feb. http://www.imf.org/external/pubs/ft/spn/2010/spn1003.pdf

broadly speaking IMF policy still amounts to austerity coupled with liberalisation of the economy.

The problem with inviting the IMF to deal with Greece – and potentially others – is that the eurozone issues the euro which purports to be an alternative to the dollar as world money. The damage to the standing of the euro as a result of IMF intervention would be palpable. The first option for core countries, therefore, has been to foster austerity on the periphery and to attempt to manage the process of adjustment from within. However, the eurozone has lacked well-established mechanisms through which to replicate the approach of the IMF. Providing rescue loans, for one thing, has been expressly forbidden by the treaties establishing the euro. As a result, the eurozone initially exercised persistent political pressure on peripheral countries to adopt austerity policies, but without advancing the requisite finance. The costs of adjustment have been shifted disproportionately onto peripheral countries, inevitably leading to clashes of national interest.[22]

In this context, the governments of peripheral countries have begun to introduce austerity policies in the hope of bringing down borrowing costs in the open markets. The strategy was first adopted by Ireland, but then also by Portugal and Spain, and with increasing alacrity by Greece in early 2010. In effect, peripheral countries were forced to adopt IMF conditionality, without the IMF loan, with a view to persuading bond markets that public finances could be brought under control through the actions of peripheral governments.

Thus, the government of George Papandreou in Greece, newly elected in October 2009, introduced ever tougher austerity measures, including general reductions in public spending, direct cuts of public sector wages, and worsening of pension rights. The impact of these measures inevitably spread to the private sector as employers took the opportunity to impose worse conditions on labour. The government also imposed higher indirect taxes, while taking steps to reduce tax evasion.

The same approach had already been tried in Ireland in 2009, bringing down borrowing costs to a degree, as is shown by CDS spreads in figure 32. However, it

---

22 IMF intervention, the advance of rescue loans and the imposition of conditionality occurred, of course, in May 2010 in Greece and eventually applied to Ireland and Portugal. The implications are discussed in detail in Parts 2 and 3.

faced many more tribulations in Greece. The country's borrowing requirements were higher, and there had been a profound loss of credibility for the Greek state in financial markets. Furthermore, speculative fever was far more advanced in early 2010 compared to 2009, making it unlikely that speculators would desist from attacking Greek government bonds for long. With good reason too, since the self-declared aim of the Greek government to reduce its budget deficit by 4 percent in the course of 2010 seemed implausible. Even worse, austerity measures would probably intensify the recession, bringing government revenues under further pressure and making the targets even harder to achieve.

Greece thus found itself in a very difficult position in early 2010: imposing cuts and raising taxes in order to pay high interest rates to buyers of its public debt. The country was able to access markets in January and March 2010, but the rate of interest was high on both occasions, well in excess of 6 percent. This represented a transfer of income on a grand scale from the many to the few. Greece had a substantial volume of debt to refinance in the rest of 2010; if commercial interest rates did not decline, it was apparent that the policy could not last for long, given the huge social costs involved. What the government would cut from its people, it would pass directly to lenders. Under these conditions, external help would be necessary, which could come either from the eurozone, or from the IMF.[23]

The political economy of a eurozone rescue loan, however, would be far from simple. In the first instance, the constitution of the eurozone forbids formal advance of such loans. Yet, the EU has been highly inventive under pressure in the past. It might be possible, for instance, to make bilateral loans to Greece, possibly in the form of guarantees of Greek debt. The real difficulty would not be formal arrangements but political relations within the eurozone. Germany, which would probably bear the main burden, has gone through sustained austerity for almost two decades. It has also expressly and repeatedly opposed the notion of bailing out states within the eurozone. There would be significant political costs for any German government in making money available to other states. Furthermore, lending to Greece might open the gates to other peripheral countries.

---

23 This event transpired in May 2010. The austerity that followed was incomparably harsher than the measures imposed by the Papandreou government in the preceding period.

On the other hand, there would be significant risks to avoiding a European loan and thus forcing Greece to go directly to the IMF. Technically the country would remain within the monetary union, particularly as there would be no legal mechanisms to force it out. But its membership would in effect become second tier, and the long-term implications for its ability to borrow at standard sovereign rates within the eurozone would be entirely unclear. More significantly, going to the IMF would create a precedent for other peripheral countries, and might invite further speculative attacks. The risks posed for the euro as world money would be multiplied, particularly given the high exposure of core banks to peripheral countries.[24]

The Greek ruling establishment has been fully aware of these complexities. Though its preferred choice has been to tie its mast to a 'European' solution, it has also raised the threat of unilaterally going to the IMF. On the whole, the dominant opinion has been that the country needs to do whatever it takes in order to remain within the monetary union. Nevertheless, austerity imposed from the top runs the risk of generating stiff resistance from trade unions, popular organisations, and political parties. Greece looked ahead at a period of political strife. The government could, however, expect to draw some support from widespread popular fear of national bankruptcy as well as from (misplaced) national pride in remaining a member of the 'rich club' of the euro.

The deeper weakness of the strategy of austerity, however, is neither the imposition of austerity on working people, nor the difficulty of securing rescue loans from the eurozone. It was, rather, that its prospects of dealing with the underlying causes of the crisis were minimal. As was shown above, the underlying structural problem of the eurozone is that German competitiveness has surged ahead during the last decade. Greece and other peripheral countries have not succeeded in raising productivity sufficiently to overcome the pressure that Germany has applied onto its workers.

A policy of austerity would do very little to tackle the underlying problem of competitiveness. It might succeed in lowering nominal and real wages for a period, but it is apparent that this cannot be a long-term competitiveness strategy for countries that already have substantially lower wages than Germany.

---

24 In the end, of course, there was both a rescue loan from the eurozone and IMF intervention in 2010–11.

Given the flatness of German nominal remuneration, austerity would simply mean falling wages for years ahead. The answer would then have to be policies to raise productivity, and in this regard the ideas that typically accompany IMF-related packages are equally disastrous.

The standard prescription, still touted after years of persistent failure, is liberalisation. In the context of the eurozone, liberalisation would amount to the full unfolding, and even intensification, of the underlying ideas of the European Employment Strategy. Key elements might be: further weakening of labour protection, particularly through reducing trade union power; abolishing collective bargaining on wages; facilitating the entry of women into the labour force, especially in part-time and temporary jobs; removal of barriers into certain closed professions; reducing the tax burden on capital by introducing heavier indirect taxes; introducing privatisation into the education system; and significantly raising the pension age, while facilitating a funded system that promotes the activities of financial institutions.[25]

There is no reason to think that such measures, or similar, would lead to sustained growth of productivity, and thus allow for genuine convergence with the countries of the core. Productivity growth requires investment, new technologies, and opening fresh fields of activity. In the case of Greece it also means moving the country away from a pattern of growth that has rested on consumption with rising household debt. These changes are unlikely to come from liberalising markets, and nor is there any evidence that Greek capitalists have the capacity to perform the required miracle. In the medium term liberalisation measures would probably lead to stagnation, with systematic transfers of income from labour to capital. Meanwhile, Greek society – the second most unequal within the eurozone – would probably become even more polarised and callous toward social deprivation. The policy of remaining within the eurozone at all costs by deploying austerity and liberalisation is likely to have grim results.

Reform of the eurozone: Aiming for a 'good euro'
The second alternative involves making structural changes to the institutional arrangements of the eurozone. A distinction should be drawn here between,

---

25 Most of these have been indeed adopted by peripheral and other countries in 2010–11.

on the one hand, reforms that would not alter the fundamental character of the eurozone and, on the other, reforms that would go against economic and social relations at the heart of the monetary union.

The former have been extensively discussed in the academic literature as well as in the popular press.[26] There has been, after all, manifest failure of the institutions of the eurozone, extensively discussed in the earlier parts of Part 1. Above all, there has been a disjuncture between unitary monetary policy and fragmented fiscal policy. The rules under which the ECB operates have been unnecessarily restrictive, including exclusive focus on inflation targeting and forbidding the acquisition of public debt. Furthermore, there has been no provision for centralised fiscal transfers that could alleviate some of the tensions created by the single monetary policy. There has also been lack of an established mechanism of fiscal intervention in crises, as became abundantly clear in 2007–9, when each nation state was left to fend for itself and for its domestic economy. The absence of such a mechanism became glaring as Greece neared default in 2010.

There is nothing in principle to stop the gradual introduction of some of these reforms in the future. It is possible, for instance, for the eurozone to develop a properly functioning Public Debt Office that could coordinate the issuing and handling of public debt in cooperation with the ECB. It is also possible for the rules applying to the ECB to be relaxed, for instance, allowing the ECB to acquire state debt directly and thus more closely resemble a normal central bank. Perhaps the ECB might be supplemented by a European Monetary Fund that would lend to eurozone states facing crises on the basis of established proportional rights. It is even conceivable that a centralised system of fiscal transfers might be established within the eurozone.[27]

---

26 For a critical perspective, see: Arestis, P. and Sawyer, M. (eds.) (2006), *Alternative Perspectives on Economic Policies in the European Union*, Palgrave/Macmillan. For reform that aims to maintains the eurozone status quo see Gros, D. and Mayer, T. (2010), 'Towards a Euro(pean) Monetary Fund', Centre for European Policy Studies, 8 February, http://www.ceps.eu/book/towards-european-monetary-fund. Gros and Mayer's arguments were run as guest article in *The Economist* of 18 February 2010.

27 The ECB has indeed been allowed to purchase public debt in the secondary markets in 2010. Other reforms with regard to public debt have proven much more difficult for reasons discussed in detail in Part 3.

It is, however, extremely unlikely that fiscal policy would become unified as that would amount to wholesale restructuring of sovereignty across the eurozone. There is a hierarchy of states within the eurozone and close calculation of national interest. Legitimacy for each state derives from its own history, but also from the structures of power and popular assent, including democratic elections. There is no prospect of a single European state, and hence no prospect of unified fiscal policy. The reforms that could take place would occur within an existing hierarchy of power, dominated by the core countries and Germany.

Consequently, such reforms would amount, at most, to palliative adjustments of fiscal policy and improved articulation of fiscal with monetary policy. For the same reason, they are unlikely to challenge directly the principles encapsulated in the Maastricht Treaty, the Stability and Growth Pact and the Lisbon Strategy, that is, fiscal and monetary conservatism that shifts the pressure of competitive adjustment onto workers.

Even so, there is a risk that mild reforms would lead to lower acceptability of the euro internationally, hence a drop in its value relative to the dollar. But if the underlying principles of monetary union were not challenged, a drop in the value of the euro might be acceptable to the core of the eurozone for a period. It is conceivable that a slightly weaker euro backed by reformed, yet still tough, mechanisms of fiscal and monetary control would be attractive to Berlin and others. If such a configuration could be achieved, Germany would still maintain its current account surplus within the eurozone, the external terms of trade would improve, and the role of the euro as world reserve currency might not be compromised.

For peripheral countries and workers across the eurozone, such a prospect would hold little attraction. German workers would continue to be squeezed, and peripheral countries would continue to generate deficits. Germany would not shift from its path of stagnation, while the economies of peripheral countries would remain precariously integrated into the eurozone. The difference would be occasional fiscal hand-outs to relieve tensions, and perhaps improved management of crises.

It is not surprising therefore that there has been a search for more radical reforms, particularly among sections of the European Left in peripheral but also core countries. An important aim has been to push for further fiscal transformation seeking the abolition of the Stability and Growth Pact. What would then follow would not be entirely clear, but the presumption is that there would be greater fiscal independence for each state, including the ability to determine budgets and national debt, but still coordinated by new European institutional arrangements.

Coordination could be reinforced by the European budget, which would be enlarged from its currently tiny size to perhaps 5–6 percent of the GDP of the EU. Coordination could also presumably benefit from sustained intervention by the European Investment Bank. Scope might thus be provided to promote ecologically sound, socially inclusive and redistributive public investment programmes that could counter-balance existing asymmetries in European development.

The European Employment Strategy would also be abandoned in preference to coordinated policies that protected labour conditions and income. A European Minimum Wage Policy (corresponding to at least 60 percent of the median wage of each country) could be instigated. This would be combined with legislation to enforce progressive working time regulation across Europe. There could also be European wage coordination mechanisms that would take into account productivity gains, inflation, and unemployment. Stabilisation of labour shares in output (from the bottom up) might narrow the differentials in competitiveness that underlie the current crisis. Finally, there could be Europe-wide unemployment insurance, perhaps financed by progressive income taxes. These measures would be expected to promote integration of the European economy that would be beneficial to workers.

A notable feature of such proposals is that they do not confront directly the issue of coordinating fragmented fiscal policy with a single monetary policy, and nor do they take into account the implications of this approach to policy for the practices of the ECB. The general presumption is that the monetary union would be preserved, but the statutes of the ECB would be changed, ending its undemocratic political independence, and allowing for easier provision of credit to states and financial systems.

This approach might thus be termed the 'good euro'. Monetary union would be supplemented by institutional reforms that would make the currency operate in favour of working people, particularly in small economies where the scope for an autonomous economic policy might be narrow. This strategy also appears to provide a political platform to unite working people in core and peripheral countries. However, the 'good euro' also faces intrinsic problems in achieving its aims.

Set aside for a moment the political difficulties of coordinating popular pressure across several eurozone countries in order to abolish the Stability and Growth Pact in the face of bitter opposition by the existing order. An underlying economic problem would be that the reforms would abandon fiscal discipline while still attempting to maintain the euro as both domestic and world money. This would be implausible for a currency that attempted to compete with the dollar. The result would probably be a fall in the value of the euro, making it impossible for large eurozone banks to operate internationally. There would also be speculative attacks on the debt of the countries with the largest deficits within the eurozone.

A common currency area, especially one that purported to issue world money, could not tolerate large and variable fiscal deficits among its constituent parts. It is not apparent that the eurozone could continue to issue a form of world money, while allowing for substantial fiscal independence among its member states. An enlarged European budget would be no answer for this problem, much as it might contribute to redistributive policies. The real answer would be to have a European budget run by a unitary or federal state with a sufficiently integrated presence across the eurozone to support a common currency. But for that to happen, the present institutional and political arrangements of the eurozone would have to be overturned.

There is no parallel between the USA and the eurozone in this respect. It is true that the USA has a federal structure that allows individual states to manage their own fiscal affairs with several degrees of freedom. But the US federal state is a federal entity that provides the ultimate guarantee for all public debt. No state could play that role within the eurozone, and there is no prospect of one emerging. Furthermore, the USA is a well-understood exception in international transactions. The dollar is already world money, and can therefore tolerate falls in its value without necessarily losing acceptability – always within limits. The euro is attempting to establish a similar role for itself, and has no comparable track record.

In other words, the strategy of radical reforms aiming at a 'good euro' does not face merely political problems, namely the enormous difficulties of constructing an alliance that could alter the structure of the eurozone. More fundamentally, it faces the problem of compatibility of means with ends. Radical reform in the fiscal sphere would probably lead to failure of the monetary union altogether as the international role of the euro would come under pressure.

Those who call for such reforms should be aware of what they are advocating and tailor their proposals accordingly. The nub of the issue is neither the abolition of the Stability and Growth Pact, nor the introduction of an expanded European Budget with a redistributive mandate. It is, rather, the compatibility of fiscal independence, and possibly rising public debt, with the international role of the euro. It is possible that radical reform would lead to collapse of monetary union. If it is not to result in chaos, therefore, radical reform would require coherent social and economic transformation of national economies, including of the monetary system. To put it differently, a 'good euro' might well lead to 'no euro' thus requiring profound transformation of European economy and society.

Exit from the eurozone: Radical social and economic change

The final alternative of exit from the eurozone is the great unmentionable in peripheral countries, or referred to as the ultimate horror by governments and the press. There is no doubt that it would have severe consequences. But note that influential economists in the Anglo-Saxon world have already raised the issue in the press. Thus, Goodhart has effectively proposed the reintroduction of the drachma for domestic purposes, which would in practice result in devaluation.[28] Feldstein has recommended a short 'holiday' of Greece from the eurozone, returning at a lower exchange rate.[29] The underlying logic of these proposals is clear: the problem originates in loss of competitiveness, which could be partly tackled through devaluation.

The suggestions made by Goodhart and Feldstein could be called 'conservative exit'. In effect, conservative exit would operate as complement to the usual IMF package by also allowing for devaluation, which is impossible within the monetary union. Austerity would still be imposed, but some of the pressure of adjustment would be taken by the fall in the exchange rate. Competitiveness would be partly revived, strengthening export demand. Liberalisation measures would presumably follow in order to improve long-term competitiveness.

---

28 Goodhart, C. (2010), 'The Californian Solution for the Club Med', *Financial Times*, 25 Jan.

29 Feldstein, M. (2010), 'Let Greece take a eurozone "holiday"', *Financial Times*, 16 Feb.

Devaluation would have costs for workers since real wages would fall to the degree to which tradables entered the wage basket. But there would also be costs for sections of the capitalist class, particularly those servicing debt abroad, including corporations and banks. Cessation of payments and restructuring of international debt would become necessary. It is no wonder, therefore, that ruling elites in peripheral countries are reluctant to consider this option.

The prospect is particularly forbidding for 'little' Greece and Portugal as their ruling elites are aware of their own impotence to confront the problem in its full complexity. Conservative exit would not by itself deal with the longer-term challenge of raising productivity growth and altering deficient economic structures. It would merely change the terms of trade, encouraging production of tradables and potentially shifting the economy away from non-tradables. It would then be up to domestic capitalists to grasp this opportunity to restructure production, expand investment, and develop new fields of activity. The free market would have to generate a burst of productive dynamism, if the underlying problem is to be resolved.

There is no evidence that private capitalists in peripheral countries would be capable of such performance. The task is particularly complicated because peripheral countries typically have productive structures of intermediate technology, while real wages are above those of competitors in Asia and elsewhere. There is a risk, therefore, that conservative exit coupled with liberalisation would lead to protracted stagnation accompanied by bouts of inflation, successive devaluations, and slow erosion of labour income. Hence the ruling elites in the periphery have generally preferred the option of remaining within the eurozone and shifting the costs onto working people.

This leaves the option of 'progressive exit' from the eurozone, that is, exit conditional on radical restructuring of economy and society. As has already been noted, exit would involve a substantial economic shock. There would be devaluation, which would release some of the pressure of adjustment by improving the balance of trade, but would also make it impossible to service external debt. Cessation of payments and restructuring of debt would be necessary. Access to international capital markets would become extremely difficult. Banks would come under heavy pressure, facing bankruptcy. The point is, however, that these problems do not have to be confronted in the standard conservative way.

Economic survival could be ensured, and a sustainable path of growth could be achieved, provided there was drastic economic and social transformation. For that it would be necessary to mobilise broader social forces capable of taking economic measures that would shift the balance of power in favour of labour. This is not the place to discuss in detail the policy that might bring about such change. But some strategic steps are clear, including the following.

To protect the banking system it would be necessary to engage in nationalisation, creating a system of public banks. Private banking in mature countries has failed systemically in 2007–9. Bank failure has threatened the provision of liquidity across the economy. Furthermore, large private banks – or Large Complex Financial Institutions – have proven 'too big to fail' in the EU and the USA. This has created major problems of moral hazard, effectively subsidising the cost of capital of large banks. Large banks currently offer expensive credit to households, while reducing loans to small and medium enterprises. They also engage in complex and often speculative transactions in open markets, of negligible economic and social value.

Placing large banks under public banks would guarantee deposits. Further, it would advance credit on reasonable terms to small and medium enterprises, thus protecting employment. Public banks would also contribute to attaining sustained growth, as well as beginning to reverse the financialisation of contemporary economies. Co-operative and not-for-profit institutions have been long-standing elements of advanced financial systems. Public ownership and control over large banks is a step that could draw on extensive public knowledge and experience.

Capital controls would also be necessary, in the first instance to prevent the outflow of liquid funds and protect the banking system. More broadly, regulation of external capital flows would be required to marshal national resources. Managing capital flows is also necessary to avoid importing instability from abroad, as even the IMF appears to have recognised of late.[30] The policy of freeing the capital account in recent decades has offered no growth advantages, while regularly generating crises.

---

30 Ostry, J. et al. (2010), 'Capital Inflows: The Role of Controls', *IMF Staff Position Note*, 19 Feb. http://www.imf.org/external/pubs/ft/spn/2010/spn1004.pdf

The combination of public banking and controls over the capital account would immediately pose the question of public ownership over other areas of the economy. The underlying weaknesses of productivity and competitiveness already threaten the viability of entire areas of economic activity in peripheral countries. Public ownership would be necessary to prevent collapse. The specific sectors taken under public ownership, and even the form of public ownership itself, would depend on the characteristics of each country. But public utilities, transport, energy, and telecommunications would be prime candidates, at the very least in order to support the rest of economic activity.

With significant areas of economic activity under public ownership and control, the rest of the economy could be shifted onto a different growth path. To that purpose it would be necessary to introduce industrial policy. Public institutions and mechanisms of promoting development, which have been steadily abolished in the years since the Maastricht Treaty, would have to be rebuilt on a new basis. In conjunction with a public banking system, they would make it possible to implement a national programme of public and private investment. There is growth potential across peripheral countries for clean energy production, more energy-efficient homes and transport, as well as improved water quality and rubbish disposal. There is also scope for public investment in housing, urban planning, roads, railways, bridges, and airports. There is, finally, scope for the much more difficult task of improving technology as well as research and development.

Progressive exit for peripheral countries would be predicated on genuine structural reform of economy and society. Such change has nothing to do with the tired shibboleths of liberalisation. If productivity is to be set on an upward path, peripheral economies have to be weaned away from consumption, low savings, individual borrowing, low investment, and speculative bubbles. Structural change requires public mechanisms that could mobilise available resources for investment. It also requires transforming education by committing additional resources and expanding its reach to the poorest. Improving education would, in time, produce gains in labour skills, thus also benefiting productivity.

It is apparent that structural change of this order cannot be undertaken using the present inefficient and corrupt mechanisms of state. Broad political and social alliances are necessary to rebuild the structures of state on the basis of grassroots control, transparency and accountability. On these grounds, the tax base would be broadened by taxing income, wealth and capital, while reducing indirect taxes. Steps would be taken to improve social provision of health and to reorganise the system of public pensions. Transfer payments would also be used directly to tackle inequality in peripheral countries, which is already the worst in the eurozone.

The political and social alliances that could deliver such change do not exist in eurozone countries at present, other than in potential form. It would be far from easy to make them real, particularly as shifting the balance of power in favour of labour is predicated upon democratic organisation of economy and society. But there is no reason to believe that, if a credible political force proposed the policy of progressive exit for peripheral countries, it would be impossible to win broad support.

Political difficulties aside, however, the strategy would also have to confront the deeper problem of attaining national development in a globalised economy. Progressive exit cannot be national autarky. It would be necessary for peripheral countries to maintain access to international trade, particularly within the EU. It would also be necessary to seek technology transfer and capital from abroad. There are no guarantees that such flows would be forthcoming, particularly as the established order in Europe would be hostile to radical change. But progressive exit also offers the prospect of different development for workers in the core countries, who have come under heavy pressure during the last two decades. Labour in core countries would be a natural ally of peripheral countries attempting a radical transformation of economy. And if the eurozone came apart in the periphery, it could also unravel at the core, allowing for genuinely cooperative relations among European countries.

To recap, peripheral countries are currently confronted with stark choices because of the crisis of 2007–9 and the structural weaknesses of the eurozone. The current crisis could be resolved in a way that served the interests of the social layers which created the disaster in the first place. This solution would involve austerity in an attempt to remain within the eurozone. It would be inequitable, imposing huge costs on working people, who are not to blame for the upheaval. It would also lead to a hardening of society, while probably failing to deliver growth and higher real incomes in the future.

Alternatively, there could be a solution that changed the current balance of social forces in Europe involving institutional and social transformation.

In this regard there is debate between those who would attempt to change the institutional arrangements of the eurozone, and those who would advocate exit from the eurozone coupled with transformation of economy and society. There would be costs to any form of radical strategy, to be sure, but the costs would be borne equitably. Unlike the option of austerity, furthermore, radical change would have the potential to put the economy on a sustainable path of development that produced benefits for all. The choice belongs to society and, as always, depends on struggle.

Part 2 THE EUROZONE BETWEEN AUSTERITY AND DEFAULT

C. Lapavitsas, A. Kaltenbrunner, G. Labrinidis, D. Lindo,
J. Meadway, J. Michell, J.P. Painceira, E. Pires, J. Powell,
A. Stenfors, N. Teles
September 2010

8. INTRODUCTION

The eurozone crisis has many aspects to it, but it is also undoubtedly a debt crisis. This Part analyses the sources, nature and reasons for debt accumulation within the eurozone, particularly following the onset of the global financial crisis. It is subsequently argued that, in the face of a growing debt mountain, governments have two choices: cease to pay for public services and reduce public expenditure (austerity) or cease to pay bondholders. The latter option is default which could, moreover, occur on terms dictated by the creditor or the debtor.

Neither of these options offers an easy route out of the crisis, and each entails different costs and benefits for different sections of society. This Part discusses both and concludes that the choice favouring the interests of working people is the latter. Heavily indebted sovereigns of the eurozone periphery should take the initiative and default on their own terms. They should then also free themselves from the trap of the euro.

The crisis that has afflicted the eurozone has two main causes, as was established in Part 1. First, it is due to the great turmoil that began in the US financial markets in 2007 and soon became a global recession. It is thus a further phase of the great crisis that began in the late 2000s, one of those rare events that mark the historical evolution of capitalism. This systemic upheaval has been called a crisis of financialisation, reflecting the rise of finance during the last several decades and the concomitant transformation of mature capitalist economies.[31]

---

31 See Lapavitsas, C. (2009), 'Financialised capitalism: crisis and financial expropriation', *Historical Materialism*, 17:2, 114–148.

Second, the crisis is due to structural biases within the eurozone. A sharp internal division has emerged between core and periphery, typified by, on the one hand, Germany and, on the other, Spain, Portugal, and Greece.[32] This division has been reflected in progressive loss of competitiveness by the periphery relative to the core. The competitiveness of the core has benefited from extraordinary pressure on workers' wages which, in Germany, has meant practically stagnant remuneration of labour for well over a decade. Loss of competitiveness has entailed systematic current account deficits for the periphery, mirrored by equally systematic surpluses for Germany. The eruption of generalised instability in late 2009 reflects these profound imbalances within the eurozone.

Nonetheless, the eurozone crisis is, in the first instance, a crisis of debt, particularly of Greek public debt. Since late 2009, financial markets have been roiled by pressures arising from the extraordinary accumulation of debt by the peripheral countries of the eurozone. It is shown in chapter 9 that peripheral debt has resulted in good measure from the unbalanced economic relations between eurozone core and periphery. Peripheral countries have been mired in debt – private and public, domestic and external – as their competitiveness has declined relative to the core. Debt has also accumulated as financialisation has proceeded apace in peripheral countries, a process that has been reflected in the growth of the financial sector and in the expansion of corporate and household indebtedness. Public debt, finally, began to accumulate rapidly once the recession of 2008–9 had emerged fully.

Irrespective of its origin, debt has its own logic, which has determined the unfolding of the crisis. Chapter 10 shows that the accumulation of peripheral

---

32 The internal periphery of the eurozone also includes Ireland, which has been as much a part of this crisis as the other three countries. However, the path of development of the Irish economy during the last two decades exhibits several peculiar characteristics, probably associated with the strong presence of multinational corporations, and the accumulation of Irish debt is best examined separately. Needless to say, there is an even sharper division between the core of the eurozone and several countries in Eastern Europe, which might be called the external periphery. Since 2008 the latter has also entered a crisis with similar characteristics to that of the internal periphery. But, once again, it is best to leave the external periphery aside in order to keep the analysis within manageable bounds.

debt has threatened the liquidity and solvency of European banks. The threat to banks has arisen for two related reasons: first, because the banks of the core have become heavily exposed to the periphery and, second, because banks have faced sustained funding problems. The debt crisis has, consequently, threatened to become a renewed global banking crisis. This is the underlying reason why eurozone authorities put together an extraordinary intervention package in May 2010, aimed at stabilising financial markets. However, banks have remained weak and their problems have not gone away.

The counterpart to rescuing banks by eurozone governments has been the imposition of austerity across the periphery, but also across much of the core. This turn of policy has had major social costs and could prove highly damaging to European economies. Chapter 11 shows that austerity has compressed the only element of aggregate demand that has shown any dynamism during the last two years, namely public expenditure. Austerity is also likely to weaken consumption, thus further hitting aggregate demand. The possibility of severe recession across the eurozone in the near future cannot be discounted.

Even worse, since austerity has spread beyond the periphery, it could lead to downward wage pressure in the countries of the core. Consequently, the competitive disadvantage of the periphery, which lies at the heart of the eurozone crisis, is unlikely to be eliminated in the foreseeable future. This is a recipe for further economic instability and dislocation, particularly for peripheral countries. Finally, austerity is also likely to change the long-term balance of power between capital and labour in favour of the former. The eurozone will probably become even more hostile to the interests of working people in the coming years.

If austerity is such a lamentable course of action, what alternatives are there? The crisis is so profound that alternatives are likely to be radical, both economically and socially. The volume of debt of peripheral countries raises the prospect of default. It is argued in chapter 12 that default has to be debtor- (rather than creditor-) led, if it is to be effective. Creditor-led default is unlikely to lead to substantial reduction of debt and it would also mean fresh profits for banks. In contrast, debtor-led default could significantly reduce the crushing burden of debt on the periphery. But debtor-led default requires full transparency as well as participation by organisations of workers and civil society in renegotiating debt. Debtor-led default, moreover, poses the issue of exiting the eurozone in order to revive economic activity in the periphery.

It is arguable that default, wholesale debt renegotiation and exit from the eurozone constitute a preferable path for countries facing intractable public debt problems. But the risks are many, including to the viability of the financial system, and thus requir decisive government action. Furthermore, such a radical policy option would have complex social implications. Appendix 2A offers some historical perspective by considering the experience of Argentina and Russia, both of which defaulted and devalued their currencies in recent years.

Chapter 12 thus concludes by briefly considering the political economy of default in the eurozone and the possible implications of exit for a single peripheral country. Discussion is preliminary and prepares the ground for fuller analysis in Part 3. The issue has obvious topicality for Greece, which has been at the forefront of the crisis, but also for other peripheral countries as well as for the core. Default poses complex questions with regard to the debtor's international position and the balance of internal social forces. Apart from foreign holders of public debt, there are also domestic holders of public debt, domestic issuers of private debt which is owed to foreigners, and domestic owners of foreign assets abroad. Default presents different opportunities and threats to all these parties, requiring decisive action, if the interests of working people are to be protected. Furthermore, exit would deliver the shock of changing the monetary standard thus bringing devaluation in its wake. It would thus pose major risks for the economy as a whole, above all, for the domestic banking system. But exit could also ameliorate the competitive weakness that has bedevilled peripheral countries within the eurozone.

In sum, peripheral countries face harsh choices and their predicament reflects the historic failure of the eurozone. The crisis could be managed in an undemocratic way that defends the interests of financial capital, particularly of core eurozone countries. Alternatively, the crisis could become an opportunity for radical change that would alter the balance of social forces in favour of labour in the periphery as well as the core. If appropriate political and social alliances were formed, the vice that is currently crushing Europe between debt and austerity could be removed.

9. A PROFUSION OF DEBT: IF YOU CANNOT COMPETE, KEEP BORROWING

Obtaining an accurate picture of the debt of peripheral countries is the first difficulty in analysing the crisis of the eurozone. Information on debt is hard to come by, not least because governments are not forthcoming regarding their own debt. This chapter develops a systematic picture of peripheral debt by using the information available in December 2009. It is shown that peripheral countries have become heavily indebted and their debt is domestic and external as well as private and public. But the mix varies considerably among Spain, Portugal and Greece, with significant implications for the path of the crisis in each country.

The chapter also discusses the causes of peripheral indebtedness, showing that they are related to the structure of the eurozone and, more broadly, to the global trend of financialisation. To be more precise, indebtedness is due to the loss of competitiveness by peripheral countries as well as to the rapid growth of the financial sector in recent years. Participation in the European Monetary Union has been of decisive importance in this regard, both because it has contributed to the loss of competitiveness and because it has facilitated the growth of the financial sector. Enormous accumulation of debt by peripheral countries has been the counterpart to adopting the common currency.

The actual pattern of indebtedness also reflects the particular economic, social, institutional and political conditions in each country. Thus, the chapter considers in some detail the evolution of debt in Spain, Portugal and Greece. It is shown that by far the strongest growth has been in private, not public, debt. Furthermore, the heaviest holders of peripheral debt are countries of the core. But the balance between private and public debt varies considerably, as does the mix between external and domestic debt. Therefore, the threat posed by debt is significantly different for each of the three countries.

The magnitude of peripheral debt

Table 1 provides a picture of aggregate Spanish, Portuguese and Greek debt as of 31 December 2009.[33]

Several aspects of peripheral indebtedness stand out and call for explanation.

---

33 For a summary of the sources, the methods and the assumptions involved in the calculation of table 1, see Appendix 2B.

First, in absolute terms, Spanish debt was roughly three and a half times the sum of Portuguese and Greek debt, the last two being fairly similar to each other in size. Thus, any suggestion of Spanish insolvency would have posed a threat of an entirely different order to global financial markets compared to Greece and Portugal. As a proportion of GDP, however, aggregate Spanish indebtedness was very similar to Portuguese, and both were significantly higher than Greek indebtedness. On this basis, the financialisation of the Greek economy appears to have been less advanced than that of the other two, as will also be shown below.

TABLE 1 Aggregate peripheral debt (end 2009)[34]

	SPAIN		PORTUGAL		GREECE	
	EUR bn	%	EUR bn	%	EUR bn	%
TOTAL DEBT						
EUR bn	**5,274**		**760**		**703**	
% GDP	**502 %**		**464 %**		**296 %**	
By Issuer						
General government	676	13 %	121	16 %	293	42 %
Financial corporations	1,628	31 %	214	28 %	120	17 %
Non-financial corporations	2,053	39 %	246	32 %	165	23 %
Households	918	17 %	178	23 %	123	17 %
		100 %		100 %		100 %
By Instrument						
Short-term	**1,544**	**29 %**	**247**	**33 %**	**189**	**27 %**
Non-resident deposits	508		122		106	
Bonds	156		44		11	
Loans	258		49		72	
Trade credit	623		32			
Long-term	**3,730**	**71 %**	**512**	**67 %**	**514**	**73 %**
Bonds	1,472		173		301	
Loans	2,258		339		212	
		100 %		100 %		100 %

34 The size and the composition of peripheral debt has changed substantially in 2010–11, not least because Greece and Portugal have found themselves in receipt of rescue packages that effectively swapped privately-held for officially-held public debt. Some of these changes are considered in Part 3. However, the table continues to cast light on the causes and components of peripheral indebtedness.

	SPAIN		PORTUGAL		GREECE	
	EUR bn	%	EUR bn	%	EUR bn	%
EXTERNAL DEBT		% of total debt		% of total debt		% of total debt
EUR bn	**1,737**	**33 %**	**357**	**47 %**	**385**	**55 %**
% GDP	**165 %**		**218 %**		**162 %**	
By Issuer		% of ext debt		% of ext debt		% of ext debt
General government	299	17 %	98	27 %	206	53 %
Financial corporations	781	45 %	187	52 %	112	29 %
Other sectors	645	37 %	73	20 %	68	18 %
		100 %		100 %		100 %
By Instrument						
Short-term	**644**	**37 %**	**158**	**44 %**	**127**	**33 %**
Non-resident deposits	508		122		106	
Bonds	75		25		7	
Loans	17		1		13	
Trade credit	45		10		1	
Long-term	**1,093**	**63 %**	**198**	**56 %**	**258**	**67 %**
Bonds	739		141		206	
Loans	354		58		53	
		100 %		100 %		100 %
Sources:	Bank of Spain, Statistical bulletin – National Financial Accounts and Balance Payments – International Investor Position		Bank of Portugal, Statistical bulletin – National Financial Accounts and Balance Payments – International Investor Position		Bank of Greece, QEDS, IMF, Eurostat	

Second, the composition of aggregate debt was quite different among the three countries. The proportion of domestic to external debt stood at 67 percent to 33 percent for Spain, compared to 53 percent to 47 percent for Portugal and 45 percent to 55 percent for Greece. It seems that Portugal and Greece were similarly indebted externally and domestically, while Spain carried a lower proportion of external debt. On this basis, domestic financialisation appears to have been more pronounced in the Spanish economy than in the other two. However, the salient fact was that all three countries were heavily indebted abroad relative to GDP, Spain at 165 percent, with Portugal and Greece at, respectively, 218 percent and 162 percent.

Third, the composition of aggregate debt was even more strikingly different when the proportion of private to public debt was considered. For Spain and Portugal the proportion was quite similar, standing at, respectively, 87 percent to 13 percent and 84 percent to 16 percent. But for Greece the proportion stood at 58 percent to 42 percent. The Greek state was more heavily indebted than the other two by several orders of magnitude. The difference was even more pronounced with regard to the composition of external debt. The balance of private to public external debt stood at 83 percent to 17 percent for Spain, 73 percent to 27 percent for Portugal, but 47 percent to 53 percent for Greece. However, when it came to the balance between the domestic and external components of public debt alone, the proportions were 56 percent to 44 percent for Spain, 19 percent to 81 percent for Portugal, and 30 percent to 70 percent for Greece. Both the Greek and the Portuguese state were heavily indebted abroad, the latter proportionately more than the former.

Finally, fourth, the composition of debt in terms of instruments was quite similar among the three countries, standing roughly at 1/3 short-term to 2/3 long-term debt. But there were significant differences in the composition of external debt, largely reflecting the different weight of public debt in external debt. Thus, Greek external debt was preponderantly long-term, since its dominant element was public bonds. The external debt of the other two countries tended to be shorter-term, reflecting the heavier presence of the private sector.

One final aspect of aggregate peripheral debt meriting attention was the composition of holders by nationality. The data in figures 1, 2 and 3 refer only to securities, but this was still a large part of external debt, as can be seen in Table 1. The vast bulk of peripheral securities were held by the countries of the eurozone core, primarily France and Germany. There were variations and specific features, for instance, French predominance in Portugal and Greece, but the fundamental point was clear: the periphery was indebted mostly to the core of the eurozone.

To sum up, all three countries carried large volumes of debt, significant parts of which were owed abroad. Domestic Spanish finance appeared to have grown more robustly, but the country remained heavily indebted abroad. Both Spain and Portugal seemed to have advanced further than Greece down the path of financialisation. However, Greece carried a far heavier burden of public debt, both domestically and externally. In short, there were common patterns of heavy indebtedness across the three countries, which were borne differently in accordance with the social, historical, political and institutional character-

FIG. 1 External holders of Spanish debt securities (end 2008)

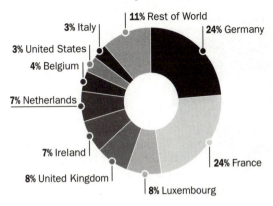

Source: *CPIS*

FIG. 2 External holders of Portuguese debt securities (end 2008)

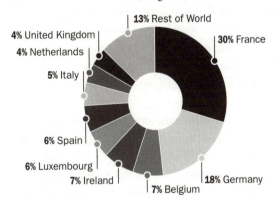

Source: *CPIS*

istics of each country. One further thing the three countries had in common was that their external debt was owed to the countries of the core, primarily France and Germany.

The rest of this chapter considers the common causes and differential patterns of indebtedness of peripheral countries. The starting point is external debt, which has been by far the most pressing element of the crisis.

FIG. 3 External holders of Greek debt securities (end 2008)

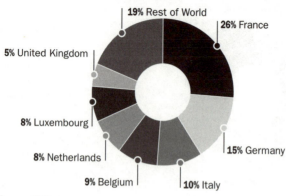

Source: *CPIS*

The economic roots of external debt

Accounting relations, summed up in Box 1, indicate that the external debt of a country corresponds to its current account deficit as well as to the financial deficit of the private and the public sector. With this in mind, pages 84–98 are concerned with establishing the analytical relations between the external debt, the current account deficit and the financial deficit of core and peripheral countries.

A striking feature of the eurozone has been the emergence of structural current account deficits in the periphery, mirrored by equally structural surpluses in the core, above all, in Germany. As was illustrated in Part 1, the cause of the imbalance has been the rise in German competitiveness due to unrelenting pressure on German wages (Germany already starting from a higher level of competitiveness, needless to say). Pressure on wages has been a general feature of eurozone countries, following the Maastricht Treaty, which has forced 'flexibility' onto the labour market thus complementing the imposition of a single monetary policy and rigid fiscal policy across the eurozone. The race to the bottom has been won by Germany, which has squeezed wages far more successfully than peripheral countries during the last decade. The result has been loss of competitiveness in the periphery, producing current account deficits that have been mirrored by current account surpluses in Germany. Figure 4 shows the divergent paths of the German, Spanish, Portuguese and Greek current accounts.

BOX 1 CURRENT ACCOUNT AND EXTERNAL DEBT ACCOUNTING

External debt can be related to the domestic components of the economy by using the framework of national income statistics. The framework deploys identities rather than behavioural relations, and hence should be treated with considerable caution. However, it can still shed light on the relations of external debt.

The financial balances of a country are given by:

$(X – M) = (S – I) – (G – T)$, or External Deficit = Private Deficit + Public Deficit (1)

Where S, I, G, T, X, M are, respectively, saving, investment, government expenditure, taxes, exports and imports.

Now, the Balance of Payments must balance, hence,

$(X – M) = F$

Where F represents total financial flows from/to abroad. In the case of the eurozone, total financial flows do not include foreign exchange reserves, which is one of the few advantages offered by the common currency. Consequently,

$F = FDI + BL + PF$

Where FDI, BL, PF are, respectively, foreign direct investment, bank lending, and portfolio flows. Thus,

$(X – M) = FDI + BL + PF$ (2)

In short, a deficit on current account (for simplicity taken as the difference between exports and imports) must be matched by financial inflows from abroad. These can be either debt-creating, as for bank lending and portfolio flows (if they are directed to bonds), or non-debt-creating, as for foreign direct investment and portfolio flows (if they are directed to shares). Typically portfolio flows are debt-creating, and this is how they will be interpreted in the rest of this report.

Combining (1) and (2):

$(X – M) = FDI + BL + PF = (S – I) – (G – T)$ (3)

That is, current account deficits correspond to debt-creating and non-debt-creating financial inflows from abroad, which further correspond to the deficit of the private sector plus the deficit of the public sector. Used with caution, these identities can help analyse the relationship between the components of domestic demand, the current account, and the accumulation of external debt.

FIG. 4 Current account balance (percent of GDP)

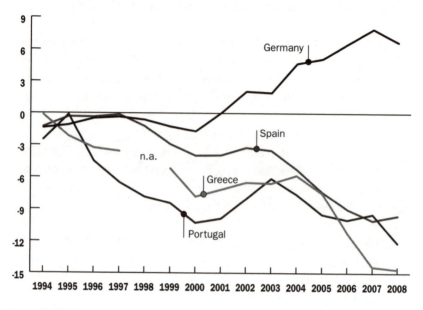

Source: *IMF BOP*

Peripheral current accounts worsened steadily since the mid-1990s on the approach to European Monetary Union, and the deficits became entrenched once the euro was adopted. Germany, meanwhile, has registered regular surpluses since the introduction of the euro. The deficits of the periphery reached extraordinary levels in the second half of the 2000s, nearing 15 percent in Greece in 2007 and 2008.

Current account deficits must be matched by flows of external finance, as is shown in Box 1. For peripheral countries, such finance has not come from flows of Foreign Direct Investment (FDI), which have remained weak throughout this period. Consequently, current account deficits have been financed through bank loans (BL) and portfolio flows (PF) from abroad (bonds). Figures 5, 6 and 7 show the composition of capital inflows into peripheral countries by splitting them into FDI (which do not create debt) and non-FDI (which do). Debt-creating flows are heavily preponderant. This feature of capital flows lies at the root of the external indebtedness of the

FIG. 5 Composition of capital flows: Spain ($ mn)

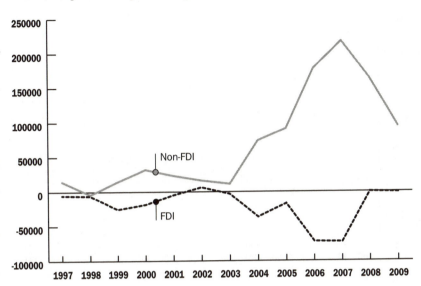

Source: *IMF IFS*

periphery, depicted in Table 1. Unsurprisingly, the funds have originated with banks and other lenders at the core.

Current account deficits correspond to the financial deficits of the private and the public sector, as was shown in Box 1. As far as the public sector of peripheral countries is concerned, the conclusion is unambiguous: the rising current account deficits of peripheral countries were not matched by rising public sector primary deficits. Figure 8 establishes the point clearly.

Portugal maintained a broadly balanced budget, with modest deficits for short periods of time, and the same holds true, more or less, for Greece. On the other hand, Spain ran steady primary balance surpluses throughout the period. Fiscal deficits rose across the three countries in 2008-9, but that was clearly the result of falling tax revenues due to the recession as well as states attempting to maintain demand. There was a bulge in public deficits in 2008-9 that has certainly accounted for the sharpening of peripheral indebtedness, but not for the accumulated volume of debt. To put it differently, the Stability and Growth Pact, which is an integral part of European Monetary Union, might have been

FIG. 6 Composition of capital flows: Portugal (\$ mn)

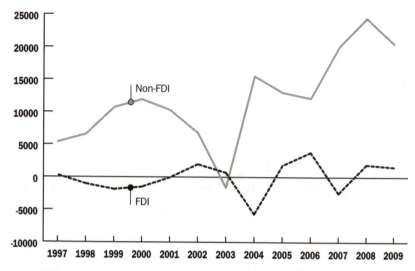

Source: *IMF IFS*

FIG. 7 Composition of capital flows: Greece (\$ mn)

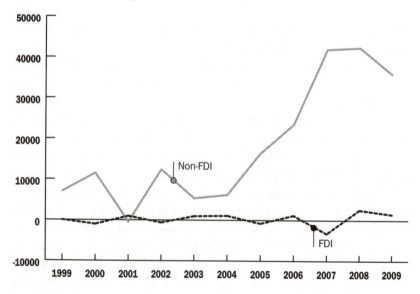

Source: *IMF IFS*

FIG. 8 Government primary balance (percent of GDP)

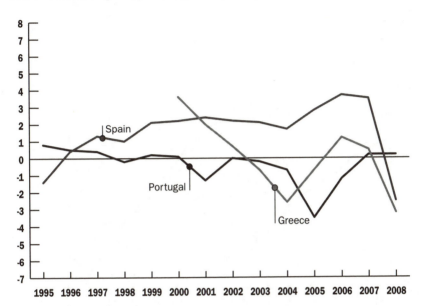

Source: *Eurostat*

occasionally breached but, on the whole, forced peripheral countries to comply with fiscal conservatism. The Spanish state has proven more conservative even than the German state, though it has not received much of a reward for its virtue.

Inevitably, then, current account deficits in the periphery have been matched by financial deficits of the private sector. The deficits of the private sector in Spain have corresponded partly to rising investment spending, much of it related to real estate. In Greece and Portugal, however, there was no upsurge of investment in the 2000s, except for a brief period prior to the Olympics in Greece. The financial deficits of the Greek and Portuguese private sectors corresponded largely to the collapse of saving, particularly after the adoption of the euro. At about the same time, Spanish saving also began to decline, thus exacerbating the financial deficit of the private sector. Figure 9 sums up trends across the three peripheral countries.

The key macroeconomic factors contributing to the accumulation of external debt by the periphery are now clear. Peripheral countries lost competitiveness

FIG. 9 Private sector saving less investment (percent of GDP)

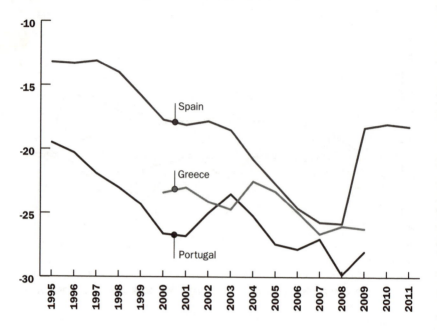

Source: *Eurostat*

relative to the core, and thus faced current account deficits which were financed from abroad. The current account deficits had little to do with the public sector of peripheral countries, which did not generate systematic financial deficits, even though it has often been described as profligate and inefficient. Rather, the current account deficits were associated with private sector financial deficits.

Unable to compete with the core countries of the monetary union, the private sector of peripheral countries reacted in ways that produced systematic financial deficits. Thus, in Spain, there was an investment bubble pivoting on real estate, while in Greece and Portugal, private saving collapsed as consumption remained at high levels. The financial deficits of the private sector matched the accumulation of external debt, which financed the current account deficit.

In other words, rising external indebtedness has reflected the biased integration of the periphery into the eurozone. Generalised pressure on wages has allowed the core to gain competitiveness, thus leading to rising indebtedness of the periphery to the core. Far from promoting convergence among member states, the European Monetary Union has been a source of unrelenting pressure on workers that has produced systematic disparities between core and periphery resulting in vast accumulation of debt in the latter.

The composition of peripheral debt: Domestic financialisation and external flows

The causes of debt accumulation in the periphery, however, should be considered further by examining the composition and the trajectory of debt during the last decade and more. A significant part of the debt has been external for reasons explained above. Note that as the pressures to accumulate external debt kept rising in the 2000s, so did the opportunities to obtain international credit, particularly for the state. Membership of EMU appeared to confer to peripheral countries the creditworthiness of Germany at a stroke.

On the grounds that the strong would provide support for the weak, international financial markets implicitly assumed that members of EMU simply would not go bankrupt. This assumption was enough to raise the credit ratings of the periphery to levels that were hardly justified by track record and economic performance. Self-evidently, financial markets and eurozone banks failed to assess risks appropriately. The error of their assumptions became apparent as the crisis of 2007 unfolded, and hit with a vengeance in late 2009.

But the domestic debt of peripheral countries has also risen spectacularly during the same period. There are similarities in this respect among all three countries, particularly with regard to household debt which has increased steadily. Speaking broadly, the accumulation of domestic debt bespeaks of advancing financialisation of peripheral economies, that is, of a structural transformation that has increased the weight of finance within the economy.

Financialisation has affected the corporate sector, the financial institutions, and households in mature and developing countries in recent years. In peripheral countries of the eurozone financialisation has been directly related to the common currency for the following reasons.

First, the euro has offered substantial advantages to banks, particularly as it has exhibited a persistent appreciation bias relative to dollar.[35] Eurozone banks

---

35 As was shown in Part 1 of this book.

FIG. 10 Spanish debt by sector of issuer (euro bn)

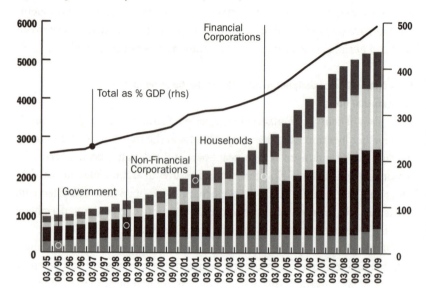

Source: *Bank of Spain, authors' calculation*

have been able to expand their international activities, while also funding their domestic activities cheaply.

Second, the loss of competitiveness has forced peripheral countries to focus on boosting domestic demand, above all, through investment in real estate and consumption. Support for demand has been provided by credit generated by the growing banks, thus leading to the accumulation of domestic debt by the periphery.

Third, and most significant, the eurozone has offered the opportunity to the private sector to borrow at cheap rates, both domestically and externally. The application of a common monetary policy across the zone brought interest rates down to German levels. Indeed, since inflation has tended to be higher in the periphery compared to the core, real interest rates in the periphery have tended to be even lower. Banks were able to meet the rising domestic demand for credit on cheap terms.

Consider now the trajectory of aggregate debt in the three peripheral countries in recent years, starting with Spain in figure 10.

FIG. 11 Spanish debt by sector of issuer (percent of total)

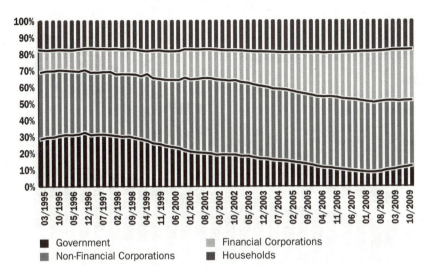

Government   Financial Corporations
Non-Financial Corporations   Households

Source: *Bank of Spain, authors' calculation*

Aggregate Spanish debt has risen dramatically as a proportion of GDP since the late 1990s. The bulk of growth has been in private debt, driven mostly by rising debt of the financial sector. The breakdown of Spanish debt by sector (figure 11), reveals the relative rise of Spanish bank indebtedness and the relative decline of Spanish public debt during the period. Spanish banks have been avid participants in financialisation, taking advantage of the opportunities opened up by EMU membership.

Aggregate Portuguese debt has also risen substantially as a proportion of GDP during this period, as is shown in figure 12.

Once again, public debt has declined as a proportion of the total, though not nearly as much as in Spain. Corporate indebtedness has declined proportionately, but this has been more than made up by the relative rise in indebtedness by the financial sector. Domestic financialisation has developed steadily in Portugal during this period.

Greek aggregate debt has approximately doubled as a proportion of GDP during this period, driven again by private indebtedness, as is shown in figure 14.

FIG. 12 Portuguese debt by sector of issuer (euro bn)

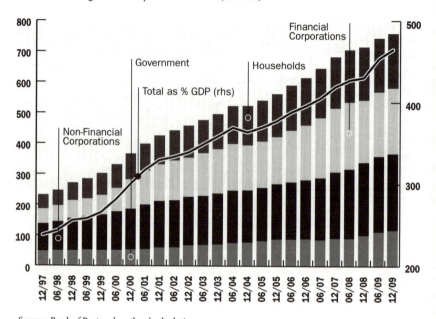

Source: *Bank of Portugal, authors' calculation*

FIG. 13 Portuguese debt by sector of issuer (percent of total)

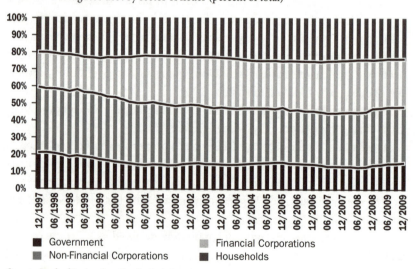

■ Government   ■ Financial Corporations
■ Non-Financial Corporations   ■ Households

Source: *Bank of Portugal, authors' calculation*

FIG. 14 Greek debt by sector of issuer (euro bn)

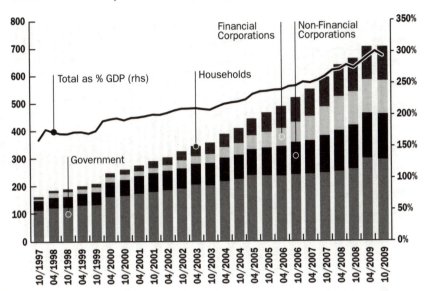

Source: *Bank of Greece, QEDS, IMF, authors' calculation*

Greek public debt has declined significantly as proportion of the total debt, though it has remained considerably higher than in Spain and Portugal, as is shown in figure 15. The sectors whose debt has risen significantly in proportionate terms were banks and households. For Greece, joining the EMU has brought rapid financialisation, more opportunities for Greek banks to engage in lending, and growing household indebtedness to support consumption.

It is striking, however, that Greek public debt has been a far more significant part of aggregate debt than in Spain and Portugal. This has been a feature of the Greek economy since the 1980s, the initial growth of public debt being an outcome of the redistribution policies followed by the social-democratic government of PASOK led by Andreas Papandreou. The point is, however, that the tremendous growth of aggregate Greek debt during the last decade has not been driven by public debt. On the contrary, it has been the result of advancing domestic financialisation that has brought rising banking and household debt in its wake.

FIG. 15 Greek debt by sector of issuer (percent of total)

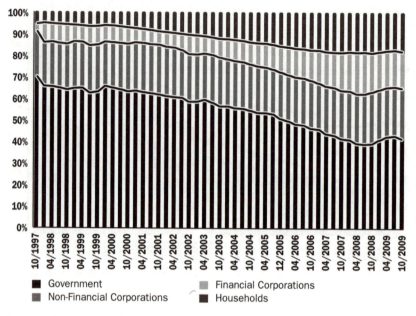

Government | Financial Corporations
Non-Financial Corporations | Households

Source: *Bank of Greece, QEDS, IMF, authors' calculation*

FIG. 16 Spanish debt by holder: Resident / non-resident (percent of total)

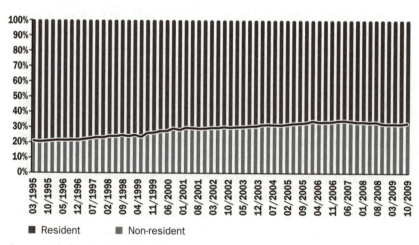

Resident | Non-resident

Source: *Bank of Spain, authors' calculation*

FIG. 17 Portuguese debt by holder: Resident / non-resident (percent of total)

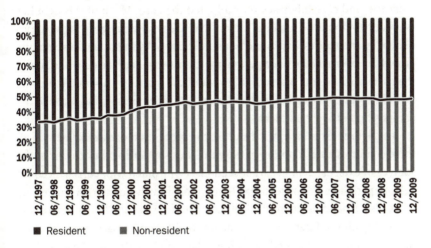

Source: *Bank of Portugal, authors' calculation*

FIG. 18 Greek debt by holder: Resident / non-resident (percent of total)

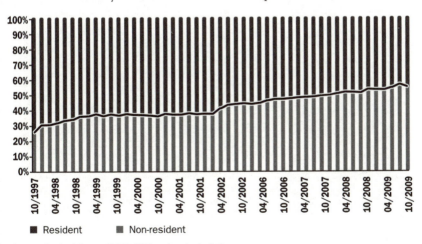

Source: *Bank of Greece, QEDS, IMF, authors' calculation*

To recap, peripheral economies have been driven by debt for more than a decade, and certainly since they adopted the euro. Much of this debt has been due to domestic financialisation that has resulted in growing volumes of debt by enterprises, banks and households. Equally important has been the growth of external debt once peripheral countries joined the euro and found themselves within the biased framework of the monetary union. Figures 16, 17 and 18 bring out clearly the change that EMU membership has made to the composition of aggregate debt.

The figures show an upward shift in the proportion of external debt in all three countries after adoption of the euro, thus supporting the analysis of the sources of external debt in earlier sections. Confronted with current account deficits, peripheral countries began to rely more heavily on external borrowing, while also expanding domestic debt. Low interest rates and falsely-improving credibility allowed peripheral countries to obtain necessary funds without undue difficulties for several years. But in late 2009 the structural biases of the eurozone finally met the inefficiency of financial markets and the results were catastrophic for the periphery.

10. RESCUING THE BANKS ONCE AGAIN

Banks in the eye of the storm

The accumulation of debt by the countries of the periphery eventually led to a major sovereign debt crisis in late 2009, starting with Greek public debt. Escalating public deficits and manipulation of statistical data in Greece led to downgrades by ratings agencies, rising spreads and eventually loss of access to financial markets by the Greek state. The sovereign debt of Spain and Portugal also came under heavy pressure during the same period. But the real threat posed by the sovereign debt crisis has been to the banks of the core. In early 2010 there emerged the danger of a full-blown crisis for the banks of the core that held significant volumes of peripheral debt. It thus became clear that the sovereign debt crisis was a continuation of the great upheaval that began in 2007.

The subprime crisis that burst out in the USA in August 2007 turned into a gigantic banking crisis and then a global recession. Unprecedented state intervention in 2008–9 rescued the banks in the USA and Europe, ameliorated the worst of the recession, and shifted much of the cost of the crisis onto the public. But the recession placed state finances under strain across mature capitalist countries, and nowhere more than in the periphery of the eurozone. As deficits escalated, the burden of accumulated debt became increasingly severe, above all, in Greece. The resulting sovereign debt crisis once again put the banks under enormous strain, particularly in Europe. The crisis had come full circle – starting with banks in 2007 and threatening to return to banks in 2010.

The vulnerable position of European banks was directly related to the accumulation of debt – both public and private – by peripheral countries. The chief providers of credit to the periphery were the banks of the core, which had taken advantage of the single currency and the associated removal of capital controls. Core banks exploited the new markets, generating revenues by lending to corporations and governments as well as to households for housing and consumption. The exposure of core banks to the periphery consequently rose throughout this period, as is shown in figures 19, 20, and 21.

It is notable that lending by core banks to the periphery kept rising even after the crisis of 2007 had begun in earnest. Indeed, the stock of outstanding bank debt peaked in the summer of 2008, a year after the start of the crisis.

FIG. 19 Eurocore bank exposure to Spain ($ bn)

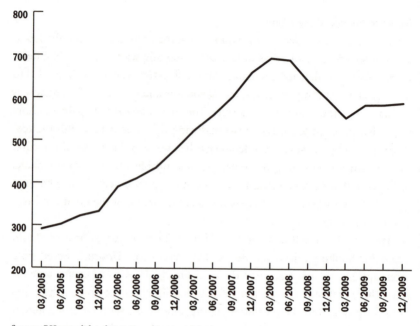

Source: *BIS consolidated statistics, ultimate risk basis*

Furthermore, lending remained at high levels throughout the rest of 2008 and 2009, despite the collapse of Lehman Brothers and the ensuing global turmoil. The reason for the perseverance of lending to the periphery by core banks even under conditions of crisis has to do with the policies of the European Central Bank (ECB).

As the crisis unfolded in 2007, interest rate spreads began to widen for peripheral countries. This development allowed banks in core countries to make attractive profits for a period. Profit making by banks was facilitated by the reaction of the ECB to events in financial markets. To be more specific, European banks started to face a pressing need for liquidity as soon as the global crisis broke out in 2007. Moreover, several European banks – above all in Germany – had made poor loans during the housing bubble in the USA and elsewhere. Consequently, in 2007–9, there was a significant danger of a banking crisis, which led the ECB to intervene by providing large volumes of liquidity to banks

FIG. 20 Eurocore bank exposure to Portugal ($ bn)

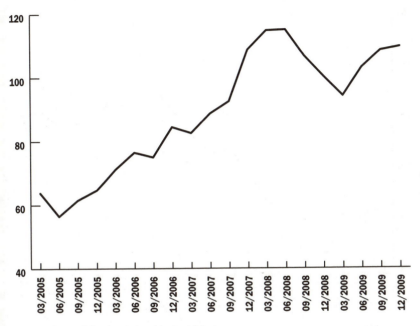

Source: *BIS consolidated statistics, ultimate risk basis*

(denominated in euro). At the same time, the Federal Reserve provided bilateral foreign exchange swap lines thus also expanding the supply of liquidity to banks (denominated in dollars). Eurozone banks used the liquidity provided by the ECB and the Federal Reserve in order to increase their lending to peripheral countries, thus taking advantage of the rising returns.

Much of the fresh business for banks was provided by public debt. In 2008–9, states across the developed world arrived in financial markets seeking extraordinary volumes of fresh funds, perhaps close to a trillion euro.[36] The pressing need for public borrowing had been created by declining tax revenue due to the recession as well as by the attempt to rescue the financial system and to avoid a depression. The result was to drive up yields for most types of

---

36 As was shown in chapter 6.

FIG. 21 Eurocore bank exposure to Greece ($ bn)

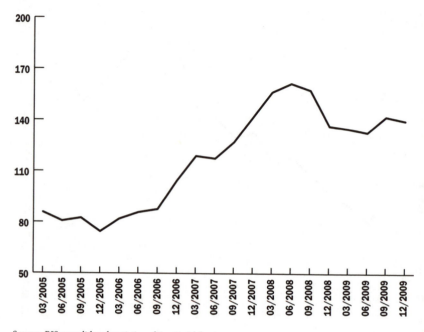

Source: *BIS consolidated statistics, ultimate risk basis*

public debt. With cheap and abundant funding from the ECB, European banks were able to take advantage of this opportunity. The euro became the new funding currency in a peculiar "carry trade", whereby banks obtained funds at low rates from the central bank to lend at much higher rates to states. During that time, banks showed no real concern about exposure to sovereign debt in peripheral countries. The assumption was that default within the eurozone was impossible.

Unfortunately, good things do not last forever, even with the ECB doing its best. The escalating Greek budget deficit in late 2009 and the downgrading of Greek public debt brought an end to easy profit-making for core banks. They were forced to re-examine their balance sheets, particularly the value of their loans to peripheral countries as well as the sources of their funding. It then became clear that core eurozone banks faced an incipient crisis that directly threatened their survival.

Detailed information on the exposure of core banks to the periphery is not available. However, the Bank for International Settlements (BIS) estimated that eurozone banks, as of December 2009, had exposure of $727 bn to Spain, $244 bn to Portugal, $206 bn to Greece, and $402 bn to Ireland.[37] The sum total of exposure to the four countries came to $1579 bn, of which $254 bn, or approximately 16 percent, was government debt. The bulk (both private and public) was held by French and German banks. With regard to public debt, the BIS estimated that French and German banks held, respectively, $48 bn and $33 bn of Spanish debt, $31 bn and $23 bn of Greek debt, and $21 bn and $10 bn of Portuguese debt. These figures are consistent with the calculations of debt in chapter 9. Total exposure of core banks to the public sector was, of course, dwarfed by exposure to the private sector, particularly in Spain.

Predictably enough, when the threat to the solvency of core banks became clear in the spring of 2010, European governments and the ECB intervened once again. Two support packages were put in place in May 2010, a relatively modest one for Greece and a far larger one for the eurozone in general. The ostensible purpose of the packages was to deal with the sovereign debt crisis by allowing peripheral countries to continue financing their public debt. In reality the aim was to protect the banks of the core from the banking crisis that had just reared its head.

Funding pressures on European banks

Financial markets in the eurozone signalled the gradual rekindling of the banking crisis in late 2009. As the Greek sovereign debt crisis gathered momentum, threatening contagion across the periphery, Credit Default Swaps (CDS) on government bonds began to rise rapidly, reaching levels unprecedented since the introduction of the common currency (fig. 22). As sovereign default suddenly became plausible, banks became wary of each other's exposure to the debt of peripheral states, thus raising bank CDS.

Banks were also concerned that the fall in the price of sovereign bonds would affect the value of the parts of their balance sheets that were marked-to-market. Consequently, lending among banks became tighter in the money markets. Fig-

---

37 BIS (2010) 'International banking and financial market developments', *BIS Quarterly Review* 18:9, June.

FIG. 22 Sovereign CDS spreads: 5 years (basis points)

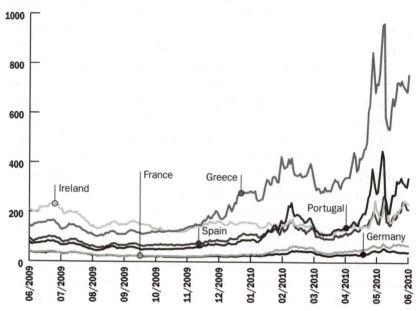

Source: *Bloomberg*

ure 23 shows the rising costs for banks in the interbank markets in terms of LIBOR-OIS and EURIBOR-EONIA spreads.[38] In the spring of 2010 both spreads widened, indicating that borrowing both dollars and euro in the interbank market had become more expensive. Borrowing dollars, in particular, was much more expensive than borrowing euro. A banking crisis was in the offing.

Borrowing costs rose sharply because European banks were exposed to peripheral debt but also because they faced complex funding problems. A specific funding gap arose due to banks taking positions in dollar-denominated

---

38 LIBOR (or EURIBOR in the eurozone) is a rate of interest closely linked to the interbank money market for maturities between 1 month and 1 year. OIS (or EONIA in the eurozone) relates to the rate of interest for overnight cash. Under normal conditions the spreads would be negligible, but in a crisis they begin to widen, acting as a gauge for the shortage of liquidity in money markets.

FIG. 23 Credit spreads: 3 month US LIB-OIS & EUR-EON (basis points)

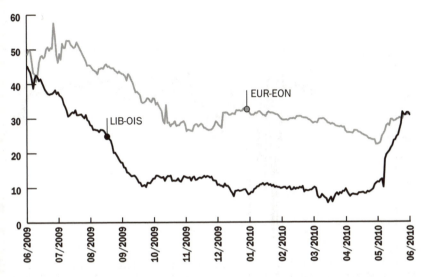

Source: *Datastream*

assets funded through borrowing in euro. The borrowed funds in euro were then swapped for dollars by using short-term foreign exchange swaps.

The funding gap had declined significantly since September 2008, but still amounted to, perhaps, $500 billion in mid-2010. European banks were able to fund the gap cheaply by borrowing euro from the ECB, which were then swapped for dollars through short-term foreign exchange swaps. But as the euro weakened in 2009–10, the banks were forced to borrow more euro in order to match the dollar gap. By the same token, the banks were forced to rely increasingly on the foreign exchange swap market. The resulting higher dollar funding costs, or "US dollar premium", are shown in figure 24 in the form of increasingly negative cross-currency basis swaps that prevailed since late 2009.[39]

---

39 The dollar premium is the cost of borrowing at floating rates in dollars compared to other currencies. This is reflected in cross-currency basis swaps which are, in effect, a string of 3 months FX forwards for a longer duration expressed in basis point differentials.

FIG. 24 Cross-country basis swap: euro/US$ (basis points)

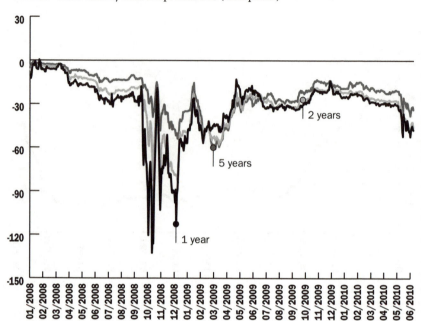

Source: *Bloomberg*

Funding pressures also rose as bank deposits became more expensive after the collapse of Lehman Brothers, as is shown in figure 25 below. Specifically, the spread between 3 month EURIBOR and the rate that banks paid for new deposits actually became negative in the second half of 2009. Furthermore, banks faced difficulties in issuing bonds because conditions in the financial markets remained tense, particularly in view of substantial volumes of banking debt due to be rolled over by 2012.

Increasing funding problems and rising credit risk from peripheral sovereign debt inevitably led to a sharp rise to CDS spreads for European banks compared to other sectors, as is shown in figure 26. European banks were in deepening trouble.

The budding crisis among European banks could hardly leave the US banking system unaffected. Figure 27 shows that US banks were heavily exposed to the European banking system, their exposure roughly doubling

FIG. 25 Bank funding: 3-month Euribor – average rate for new deposits (basis points)

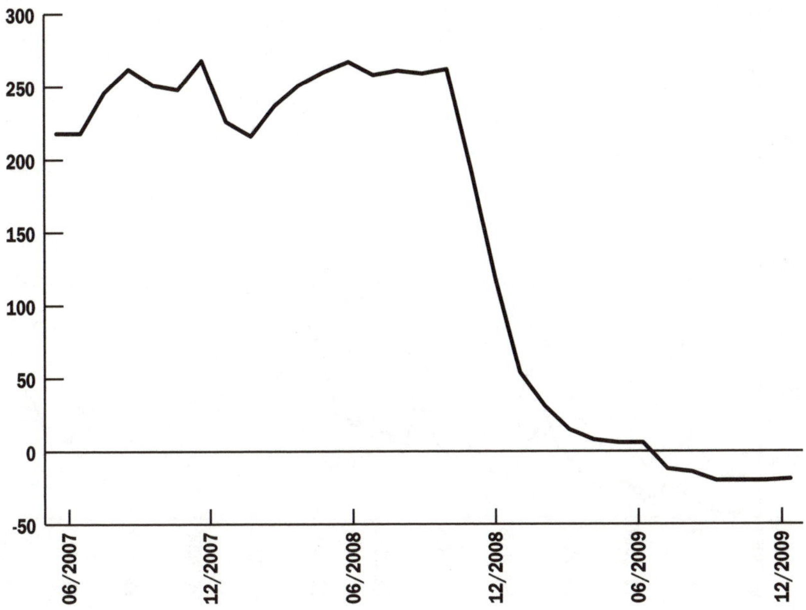

Source: *IMF FSR*, April 2010, Fig. 1.18

during the last five years. If a full-blown banking crisis materialised in Europe, there would be ripple effects across the US banking system, and indeed across global finance. The threat of a global banking crisis had become real during the early part of 2010.

The European support package and its aims

On 2 May 2010, after much procrastination and internal wrangling, the European Union announced a support package for Greece of 110 bn euro, jointly put together with the International Monetary Fund. The Greek intervention acted as pilot for a far larger package, announced on 9–10 May, of roughly 750 bn euro. The second package was aimed at European financial markets in general, and was put together by the EU, the IMF, the ECB and other major central banks. The underlying approach of the two packages was the same.

FIG. 26 Eurozone 5-year CDS spreads by sector (basis points)

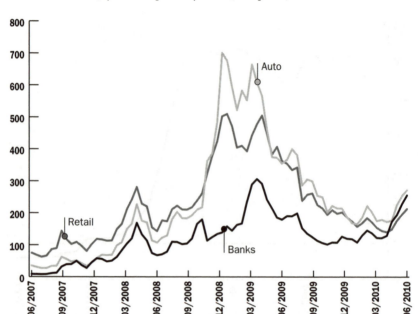

Source: *Datastream*

Although the rhetoric of European leaders was about saving the European Monetary Union by rescuing peripheral countries, the underlying aim was to deal with the parlous state of the banks of the core. The intervention was less concerned with the unfolding disaster in Athens and more worried about European (mainly German and French) banks facing a wave of losses and further funding difficulties. A weaker euro would also become less acceptable as international reserve currency, thus harming the potential for expansion of European financial capital. Not to mention that it would further worsen the funding problems that European banks faced on their balance sheets.

The EU contributed to the package by establishing the European Stabilisation Mechanism. This resulted in a new lending facility of 60 bn euro available to all EU member states. The facility was financed through the issuing of European Commission debt and could be advanced without the approval of national parliaments. Clearly, the sum was small, reflecting the limited

FIG. 27 EU–US and US–EU banking exposure ($ trillion)

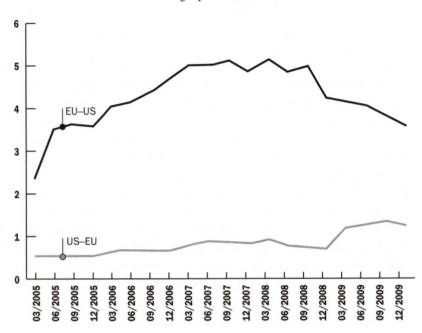

Source: *BIS IBS – Consolidated foreign claims of reporting banks – ultimate risk basis*

resources directly at the disposal of the EU. Potentially much more significant was the establishment of the European Financial Stabilisation Facility (EFSF). This would have up to 440 bn euro, and be available only to eurozone members.

The mode of operation of the EFSF was not made clear for a long time, but it appeared that it would be, in effect, a Special Purpose Vehicle (SPV) funded through the issuing of bonds guaranteed by eurozone members on a pro rata basis.[40] The guarantees had to be approved by national parliaments, and would come into force only after approval by countries representing at least 90 percent of the shares of the EFSF. Thus, the EU demonstrated a strong preference for market-based solutions to its financial problems, even to the

---

40 The functioning of the EFSF is discussed in fuller detail in Part 3 of this book.

extent of creating an institutional vehicle similar to those that had caused the gigantic crisis of 2007–9. The EFSF further rested on dominance by the core countries. In short, the package has shown a profound lack of solidarity among the members of the eurozone.

The IMF also announced that it would cooperate with the EU by making available the equivalent of 250 bn euro of its own financial assistance to supplement the European Stabilisation Mechanism. The price of its assistance would, of course, be economic and fiscal adjustment programmes. In short, austerity would be imposed on member states in trouble, as happened immediately in Greece. The nature and possible implications of the shift toward austerity are examined in chapter 11. Suffice it to state here that the intervention of the IMF in eurozone affairs bespeaks of reliance on US power to support the common currency. The euro has already lost credibility in its attempt to become world money.

More relevant for our purposes in this section, and vitally important for the stabilisation of financial markets, were the remaining parts of the package. Above all, the ECB announced that it would start purchasing public securities of eurozone countries in the secondary markets. This was a remarkable step, contravening the ECB's founding principles. Thus, the ECB suspended the application of the minimum credit rating threshold in collateral eligibility requirements, starting with marketable debt instruments issued or guaranteed by the Greek government. Moreover, it began to conduct interventions in secondary markets that were sterilised by altering time deposits. To tackle the funding problems of banks, the ECB adopted a procedure of fixed rate tenders with full allotment in its regular 3-month longer-term refinancing operations; it also increased liquidity provision through long-term repo operations. Finally, the ECB resumed dollar liquidity-providing operations.

It is apparent that these extraordinary actions by the ECB were aimed at gaining time for banks. By purchasing European public debt in the secondary markets (even if sterilised) the ECB acted as market maker of last resort, despite not being allowed to buy public bonds directly in the primary markets. A clear signal was given to banks that they could continue to dispose of poor quality peripheral public debt. However, the ECB was allowed to buy such bonds only from the banks themselves. The chief aim of the exercise was to help banks strengthen their balance sheets, rather than to support struggling peripheral states.

Finally, the rescue package involved the Federal Reserve, which reinstated temporary dollar swap lines with the ECB and a range of other major central banks, authorised until January 2011. The US has emerged as ultimate guarantor of the euro, particularly as no limits were placed on the swap lines. In doing so, the US authorities were trying to protect US banks, while avoiding the re-emergence of a global banking crisis. As was shown above, the exposure of US banks to eurozone banks had risen steadily during the last few years. Generalised crisis in the European banking sector could have important consequences for US banks, thus forcing the Federal Reserve to take action in support of European banks. Once again, the euro was shown to pose an ineffectual challenge to the dollar as world money.

The chances of success of the rescue package

The rescue package did not immediately reassure financial markets. It was thus followed by some desperate reactions on the part of European governments, none more so than the intervention by BaFin, the German financial regulator. In March 2010 BaFin had argued against the notion that the root of the crisis lay in speculative transactions in the market for Greek CDS. But under pressure from the German government, BaFin reversed its position and banned short-selling of key German financial stocks, European bonds and CDS. The action appeared hostile to financial markets and coincided with a broader discussion on adopting tougher European regulation of hedge funds. In practice, the clumsy intervention by BaFin aimed at protecting German banks, which had been at the receiving end of some CDS speculation.

Nonetheless, even by July 2010, the package had not fully restored confidence in the health of the European banking sector. During the same month the results of stress tests on 91 European banks were announced, indicating that only seven did not have adequate capital (at least 6 percent Tier 1 capital).[41] The tests had been undertaken over a period of months and were designed to restore confidence in the banking sector. Remarkably, the tests assumed that there was no possibility of default on sovereign debt, even by Greece. Confi-

---

41 See Committee of European Banking Supervisors (2010), 'Aggregate outcome of the 2010 EU wide stress test exercise coordinated by CEBS in cooperation with the ECB'. http://stress-test.c-ebs.org/documents/Summaryreport.pdf

dence appeared to improve, but financial markets remained sceptical. They had good reason for scepticism, in view of the haphazard nature of the rescue package and the deep-seated nature of the problem.

The bulk of the funding (440 bn euro) comprised guarantees backing the issuance of debt by EFSF, subject to approval by national parliaments. There remained some lack of clarity, therefore, on how the package would be financed, and by which governments. In addition, intervention in the secondary market by the ECB could affect securities prices in the short-term, but judgement of long-term prices was left to markets. Moreover, the more that the ECB intervened in the public debt market, the greater the volume of potentially 'toxic' sovereign bonds that it would be likely to acquire. Who would carry the ultimate risk of these bonds? Finally, few European banks appeared to take advantage of the currency swap lines immediately after the introduction of the package.[42] This was, perhaps, due to the lines being very expensive as they were set at 100 basis points over the overnight indexed swap rate. The maturity of the lines (between 7 and 84 days) was also quite short for the needs of banks.

In short, there were several reasons for concern arising from the technical features of the rescue package. But the deeper causes of concern had to do with its impact on the European economies, both core and periphery. The package had come at the price of austerity, the implications of which were unclear. To rescue banks, Europe had found itself in the grip of contractionary government policies, which run the risk of exacerbating recession. The next chapter considers in detail the costs and risks posed by austerity across Europe.

---

42 As is evidenced by the balance sheet of the ECB between the middle of May and June, see http://www.ecb.int/press/pr/wfs/2010/html/index.en.html

11. SOCIETY PAYS THE PRICE: AUSTERITY AND FURTHER LIBERALISATION

The counterpart to the rescue package has been the imposition of austerity on the periphery, and increasingly on the core. Confronted with a shaken monetary union, renewed banking crisis, and continuing recession, several governments of the eurozone have opted for contraction of public expenditure. In effect, the costs of rescuing the euro and the banks have been shifted onto society at large. At the same time, and partly at the behest of the IMF, liberalisation measures have been imposed on peripheral countries, above all, in the labour market. The ostensible aim has been to strengthen growth potential.[43]

The response of the eurozone has been consistent with entrenched neoliberalism within the EU. The overriding concern of policy has been to rescue the financial system. The practices and the institutional framework of the eurozone were accordingly altered. Thus, contrary to all previous assertions, a bailout of member states was organised, first for Greece but also potentially extending to others. Along similar lines, the statutes of the ECB were ignored, allowing it to buy public debt from banks. There was even talk of establishing a European Monetary Fund. Yet, at the same time, fiscal conservatism re-emerged triumphant. It was even proposed that the Stability and Growth Pact should be hardened by introducing severe penalties for countries that contravened its strictures.[44] In short, the eurozone has certainly shown a capacity to change. But it has all been change in the same conservative and neoliberal direction, favouring capital over labour.

The mix of austerity and liberalisation within the eurozone has been harsh on working people but also dangerous for economy and society. In the midst of a severe recession, policy-makers appeared to believe that European economies needed a good dose of cleansing medicine plus more flexibility to ensure growth. This was a return to the hoariest economic ideas of pre-Keynesian vintage. It is shown in this chapter that the policy shift within the eurozone posed major economic risks, and could have disastrous implications across the continent.

---

43 In other words, eurozone governments opted for austerity out of the three options described in Part 1. This was hardly a surprise.

44 A change that was eventually instigated in early 2012.

FIG. 28 GDP growth by aggregate demand category – Germany (percent)

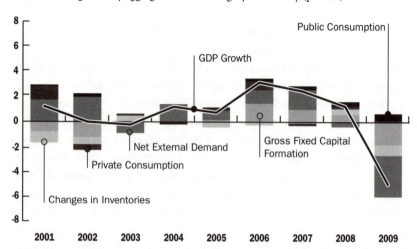

Source for figures 28 to 33: *Ameco*

The spread of austerity and its likely impact

The global recession of 2008–9 emerged in Europe mainly in the form of collapsing aggregate demand. Figures 28, 29, 30, 31, 32, and 33 trace the evolution of the components of aggregate demand in three major eurozone economies (Germany, France, Italy) as well as in three peripheral economies at the epicentre of the public debt crisis (Spain, Portugal, Greece).[45]

Differences in the pattern and composition of growth during the last decade are immediately apparent. Thus, Germany, Italy, France and Portugal showed poor growth throughout the 2000s, while Greece and Spain performed much better, fuelled by credit, as was shown in chapter 9. The main source of growth for Germany was net external demand, reflecting its rising competitiveness within the eurozone. Private consumption played an important role in France, Portugal, and Spain, but above all in Greece. Private investment was signifi-

---

45 It is never an easy task to place Italy within the eurozone accurately. In this context it is located within the core for obvious reasons of population size and relative economic weight. Details on the construction of these figures are given in Appendix 2C.

FIG. 29 GDP growth by aggregate demand category – France (percent)

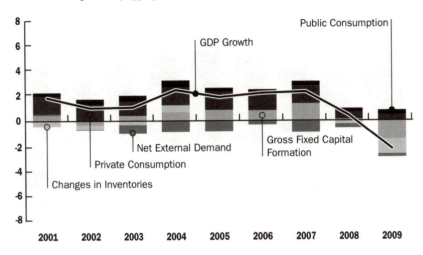

FIG. 30 GDP growth by aggregate demand category – Italy (percent)

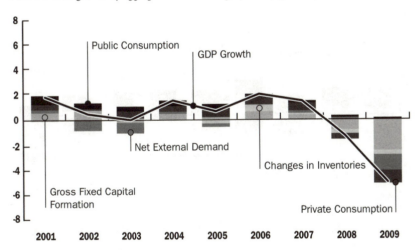

cant in Spain, partly reflecting the real estate bubble, but it was generally weak across the sample. Italy was the picture of stagnation in all respects.

More relevant for our purposes is that growth rates turned downward in 2008 as the crisis began to bite, and became strongly negative in 2009 as

FIG. 31 GDP growth by aggregate demand category – Spain (percent)

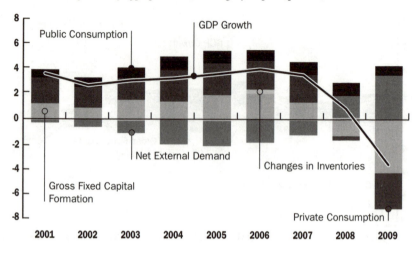

FIG. 32 GDP growth by aggregate demand category – Portugal (percent)

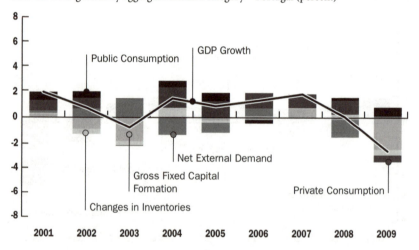

recession materialised. The main cause of negative economic growth in 2009 was the general collapse of private investment, as is typical of capitalist crises, but also the collapse of exports in Germany. In an environment of radical uncertainty and tightening credit, the private sector postponed or cancelled

FIG. 33 GDP growth by aggregate demand category – Greece (percent)

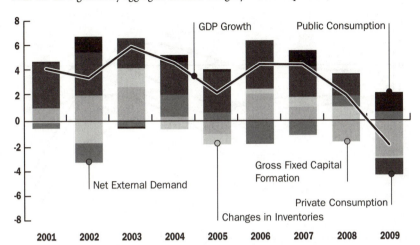

investment projects. Private consumption remained broadly stable, partly due to remaining labour protection in Europe. Complete collapse of aggregate demand was prevented through rising public expenditure, which reflected the role and weight of the state in the economy.[46]

The impact of the recession on public finances was inevitable and predictable. As tax revenues fell, the attempt by the state to prevent depression led to record-breaking public deficits in most eurozone countries, easily exceeding the limit of 3 percent of GDP imposed by the Stability Pact. Even France, Italy and Germany exceeded the limit (deficits for 2010 projected at, respectively, 8 percent, 5.3 percent, and 5 percent). In Spain, Portugal and Greece, where the problems of integration into the eurozone became sharply apparent, public deficits reached very high levels, as is shown in figure 34.

This is the context in which austerity was imposed across the eurozone. Pressed by financial markets, which were in turmoil at the prospect of peripheral default, even the biggest economies of the eurozone adopted austerity programmes with the aim of complying with the 3 percent limit

---

46 Positive net external demand in Spain, Portugal and Greece reflects collapsing imports as recession took hold, not rising exports.

FIG. 34 Fiscal balance (percent of GDP)

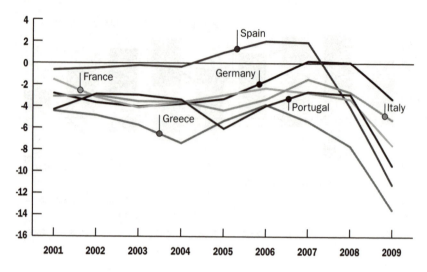

Source: *Ameco*

for the deficit within three years. Germany announced a plan to cut public spending by 80 bn euro, lowering civil servant wages, reducing the number of civil servants, reforming social security, cutting military expenditure and reducing public subsidies. France followed the same path, while remaining critical of Germany. The French government declared its intention to inscribe the limit to budget deficits in the constitution (following Germany in this respect). Public savings of up to 100 bn euro were to be made until 2013 through freezing central government spending, removing tax breaks, and considering a pay freeze for public sector workers. Even Italy, where the economy has shown no dynamism at all for more than a decade, announced an austerity programme of 24 bn euro aimed at bringing its relatively small fiscal deficit down to 3 percent by 2012.

The implications of austerity were likely to be severe since the policy put pressure on the only component of aggregate demand that showed resilience in 2009, namely public expenditure. Further pressure was also put on private consumption, which was already in trouble. The prospect of the private sector taking up the mantle of sustaining demand was not at all persuasive. Investment has been weak throughout the 2000s, while collapsing in 2009. There remained considerable uncertainty within the productive sector, while access to credit had hardly improved for private enterprises, given the parlous state of the financial sector. Meanwhile, with the global economy likely to perform indifferently in 2010–11, and given the high regional integration of European economies, it was unlikely that exports would prove the engine of growth for Europe as a whole. The policy of austerity ran the risk of resulting in major recession.

To recap, the eurozone, spurred by turmoil in the financial sector, opted for a violent adjustment of economic activity. There was a resurgence of neoliberal conservatism, even though recovery from the turmoil of 2007–9 has barely taken shape. Faced with falling aggregate demand, eurozone governments decided to cut public expenditure and to apply pressure on wages. The resulting economic purge would presumably result in overall efficiency gains, leading to robust economic growth through healthy private activity. A preKeynesian approach to economic policy appeared to take hold, as if the Great Depression of the 1930s had never taken place. Grave risks emerged for European economy and society.

The periphery takes the brunt of austerity policy

Peripheral governments in Greece, Spain, and Portugal led the way in adopting austerity policy with the aim of bringing public deficits within the 3 percent limit of the Stability and Growth Pact by 2013. Greece imposed austerity already in early 2010 of its own accord, but adopted far harsher measures once its support package had been agreed with the EU and the IMF in early May 2010. With the second and far broader package agreed across the eurozone, austerity measures spread to the rest of the periphery, and indeed to the core.

The measures adopted by peripheral countries have varied widely in scale, reflecting differences in fiscal and economic outlook. They have been at their harshest in Greece, as codified in the Memorandum signed by the Greek government, the EU and the IMF.[47] The Memorandum has been passed by the Greek parliament and thus has the force of law. It is notable that, in addition

---

47 See: http://www.mnec.gr/export/sites/mnec/en/press_office/DeltiaTypou/Documents/2010_05_04_GreecexLOI.pdf

to specific measures described below, the Memorandum also contains explicit clauses requiring the government to do whatever else might be necessary to attain fiscal balance. Open field has been effectively declared on Greek economy and society in order to reduce the fiscal deficit. Greece has been obliged to undertake violent cuts in public spending and raise taxes. At the same time it has been forced to introduce new legislation in labour markets and to engage in ambitious privatisation.

Spain has withdrawn the extraordinary measures that it had put in place after 2007 to ameliorate the impact of the financial crisis and the recession. Further austerity measures were announced in May aiming to reduce public sector expenditure by cutting wages, pensions, and transfers to local authorities. Nonetheless, Spanish measures were milder than those introduced in Greece. On the other hand, Portugal appeared to have positioned itself in between the other two countries. Public spending cuts were announced affecting wages and pensions but also social spending. Tax rates were generally raised, while new taxes were introduced. As for Greece, a programme of further privatisation of public enterprises was put in place.

The austerity measures in all three countries were heavily directed against labour, as is shown in Box 2. The aim of wage cuts and freezes, reductions in social spending, contraction of employment, and harsher pension terms was not simply to reduce public expenditure but also to lower the cost of labour in the public sector. If labour costs were lowered in the public sector, the effect would be likely to spread across the rest of the economy. The aim of lowering labour costs in general has been quite explicit in Greece, but was also present in other peripheral and even core countries.

The austerity drive would thus place workers in a weaker position in the labour market, allowing capital to benefit. The pressure on labour was also apparent in the regressive character of the tax increases incorporated in the austerity programmes, which relied on raising VAT and income tax, rather than corporate tax. Finally, the privatisation programmes in Greece and Portugal would probably lead to a retreat of public provision, while worsening the conditions of labour in the newly privatised enterprises.

In short, the shift toward austerity was partly intended to cut fiscal deficits, and partly to compress labour costs. Working people would bear the burden of adjustment, while capital would benefit. Furthermore, austerity would set in motion a formidably regressive redistribution of income. The impact would be at its sharpest in Portugal and Greece, the poorest and most unequal countries of the eurozone.[48]

Mission impossible?

Austerity policy would compress demand, while cutting wages and paving the way for the introduction of a radical liberalisation programme. The role of the state in the economy would be redefined, also promoting a more regressive distribution of income that would appease the ruling social layers in eurozone countries. But austerity policy represents a huge gamble for eurozone governments, particularly for those in the periphery. For the policy rests on the hope that exports and private expenditure would pick up, thus avoiding deep recession. Things could turn out to be very different. Allowing bond markets to dictate a neoliberal shift of policy across the eurozone carries major risks for the economy as a whole. Given the weak state of private consumption and investment in 2010, contraction of public expenditure is fraught with danger.[49]

It is worth pursuing the argument further by deploying Parenteau's recent analysis of Sector Financial Balances.[50] Its point of departure is the identity that was also used in Box 1:

Domestic Private Sector Financial Balance + Fiscal Balance
+ Foreign Financial Balance = 0

Parenteau's use of the framework allows for penetrating conclusions. Namely, if the foreign financial balance does not change radically, then changes in the fiscal balance must be matched by an equal and opposite adjustment of the private sector's financial balance. Given that current accounts are unlikely to shift dramatically in Europe in the foreseeable future, it follows that the

---

48 The validity of this broad assessment was broadly confirmed in the year that followed the time of writing (September 2010).

49 Greece has indeed entered a full-scale depression in the year that followed this analysis. Some of the disastrous implications of Greek austerity are considered in Part 3.

50 See Parenteau, Robert (2010). 'On Fiscal Correctness and Animal Sacrifices (Leading PIIGS to Slaughter)'. http://www.nakedcapitalism.com/2010/03/parenteau-on-fiscal-correctness-and-animal-sacrifices-leading-the-piigs-to-slaughter-part-1.html

BOX 2 AUSTERITY MEASURES IN 2010, OR SHIFTING THE BURDEN ONTO LABOUR

i) Wages, social spending, and conditions of labour
In Greece there would be a reduction of public sector wages by, perhaps, 20-30 percent. There would be a cut of nominal wages that could be as high as 20 percent, while the so-called 13th and 14th salaries would be replaced by an annual lump sum the size of which varies with the wage. Wages and salaries are to be frozen for the next three years. Employment in the public sector is to be reduced on the basis of one-for-five, that is, one worker hired for every five workers who retire. Unemployment benefits have been cut, while a poverty support scheme that had been put in place in December 2009 has been suspended. It is more than likely that the pressure on the income of labour would also spread to the private sector.

In Portugal public sector wages were frozen for 2010, and are expected to remain frozen for the next two years. Public sector employment will be cut on the basis of one-for-two. Social spending was capped through limiting transfer payments, and unemployment benefits were reduced. The freezing of public sector wages was expected to act as a benchmark for private sector wages. In Spain the first austerity package introduced a wage freeze for the public sector, while halting new employment in the public sector. The second austerity package introduced a cut of 5 percent in public sector wages. Social spending has also been cut, for instance, by withdrawing the subsidy for newborn babies that had been put in place in 2007.

Equally important were plans to abolish collective bargaining in Greece, replacing it with individual contracts. The existing practice of internships for very low paid or even unpaid workers has been given the force of law. The provision of temporary labour via specialist agents has also been established by law, and it has been made possible to supply temporary workers to the public sector. The so-called 'closed professions', i.e., mostly self-employed businesses or professionals operating under restrictive internal regulations, were due to be liberalised. Similarly, in Spain, labour market reforms have been approved aiming for greater flexibility in paid work hours, reducing negotiation time in labour disputes, and aiming to create an unemployment fund out of workers' own contributions.

ii) Tax

In Greece there were increases across a range of indirect taxes, including VAT from 19 percent to 23 percent and the imposition of Special Consumption Taxes on fuel, tobacco and alcohol. Income tax was also raised for the middling band of incomes. Corporate taxes, on the other hand, were reduced. Attempts have also been made to reduce tax evasion and to expand the tax base. In Portugal VAT was increased by 1 percent across all categories of goods and services. Income tax has also been raised, as has corporate tax. In Spain, similarly, VAT was increased by 2 percent across all categories of goods and services, while income tax has also been raised.

iii) Privatisation

A broad-ranging privatisation programme was proposed for Greece, including ports, airports, railways, finance, the water supply and energy as well as public land. A similarly ambitious privatisation programme has been introduced in Portugal, including energy, defence and naval construction, transport, finance, the postal service and mining.

iv) Pension systems

Greek pensions would be lowered substantially and then frozen, though it was difficult to estimate the losses, particularly as further decisions were to be taken in late 2010. The retirement age would be raised significantly, ranging from three to seventeen years, and the worst affected workers would be women. It would be necessary to complete forty years in employment before claiming a pension. In Portugal the convergence period for public and private sector pensions was shortened. Spanish pensions would be practically frozen.

FIG. 35 Nominal unit labour costs (2000=100)

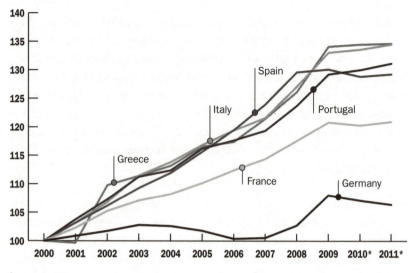

Source: *Ameco*

effort to reduce public deficits must be matched by increased private spending. Hence, the private sector must totally reverse its recent behaviour that was summed up in pages 114–119. But how likely would it be for private investment and consumption to rise significantly, given wage cuts and freezes, rising unemployment, and considerable uncertainty? And that is without even mentioning the weak state of European banks, which has resulted in expensive and tight credit for enterprises. Austerity was much more likely to lead to contraction of GDP, rising unemployment and wage deflation.

Even worse, the austerity strategy suffered from a deep flaw that boded ill for its future. The opposition between core and periphery within the eurozone and the resulting debt problems of peripheral countries ultimately derive from the loss of competitiveness by the periphery, as was shown in Part 1. The core has enjoyed sustained competitive gains due to wage repression, particularly in Germany. The adoption of austerity across the eurozone, including by the core and especially Germany, was likely to entrench the divergence in competitiveness for the foreseeable future. Austerity represents an attempt by peripheral countries to improve competitiveness through repressing wages, but similar, if milder, policies have also been applied by the core. The handicap of the periphery was unlikely to go away.

Support for this argument was given by the forecast of nominal unit labour costs for 2010 and 2011 by the European Commission, shown in figure 35. Even if peripheral economies succeeded in freezing nominal costs, which would imply a fall in real income for workers, the projection was for Germany to decrease its own nominal labour costs. On this basis, Germany was set once again to win the race to the bottom that EMU has brought in its trail. The result would be further current account deficits for the periphery and surpluses for Germany. Far from solving the underlying problem, austerity was likely to make it even more intractable, despite imposing huge costs on working people.

The prospects for peripheral countries of the eurozone were grim in late 2010. Given the spread of austerity policies, the public and private debts that were accumulated during the last decade were unlikely to be significantly reduced. It was even possible that peripheral countries could enter a deflationary spiral in which the contraction of GDP as well as of prices and wages would lead to a rise of debt relative to income. This would in turn exacerbate the difficulties of both public and private sector in servicing debt. The eurozone threatened to engulf peripheral countries in long-term recession that would lead to an even sharper contrast between core and periphery.

12. THE SPECTRE OF DEFAULT IN EUROPE

Default, debt renegotiation and exit

Part 1 of this book identified three strategic options for peripheral countries confronted with the eurozone crisis. Namely, first, austerity imposed by the core and transferring the costs of adjustment onto society at large, second, broad structural reform of the eurozone in favour of labour and, third, exit from the eurozone accompanied by default that would shift the social balance in favour of labour. Not surprisingly, the preferred policy of eurozone governments – at the behest of the IMF – has been austerity. There has also been some reform, all of which has been in a neoliberal direction, as was discussed in chapters 10 and 11.

This course of action is consistent with the nature of the eurozone and the entrenched neoliberal ideology at its core. And nor is it surprising that the second option has found little favour, either in official discussions or in policy-making. The nature of the crisis has required immediate measures leaving little room for long-term reforming initiatives, quite apart from the inherent difficulty of reforming the eurozone in favour of labour. Indeed, the eurozone has become even more conservative during this period.

Nevertheless, as the policy of austerity has spread, the idea of default on public debt has also made significant headway. Austerity is a highly fraught path for the economies of both periphery and core, as was shown in chapter 11, and it might even worsen the problem of indebtedness. In the global financial markets it was widely expected in 2010 that Greece, at least, would face default in the future. Voices were heard within the mainstream already in 2010 claiming that austerity might be a dead-end, particularly for Greece, and thus favouring controlled restructuring of public debt.[51] At the radical end of the political spectrum in Greece and elsewhere there have also been calls for default. It is probable that even governments have considered the possibility, though in hermetically sealed rooms.

---

51 See Roubini, N. (2010), 'Greece's best option is an orderly default', *Financial Times*, 28 June; or Beattie, A., 'Why Greece should default, lecture delivered at the LSE, 14 July 2010'. Podcast available at: http://richmedia.lse.ac.uk/publicLecturesAnd Events/20100714_1830_whyGreeceShouldDefault.mp3

The concluding chapter of Part 2 tackles default and debt renegotiation in view of the preceding analysis. Since default inevitably raises the issue of eurozone membership, the possibility of exit by peripheral countries is also considered. The focus of discussion lies on the political economy of these options, all of which involve complex social changes and different sets of winners and losers, both domestically and internationally. It is not easy to ascertain what is in the interests of working people in the periphery, not to mention the core. The approach adopted here is that, if the path of default, renegotiation and exit was entered, it should lead to a change in the social balance in favour of labour. By the same token, it should break the grip of conservatism and neoliberalism on the eurozone as a whole.

Discussion below is conducted under the rubrics of creditor-led and debtor-led default. Distinguishing between the two is useful in order to ascertain the social interests involved in default, renegotiation and exit. Creditor-led default is likely to be a conservative policy path that would still impose the costs of adjustment onto working people, while leaving unchanged the underlying nature of the eurozone. Debtor-led default, in contrast, could bring significant benefits to peripheral countries, while creating room to shift the social balance in favour of labour. Debtor-led default would immediately pose the question of exit from the eurozone, thus inviting analysis of the implications for economy and society.

Default, renegotiation and exit are discussed below mostly as they would apply to a single peripheral country. It is natural to make this assumption, given that the pressures of crisis have been overwhelmingly heavier in Greece compared to other peripheral countries. Greece has been at the sharp end of the eurozone crisis, and is likely to remain in that position for the foreseeable future. But even for analytical purposes alone, it would still have been necessary to make the assumption that default, renegotiation and exit occurred in a single country. Only then could the balance of social forces, the levers of economic policy and the international economic context be taken as given with any degree of precision.

Needless to say, if these decisive events occurred in one peripheral country, there would be major repercussions on the rest of the eurozone. For one thing, what holds individually for Greece, also holds individually for Spain and Portugal (and probably for Ireland, though it has not been considered in Part 2). There are significant differences among the three, as was established above, but their predicament as peripheral countries of the eurozone is similar. If one was to adopt default, renegotiation, and exit, the demonstration effect on the others would be great. Each would naturally approach the issue from the perspective of its own social, political and institutional outlook, but the underlying economic compulsion would be similar. The tale might be told primarily for Greece, but Spain and Portugal would also recognise themselves.

It should finally be mentioned that default, renegotiation and exit could, at the limit, lead to fracturing, or even collapse, of the eurozone as a whole. It is impossible to analyse with any credibility the repercussions of such a cataclysmic event, other than to state that the costs for both periphery and core would be great. Yet, even this outcome would ultimately be the result of the nature of the eurozone – exploitative, unequal, and badly put together. The fault would not lie with peripheral countries but with the monetary union as a whole, which has placed the periphery in an impossible position. Working people in peripheral countries have no obligation to accept austerity for the indefinite future in order to rescue the eurozone. Moreover, if the eurozone collapsed under the weight of its own sins, the opportunity would arise to put relations among the people of Europe on a different basis. Solidarity and equality among European people are certainly possible, but they require grassroots initiatives. The eurozone in its present form is a barrier to this development.

Creditor-led default: Reinforcing the straitjacket of the eurozone

Austerity is a very risky strategy when dealing with public debt because it restricts economic activity, as was shown in chapter 11. Even official projections in 2010 expected the ratio of public debt to GDP to continue rising in all peripheral countries until 2012–3, reaching 149 percent in Greece. The dynamic of debt could become unsustainable, if there was a deeper than expected domestic recession, if social and political unrest occurred on a large scale, or if the European and the world economies took a turn for the worse. The pressures would be greatest in Greece because of the extent of austerity measures and the volume of public debt; but the danger would be present for all peripheral countries.[52]

If it became clear that austerity had begun to fail in Greece – and elsewhere – the prospect of creditor-led debt restructuring would raise its head.

---

52 As indeed occurred in 2011 in ways that are discussed in Part 3.

Creditor-led default would not necessarily involve a unilateral suspension of interest payments, and formal default might not be declared. Nonetheless, a controlled form of default could occur in practice, involving the exchange of old for new debt, perhaps along the lines of Argentina in the period immediately before its final default, discussed in Appendix 2A. This process would obviously take place under the aegis of banks and within the framework of the eurozone. It would mean, at best, a mild 'haircut' for lenders accompanied by a lengthening of maturities and possibly lower interest rates. The banks that organised such a restructuring could expect to earn substantial fees.[53]

Creditor-led default would be in the interests of lenders, particularly banks. It should be stressed that this includes domestic lenders, for instance, domestic banks that hold significant volumes of public debt. Lenders would benefit because the institutional mechanisms of the eurozone would be brought to bear on borrowing states with the aim of minimising lender losses. Banks would also benefit since they would continue to have access to ECB liquidity, in effect using the mechanisms of the ECB to facilitate the default. Above all, lender banks would benefit by accepting the already-known fact that some of the public debt on their books is bad, subsequently shifting it off the balance sheet on favourable terms. In that context, domestic banks would also attempt to swap old for new public debt on terms that transferred onto the state as much of the cost as possible.

Is it conceivable that creditor-controlled default could occur together with radical reform of the eurozone? Some in Greece and elsewhere continued to hope for an associational approach to the problem of debt whereby the countries of the core would offer genuine support to the countries of the periphery. Could there be eurozone action that decisively lightened the burden of debt on the borrowers within the framework of the eurozone, while also allowing for fiscal transfers from rich to poor, a larger European budget, wage protection, and so on?

The enormous difficulties of reforming the eurozone in a pro-labour direction have been made clear in the course of the current crisis. Default and debt renegotiation have pressing urgency, requiring counter-measures of equal urgency. The eurozone has introduced a rescue package at the cost

---

53 In broad terms this is exactly what transpired in late 2011 and early 2012.

of austerity, first in Greece but then across much of the rest of the union. Faced with turmoil, it has opted for more pressure on working people, greater fiscal rigidity and punitive terms imposed on indebted countries. At the same time, it has taken strong steps to rescue banks. These actions are consistent with the nature of the euro as world money serving primarily the interests of financial capital in Europe. The actions are also consistent with entrenched neoliberalism at the heart of the eurozone. This is not a system that would admit of pro-labour reform within the timescale of a debt crisis, if at all.

In sum, creditor-controlled restructuring of debt within the framework of the eurozone is a conservative approach that would be consistent with the current policy of austerity. For this reason, it is unlikely to prove a long-term solution for the crisis, and nor to bring significant benefits to working people in peripheral countries. The burden of debt would remain substantial and austerity policies would probably continue. The long-term outlook for Greece and other peripheral countries would remain poor.

Debtor-led default and the feasibility of exit from the eurozone

Debtor-led default is potentially a more radical option, though its outcomes would vary depending on how it took place.[54] If, for instance, austerity failed and creditor-led restructuring did not produce decisive results, the option of debtor-led default would emerge even for the current crop of peripheral governments. But the prospect of debtor-led default would then arise in the midst of social and economic chaos caused by failed austerity. Thus, the deeper danger of the current policies of the EU and the IMF is that they might lead to a repetition of the experience of Argentina, discussed in Appendix 2A. From this perspective, if peripheral countries were to adopt debtor-led default, they ought to do so on their own accord, decisively, in good time, and while setting in train profound social changes.

Debtor-led default would mean, in the first instance, unilateral suspension of payments. The latter would usher in a period of intensified domestic social struggle as well as major tensions in international relations. Thus, the country would have to decide which among its foreign obligations to hon-

---

54 The modalities and implications of debtor-led default are analysed in detail in Part 3.

our, and in what order. Even more complexly, domestic banks, institutional investors, and other holders of public debt would seek to protect their own interests.

From the perspective of working people, but also of society as a whole, it is imperative that there should be a public audit of debt following suspension of payments. Transparency is a vital demand in view of the cloak of secrecy that envelops government borrowing. Auditing the debt would allow society to know what is owed to whom as well as the terms on which debt contracts were struck. It would also show whether parts of the debt were 'odious' or illegal, allowing the debtor to refuse to honour such debts outright. The future direction of default and its ability to produce benefits for working people would depend on whether transparency prevailed regarding the stock of debt. This would be prime terrain of internal social struggle once default materialised.

Negotiations to settle the debt would follow at the initiative of the debtor, with a view to being concluded as rapidly as possible. The objective could only be to achieve a deep 'haircut' for lenders, thus lifting the crushing weight of debt on borrowing countries. It is impossible to ascertain the extent of the 'haircut' in advance and prior to auditing the debt but, for Greece, it is unlikely to be less than for Russia or Argentina, some details of which are given in Appendix 2A.

Two thirds of Greek public debt is held abroad, while the rest is held domestically.[55] The largest holders, both domestically and abroad, are banks. Note further that the great bulk of public bonds appear to have been issued under Greek law, thus possibly allowing the country to avoid extended legal wrangles in US and UK courts, as would have happened for other middle income countries.[56] Given that core banks are substantially exposed to Greece (and even more heavily to the periphery) as was shown in chapter 9, there are some advantages to Greece in renegotiating its public debt. A government that reflected popular will and acted decisively might be able to secure deep 'haircuts' in a fairly short order of time.

---

55 The composition of Greek public debt has changed in 2010–11 as a result of the rescue packages but the points made in the text remain valid.

56 See Buchheit L. and Gulati, G. Mitu, 2010, 'How to restructure Greek debt', http://papers.ssrn.com/sol3/papers.cfm?abstract_id=1603304there

But debtor-led default would also carry significant risks. The most immediate risk would be of becoming cut off from capital markets for a period. More complexly, default might lead to trade credit becoming scarce as international and domestic banks would be affected, thus hurting the debtor's exports. Even more seriously, default would run the risk of precipitating a banking crisis, since substantial volumes of public debt are held by both domestic and foreign banks.

International experience shows that the period of being cut off from capital markets does not last long, and there are always alternative sources of funding. Typically, countries regain credibility within a short space of time, and capital markets exhibit a very short memory. The threat to trade credit, on the other hand, would probably be of greater consequence, and the government would have to intervene to guarantee trade debts. But the gravest danger would be posed by the threat of a banking crisis, which could greatly magnify the shock of default. To avert a banking crisis, there would have to be extensive and decisive government intervention. In Greece this would certainly mean extending public ownership and control over banks, thus protecting the banks from collapse and preventing depositor runs. Under public ownership, the banks could act as levers for root and branch transformation of the economy in favour of labour.

Could such a drastic course of action occur within the confines of the eurozone? Note first that it is entirely unclear whether it would be formally feasible. No precedents of sovereign default exist within the eurozone, and its legal framework makes no allowance for such an event.[57] There is no firm way of ascertaining the formal response of the eurozone to a unilateral suspension of debt payments by one or more of its members. And nor is it clear what default would mean in terms of participating in the decision-making mechanisms of the eurozone, including the setting of interest rates. It is inevitable that the defaulter would become a pariah, but the formal outlook remains unclear.

---

57 See Athanassiou, P. 2009. 'Withdrawal and Expulsion from the EU and EMU: Some Reflections', *Legal Working Paper Series*, No. 10, December, European Central Bank, Eurosystem. Athanassiou thinks that exit from the eurozone would be 'inconceivable' without also exiting the EU. Suffice it to note that what is inconceivable to lawyers at one point in time could become eminently conceivable at another.

Formal feasibility aside, would it be desirable for debtor-led default to occur within the confines of the eurozone? The answer is in the negative. First, it would be more difficult for the defaulting country to confront a domestic banking crisis without full command over monetary policy. More broadly, if banks were placed under public ownership following default but continued to remain within the Eurosystem, it would be practically impossible to deploy the banking system to reshape the economy. Second, continued membership of the eurozone would offer little benefit to the defaulter in terms of accessing capital markets, or lowering the costs of borrowing. Third, the option of devaluation would be impossible, thus removing a vital component of recovery. The accumulation of peripheral country debt is inextricably tied to the common currency and as long as the defaulter remained within the eurozone the problem would reappear.

Consequently, debtor-led default would raise the prospect of exit from the eurozone. Exit would offer immediate control over domestic fiscal and monetary policy. It would also remove the constraints of a monetary system that produced embedded current account deficits for the periphery. It is reasonable to expect that devaluation would allow for recovery of competitiveness. It is also plausible that there would be a rebalancing of resources in favour of domestic industry. The outcome would be protection of employment as well as lifting the pressures of austerity on wages. As can be seen for Argentina and Russia in Appendix 2A, default and devaluation resulted in rapid recovery. To be sure, peripheral European economies are different from these resource-rich, primary commodities exporters. But there is no reason to expect that other areas of activity, such as tourism and parts of the secondary sector, would not respond positively to devaluation.

But exit would also entail costs, given the violent change of monetary system. The return to a national currency for Greece, or another peripheral country, would be more difficult than the 'pesification' of the Argentine economy, given the unprecedented degree of monetary integration within the eurozone. However, replacing the euro is not a particularly complex issue, and its basic parameters are not hard to ascertain.

The decision to exit would have to be announced suddenly in order to minimise capital flight; there would be an extended bank holiday; banks would be instructed to convert deposits and other domestic liabilities and assets into the new currency at a nationally chosen rate. When banks reopened, there would be parallel domestic circulation of the euro and the new currency, resulting in twin prices for a range of goods and services. There would also be monetary unrest as contracts and fixed obligations adjusted to the new unit of account. To prevent collapse of confidence, which could have catastrophic effects for economic activity, there must not be dithering once the policy has been adopted. Eventually prices and monetary circulation would adjust to the new currency, while the euro would be excluded from the domestic economy.

The international value of the new currency would inevitably fall, creating complex movements in the balance of domestic social forces. Banks and enterprises servicing debt abroad would face major difficulties; their immediate response would be to try to shift some of their own debt onto the state. On the other hand, those holding assets abroad would seek to speculate against the new currency. For the domestic capitalist class, the return to a national currency would represent an opportunity to transfer costs onto society, while attempting to obtain a transfer of wealth as the new currency devalued.

From the perspective of working people, but also of society as a whole, the answer would be to introduce a broad programme of public ownership and control over the economy, starting with the financial system. Public ownership over banks would guarantee their continued existence, preventing a run on deposits. Capital and foreign exchange controls would also be imposed to prevent export of capital and to minimise speculative transactions. A set of conditions would thus be created allowing for the adoption of industrial policy which would alter the balance of the domestic economy by strengthening the productive sector. The sources of growth in the medium term would be found in the decisive restructuring of the economy, rather than the expansion of exports through devaluation.

The new currency would also create inflationary pressures as import prices would surge, particularly energy prices; real wages would fall as a result. Confronting these pressures would be far from easy, but it would certainly be feasible. It is, first of all, impossible to tell what would be the pass-through from import prices to domestic prices. Furthermore, renewed command over monetary policy would allow for counter-inflationary measures, particularly during the months of the initial shock of devaluation. Support for real wages could then be provided through a policy of income redistribution effected through taxing higher incomes and wealth. After all, peripheral countries are the most unequal in the eurozone and in urgent need of redistribution. Note further that a bout of inflation would reduce the vast burden of domestic debt.

Default and exit, finally, would create problems of public finance, particularly as access to the international funds would come to an end. International experience shows that the primary balance typically returns to surpluses soon after an event of this nature has occurred. In the short term, public finance problems would be ameliorated as recovery began after default. The government could also borrow from the nationalised banking system as well as monetising the deficit to a certain extent. But for a country such as Greece, the medium term answer must be to restructure the tax system by expanding the tax base to include the rich and capital itself.

Altering the tax system would be an integral part of restructuring the Greek state as a whole, making it more democratic and accountable. There could be no permanent resolution to public finance problems in Greece, or other peripheral countries, unless there was a change in the nature of the state, reflecting an underlying shift in the balance of class forces. More broadly, there could be no rebalancing of the economy in favour of working people without a profound restructuring of the state.

In sum, there are no easy alternatives for working people in peripheral eurozone countries. The dilemma these countries face is harsh. They could acquiesce to austerity, remaining within the eurozone and putting up with recession, or stagnation, for the indefinite future. Alternatively, they could opt for debtor-led default accompanied by exit from the eurozone. The latter option could signal a radical transformation of economy and society, shifting the balance of power against capital. The distributional struggle over who would carry the costs of the crisis would continue, but more favourable conditions would have been created within which to fight for a progressive solution in the interests of the many.

Debtor-led default could prove the start of an anti-capitalist turn across the periphery of the eurozone that would lift the neoliberal stranglehold over the EU, thus pushing Europe in an associational, socialist direction. It remains to be seen whether European workers in the periphery but also the core have enough organisational and ideological strength to bring about such profound change.

APPENDIX 2A

THE CRISIS LAST TIME: ARGENTINA AND RUSSIA

The crisis in the periphery of the eurozone is only the latest in a long line of sovereign debt crises during the last three decades, mostly in the developing world. The European Union, despite asserting its promotion of convergence of per capita income and living standards, has effectively created a sharp two-tier structure of core and periphery, without even counting the broader periphery in Eastern Europe. The debt problems of the periphery of the eurozone have an inherent similarity with those of the global periphery. It is instructive in this respect briefly to consider the sovereign debt crises of Argentina and Russia in recent years.

On 24 December 2001, Argentina announced the suspension of payments on almost its entire public debt of $144 bn. The fixed exchange rate, binding the Argentine peso to the US dollar, was abandoned a short while later. GDP collapsed by 11 percent the following year. Yet the Argentine economy bounced back, sustaining growth of 8–9 percent annually from 2003 to 2007, while GDP per capita returned to its pre-crisis peak in 2008. International debt markets were reopened to Argentina in 2006, with the sale of $500m worth of five-year bonds.

Two years earlier Russia had also defaulted on its external debts, forcing an immediate devaluation of the rouble. Within months the economy had returned to growth, expanding rapidly for almost a decade. Indeed, Russia weathered the crisis far better than Argentina. The experience of the two countries is compared below, drawing out the implications for the eurozone sovereign debt crises.

THE WASHINGTON CONSENSUS BRINGS COLLAPSE TO BUENOS AIRES

In 1991 Argentina adopted the "Convertibility Plan" that included trade and capital liberalisation, privatisation of state-owned assets, tight monetary policy and, above all, the pegging of the peso to the US dollar on a one-to-one basis, overseen by a currency board.[58] The country thus spent the 1990s following the

---

58 Cibils, A. and Lo Volo, R. (2007), 'At debt's door: what can we learn from Argentina's recent debt crisis and restructuring?', *Seattle Journal for Social Justice* 5:2, p. 757.

prescriptions of the Washington Consensus, with the IMF's benign approval and extended financial support.[59] The initial rewards appeared to be substantial as hyperinflation ended and growth averaged 6 percent over 1991–1998.[60] Net capital inflows totalled $100 bn over 1992–1999.[61] Apparent success turned Argentina into the Fund's favourite emerging economy, paraded as an example for others to follow.[62] Continued IMF support helped ease borrowing conditions for Argentina, with creditors believing that the Fund would not allow such an exemplary country to fail.[63]

With hindsight, it is evident that macroeconomic stabilisation was more the product of good fortune than good policy. Low US interest rates had held back dollar appreciation, whilst a recovering US economy in the 1990s buoyed up Latin America. Once the dollar began to rise steadily in value from the mid-1990s onwards, the fixed dollar–peso link became a noose for the Argentine economy. Following the Russian crisis of 1998, Brazil undertook a devaluation of 70 percent in January 1999, worsening Argentina's terms of trade further.[64] The peso became heavily overvalued, up to

---

59 Cavallo, D.F. and Cottani, J.A. (May 1997), 'Argentina's convertibility plan and the IMF', *American Economic Review* 87:2, pp. 18–19.

60 International Monetary Fund Independent Evaluation Office (2004), *The IMF and Argentina, 1991–2001*, Washington, DC: International Monetary Fund, p. 10.

61 International Monetary Fund Independent Evaluation Office (2004), *The IMF and Argentina, 1991–2001*, Washington, DC: International Monetary Fund, p. 11.

62 See, for example, remarks by Michael Camdessus, IMF Managing Director, press conference, 24 April 1997; Camdessus, M. (1996), 'Argentina and the challenge of globalisation', speech, Academy of Economic Science, Buenos Aires, 27 May 1996; and International Monetary Fund (1998), *Country Report: Argentina*, IMF Staff Country Report 98/38.

63 Although the size of this moral hazard effect may not have been especially large in Argentina's case. See IMF Policy Development and Review Department (March 2007), 'Fund financial support and moral hazard: analytics and empirics', Washington: International Monetary Fund.

64 Sturzenegger, F. and Zettelmeyer, J. (2007), *Debt Defaults and Lessons from a Decade of Crises*, Cambridge, MA: MIT Press, p. 168.

55 percent according to the estimates of the World Bank.[65] Deflation and output contraction set in.

The incipient recession turned into a full-blown economic slump in subsequent years, and by the latter half of 2002 Argentina's GDP had declined by nearly 20 percent. The number of Argentines living below the poverty line hit 57.5 percent of the population in October 2002, while the proportion living in extreme poverty – even lacking the ability to purchase food – exceeded 27.5 percent. Inequality rose sharply and unemployment reached 25 percent.

As the slump gathered pace, the federal government's debt rose steadily relative to GDP: from 34.5 percent in 1997 to 37.6 percent in 1998, to 43 percent in 1999, to 45 percent in 2001, and to 53.7 percent in 2002. By the middle of 2001, capital markets were effectively closed to Argentina. Throughout this period, the IMF actively supported Argentine policy-making, particularly the peso–dollar peg. Indeed, the Fund moved from assessing policies under the peg, to actively endorsing the peg itself.[66] As late as October 1998, mere weeks before the debacle opened, the Fund's Managing Director described Argentina as "exemplary".[67] After capital markets had effectively closed to Argentina in mid-2001, the IMF became the only source of external loan support for the country, increasing further its leverage. Nonetheless, there was a remarkable degree of unanimity between IMF advisors to Argentina, and senior Argentine officials and ministers. The IMF imposed its prescriptions in cahoots with the ruling elite of Argentina.[68] The result was a series of chaotic policy turns that eventually led to default.

An initial round of tax increases and spending cuts reduced the government's primary deficit from 19.4 percent to 18.9 percent of GDP from 1999 to 2000. But this fiscal tightening proved insufficient particularly as the central

65 Perry, G. and Servén, L. (2003), 'The anatomy of a multiple crisis: why was Argentina special and what we can learn from it', working paper WPS 3081, World Bank.

66 International Monetary Fund Independent Evaluation Office (2004), *The IMF and Argentina, 1991–2001*, Washington, DC: International Monetary Fund, p. 37.

67 Quoted in International Monetary Fund Independent Evaluation Office (2004), *The IMF and Argentina, 1991–2001*, Washington, DC: International Monetary Fund, p.1 2.

68 Cibils, A. and Lo Volo, R. (2007), 'At debt's door: what can we learn from Argentina's recent debt crisis and restructuring?', *Seattle Journal for Social Justice* 5:2, p. 755.

government seemed to lack fiscal control over regional authorities. Promises to control the latter allowed for the release of further financial assistance from the IMF and the World Bank, totalling close to $20 bn.[69] But the fiscal targets imposed by the IMF for the first quarter of 2001 were missed, prompting the resignation of the finance minister. A new minister attempted to impose direct cuts of approximately $2 bn, but was forced to resign within a fortnight of his appointment.[70]

A further turn of policy followed, attempting to peg the peso to the average of the euro and the dollar, thus boosting the productive sector. The policy failed, opening the way for the *megacanje de deuda* ("mega debt swap") in June 2001. This was co-ordinated by a syndicate of major North American and European banks, offering longer maturities for existing debt holders through a "competitive" process. The end result was that the overall foreign debt of Argentina was actually increased and, of course, the banks that arranged the deal earned an "enormous commission".[71] The economy continued to decline rapidly and another debt swap was attempted in September 2001 with the approval of the IMF. The gains for Argentina were again modest. As spending continued to overshoot agreed IMF limits, dissent began to emerge within the Fund on whether support should continue. An expected disbursement was left unpaid, provoking a run on the Argentine banking system. The government was forced to ban deposit withdrawals, leading to massive popular unrest. On Christmas Eve of 2001 the country eventually defaulted.

In January the Convertibility Law was repealed and a new fixed dollar-peso rate was adopted. The resulting capital flight soon forced the government to announce the "pesification" of dollar-denominated financial assets and liabilities held in Argentina. Consequently, demand for dollars rose, further increasing the pressure on the peg, while the banks were rendered insolvent.[72] In March 2002 the country was forced to abandon the fixed exchange rate

---

69 Ibid., p. 170.

70 Ibid., p. 171.

71 Teubal, M. (2004), 'The rise and collapse of neoliberalism in Argentina: the role of economic groups', Journal of Developing Societies 20:3–4, p. 185.

72 Miller, M., Fronti, J.G., Lei, Z. (2004), 'Default, devaluation, and depression: Argentina after 2001', working paper.

regime entirely, and the peso fell to around 75 percent of its previous dollar rate. As a result, consumer prices rose by 40 percent. The ensuing dislocation of fundamental monetary functions contributed to an extremely sharp slump. But the substantial devaluation of the peso, alongside the government regaining control of the situation, meant that the worst of the crisis was over by April 2002. Growth for the last three quarters of 2002 was positive, and continued to accelerate over subsequent years.

In September 2003, with the crisis clearly over, the government sought a formal restructuring of its debt. Bondholders were initially offered a 75 percent reduction in capital, lower interest rates and longer debt maturities. Creditors reacted angrily, forming a pressure group that worked with the IMF to demand better conditions. The IMF refused to recognise an improved offer from the Argentine government of 45 percent capital reduction in January 2004. The government then took the unprecedented step for a developing country of proceeding with the restructuring without IMF support. By February 2005, 76 percent of Argentina's creditors had reluctantly agreed to the new credit terms.[73]

SOME LESSONS FROM ARGENTINA

The official view of default stresses its substantial costs, particularly the slide in economic output, accelerating unemployment and possible impoverishment. This is in line with much conventional economic literature, which suggests that costs act as a means to discourage governments from reneging on debts.[74] But there is also a counter view within mainstream theory, which effectively treats default as a policy option with both costs and benefits.[75]

The experience of Argentina is consistent with the view that default can be a positive step for an economy crushed by debt. The worst collapse of the

---

73 Cibils, A. and Lo Volo, R. (2007), 'At debt's door: what can we learn from Argentina's recent debt crisis and restructuring?', *Seattle Journal for Social Justice* 5:2, p. 775.

74 Eaton, J. and Gersovitz, M. (1981), 'Debt with potential repudiation: theoretical and empirical analysis', *Review of Economic Studies* 43, pp. 289–309.

75 See Reinhart, C. and Rogoff, K. (2004), 'The modern history of exchange rate arrangements: a re-interpretation', *Quarterly Journal of Economics* 119:1; Tovar, C.E. (May 2010), 'Currency collapses and output dynamics: a long-run perspective', *BIS Quarterly Bulletin.*

Argentine economy occurred in the first three months of 2002 as the government attempted to maintain a new currency peg without credibility. During the same period, it attempted to force "pesification" into a currency that lacked credibility, thus encouraging capital outflows. The economy began to recover strongly only after the illusion of a "strong" domestic currency was abandoned.

It is important to note that the Argentine debt crisis was not a product of lax fiscal discipline. The primary deficit remained "remarkably flat" relative to GDP over 1993–2001.[76] Fiscal problems began to emerge as a recession materialised in 1997–8, driving tax revenues down steeply. Indeed, many of Argentina's fiscal troubles can be traced to the privatisation of its pay-as-you-go social security system under the Convertibility Plan.[77] Government revenues declined but, astoundingly, the government retained all its existing social security liabilities. By 2001, the gap between lost social security revenues, and continued payments to pensioners with cumulative debt interest – amounted to virtually the entire primary deficit.[78]

Argentina was certainly affected by the decline in the terms of trade after the Asian crisis of 1997; by the US slowdown in 2001; and by capital flight and rising spreads across developing countries following the 1998 Russian crisis. But their impact was no more than for other Latin American countries.[79] The depth and severity of the Argentine crisis was due to the monetary framework of the country, in particular the fixed dollar peg run by a currency board. Fixing the exchange rate contributed to a current account deficit that was only closed through recession. The result was growing public and private sector debt in the late 1990s and early 2000s.[80]

---

76 Hausmann, R. and Velasco, A. (2002), 'Hard money's soft underbelly: understanding the Argentine crisis', Brookings Trade Forum.

77 Holzmann, R. (2000), 'The World Bank Approach to Pension Reform', World Bank presentation.

78 Baker, D. and Weisbrot, M. (2002), 'The role of social security privatisation in Argentina's economic crisis', working paper, Center for Economic and Policy Research.

79 Perry, G. and Servén, L. (2003), 'The anatomy of a multiple crisis: why was Argentina special and what we can learn from it', working paper WPS 3081, World Bank.

80 Cibils, A. and Lo Volo, R. (2007), 'At debt's door: what can we learn from Argentina's recent debt crisis and restructuring?', *Seattle Journal for Social Justice* 5:2, pp. 765–766.

Sticking to "respectable" "orthodox" economic policy, supervised by the IMF, also proved disastrous for Argentina. At every turn it prevented decisive policy action that could have removed the monetary bind at the heart of the problem, thus encouraging policy confusion. Finally, "orthodox" policy created room for the illicit export of capital by large sections of the Argentine ruling and middle class. Domestic capital held abroad could speculate on the prospect of "pesification", continually destabilising the economy. When "pesification" eventually arrived, it created opportunities for wealth transfers in favour of the ruling class. Default and "pesification" released the economy from the straitjacket of the Convertibility Plan, but the Argentine rich were still able to benefit.

RUSSIA'S TRANSITION FROM A PLANNED ECONOMY: COLLAPSE AND RECOVERY

Russia spent the 1990s in transition to free-market capitalism under IMF tutelage. During the 1980s, the USSR had developed substantial foreign debt exposure, which Russia, as the main successor state, took over in its entirety. Notoriously, the transition process led to economic collapse.[81] Money disappeared from much of economic life; half of industrial sales were completed through barter by early 1998. Tax collection by the central government was extraordinarily erratic, while a tiny fraction of taxes was collected in cash.[82] Russia concluded agreements with the IMF in 1995 and 1996 which, together with the adoption of a high and fixed exchange rate, appeared to be bringing inflation under control.[83] Access to international credit markets moved towards normalisation after 1996.[84]

Success was entirely fictitious. After the onset of the Asian crisis, the rouble came under speculative attack. The prices of oil and nonferrous metals,

---

81 Milanovic, B. (1998), *Income, Inequality, and Poverty During the Transformation from Planned to Market Economy*, Washington DC: World Bank, pp. 186–90.

82 Gaddy, C.G. and Ickes, B.W. (1998), 'Russia's virtual economy', *Foreign Affairs* 77:5, p. 56.

83 Chiodo, A.J. and Owyang, M.T. (2002), 'A case study of a currency crisis: the Russian default of 1998', *St Louis Federal Reserve Review*, p. 9.

84 Sturzenegger, F. and Zettelmeyer, J. (2007), *Debt Defaults and Lessons from a Decade of Crises*, Cambridge, MA: MIT Press, p. 95.

together accounting for around two-thirds of Russian exports, began to fall.[85] Political unrest followed as the economy faltered. Tax collection was extraordinarily weak and public debt began to rise relative to GDP: from 43.4 percent in 1996, to 53.6 percent in 1997, to 68.1 percent in 1998, to 90.2 percent in 1999. The fear of default and devaluation pushed up central bank lending rates to banks, and the Russian government found it very difficult to continue with its short-term borrowing operations. In an effort to support it, a $22.6 bn multilateral assistance package was announced in July, with $4.8 bn to be disbursed immediately.[86] The intention was to support the currency peg, while swapping expensive short-term for long-term bonds. The package failed within days and capital flight swelled to perhaps $4 bn between May and August.

On 17 August 1998 the Yeltsin government announced that it was devaluing the rouble, imposing a moratorium on all rouble-denominated public debt payments, and suspending payments on all foreign currency liabilities by Russian financial institutions. Renewed political unrest provoked further pressure on the rouble and all attempts to control the exchange rate were abandoned in September. The rouble plunged to less than a third of its value relative to the dollar.[87] The attempt to defend the peg from October 1997 to September 1998 had cost roughly $30 bn, about one-sixth of Russia's GDP at the time.[88]

Default produced a major banking crisis as the aggregate capital of Russia's banks was approximately equal to the volume of frozen Russian loan payments. A run on Russian financial institutions had been brewing since August 1998, with queues of worried depositors beginning to form outside bank doors. In response, the central bank injected massive volumes of liquidity into the system, lowering reserve requirements, extending loans

---

85 Chiodo, A.J. and Owyang, M.T. (2002), 'A case study of a currency crisis: the Russian default of 1998', *St Louis Federal Reserve Review*, p. 10.

86 Kharas, H., Pinto, B. and Ulatov, S. (2001), 'An analysis of Russia's 1998 meltdown: fundamentals and market signals', *Brookings Papers on Economic Activity*, p. 10. The IMF contribution was reduced from $5.6 to $4.8 bn after the Duma failed to agree to all of the conditionalities the Fund wished to impose.

87 Kharas, H., Pinto, B. and Ulatov, S. (2001), 'An analysis of Russia's 1998 meltdown: fundamentals and market signals', *Brookings Papers on Economic Activity*, p. 1.

88 Ibid, p. 3.

to major institutions, and swapping frozen bonds for cash. The measures successfully halted the run, at the cost of reinforcing the devaluation of the rouble and subsequent inflation.

Devaluation had the effect of pushing the cost of servicing dollar-denominated debt sky-high. In January 1999 credit rating agencies declared Russia to be in complete default. The Russian government quickly opened negotiations with holders of debt aiming at restructuring. By May 1999 agreement was secured with approximately 95 percent of resident, and 89 percent of non-resident debt-holders. Bondholders received haircuts estimated at around 53 percent.[89]

Swift action on the banking crisis, speedy renegotiation of debts and the devaluation of the rouble paved the way for a sharp rebound in the Russian economy. Growth resumed apace, reaching 6.3 percent in 1999 and 10 percent in 2000, never falling below 4 percent annually until the recession of 2008. Barter, arrears and non-payments were steadily eradicated.[90] The fiscal balance shifted into surplus for the first time in 2000, and Russia had repaid its debts to the IMF fully by 2005. Foreign exchange reserves topped $200 bn in 2006, the fourth largest amongst emerging market economies.[91]

Much of this success was determined by sharp rises in primary commodity prices, especially oil, from around 1999 onwards. But the recovery also helped domestic producers, as consumption shifted from expensive foreign goods into locally-produced commodities. Household consumption also recovered strongly on the back of sharp rises in real disposable incomes.[92] There is little doubt that such growth would have been impossible, even with rising oil

---

89 Sturzenegger, F. and Zettelmeyer, J. (2007), *Debt Defaults and Lessons from a Decade of Crises*, Cambridge, MA: MIT Press, pp. 105–106.

90 Ahrend, R. (2008), 'Can Russia sustain strong growth as a resource-based economy?', CESifo Forum 2/2008, Paris: Organisation for Economic Co-operation and Development, p. 3.

91 Sturzenegger, F. and Zettelmeyer, J. (2007), *Debt Defaults and Lessons from a Decade of Crises*, Cambridge, MA: MIT Press, p. 113.

92 Ahrend, R. (2008), 'Can Russia sustain strong growth as a resource-based economy?', CESifo Forum 2/2008, Paris: Organisation for Economic Co-operation and Development.

prices, had Russia still attempted to maintain the overvalued rate of the rouble. Default and devaluation, though undoubtedly carrying immediate economic costs, proved a more viable option for the Russian economy.

DEFAULT IS NOT SUCH A DISASTER, AFTER ALL

Fundamental to the crisis in both Argentina and Russia was the attempt to maintain an overvalued exchange rate, ostensibly for the purpose of stabilising prices. The result was to cripple private sector output, create current account deficits, and generate private and public debt. The problems of public finance in both countries thus resulted from the broader framework of neoliberal policy imposed by the IMF as well as from external shocks. Eventual default and devaluation, while carrying significant economic costs, created the conditions for rapid economic recovery. Both countries underwent debt renegotiation relatively smoothly, without official IMF support. Access to international capital markets was regained not long after default. It should be noted, however, that Argentina continued to rely on bilateral Venezuelan loans. Even so, default did not leave the two countries without access to credit.

Russia and Argentina handled default and devaluation quite differently. Confronted with an implausible exchange rate peg and a worsening debt position, Russia's government acted decisively to default and devalue in short order. The entire process took approximately five months, while renegotiation of the great bulk of debt finished a little more than a year later. Argentine governments, in contrast, clung to the unworkable currency board for years, while generally adopting the view that 'orthodox' methods would resolve the worsening economic crisis. Furthermore, once a banking crisis had emerged following default, Russia resolved the problem rapidly through restrictions on capital movements and by effectively nationalising bank deposits. Procrastination and policy confusion in Argentina contributed to bank runs that led to riots and deaths.

Default and devaluation certainly carry costs. But they might well be the better option for a country facing an intractable debt crisis that has been created in large measure by international monetary and financial relations. The costs can be reduced and a path can be cleared for future economic growth, if governments are prepared to act decisively, breaking the international consensus if needed.

At the same time, default and devaluation, particularly when they involve a change of monetary standard, as in Argentina, also entail wealth transfers and a rebalancing of class forces. They could re-strengthen the rule of the domestic capitalist class, but they could also create opportunities to shift the balance of power in favour of labour. They could open the way for public ownership and control over banks, regulation of capital flows, public control over other areas of the economy, industrial policy, and redistribution of income and wealth. The eventual outcome of default and devaluation, in other words, depends on social struggle. This is the challenge that is currently confronting working people in the periphery of the eurozone.

APPENDIX 2B

CONSTRUCTION OF AGGREGATE DEBT PROFILES

Data about the debt liabilities of a country tend to be dispersed over a number of sources and classified according to varying sets of criteria. The lack of data that is consolidated at the national level according to the same accounting standard presents difficulties in the analysis of data, and in particular makes international comparisons, such as those in the present report, problematic. In order to clarify the data methods used to reach the conclusions in this report, this Appendix provides an outline of the data sources, calculations and assumptions used in constructing the figures on the debt of periphery countries contained in chapter 9.

There are two primary ways in which the debt of a country may be disaggregated: by issuer, most importantly public vs. private-issued debt, and by holder, where domestic vs. foreign holding is the most significant division. With regard to the former, data about public debt is broadly disclosed, usually through the national public debt agencies which take responsibility for the production of these statistics. These agencies provide data about outstanding volumes of debt disaggregated in a number of ways, for example by instrument, maturity, currency, type and geographical location of the debt holder at the initial placement.[93] With regard to foreign holdings of debt, data about countries' external debt is disclosed through supranational institutions and is usually based on the International Investor Position statistics of the Balance of Payments, provided by home central banks.[94]

Consolidated statistics on the total volume of debt liabilities of individual countries are not published by either national authorities or international organisations. In order to calculate the level of indebtedness of periphery countries, the "National Financial Accounts", published by the central banks of each country, were used as primary sources. These data sets provide a detailed breakdown of the stocks of financial assets and liabilities of each institutional

---

93 Data about Spanish public debt can be found at http://www.tesoro.es; about Portuguese debt at http://www.igcp.pt; and about Greek debt at http://www.mof-glk.gr.
94 For Spain http://www.bde.es/homee.htm; Portugal http://www.bportugal.pt/en-US/Pages/inicio.aspx; and Greece http://www.bankofgreece.gr/Pages/en/default.aspx.

sector of an economy. The data are classified by issuing sector[95] and by type of instrument.

The total indebtedness of each country was calculated by summing over the total debt securities, loans and non-resident deposits of each of the institutional sectors. The following assumptions were made:

1. Domestically held deposits were excluded from the definition of debt, while foreign deposits were included.
2. The foreign liabilities of the monetary authorities were excluded from total indebtedness. These liabilities are the result of ECB liquidity provision operations. These repo operations take place via the home country central bank, resulting in the expansion of both sides of the balance sheet and giving rise to the appearance of increasing indebtedness at the national level. However, as these operations are essentially domestic liquidity provision by the central bank, they do not constitute an expansion of external debt.
3. In the case of Portugal, the quarterly financial accounts do not provide data about trade credit debt. Yet, those are provided for the period 2004–2009 in the annual tables. The annual figures were then used to calculate values for trade credit for the respective years. However, for the period before 2004 estimates were calculated by extrapolating the average of period 2004–2009 and applying it to period 1997–2003. It was also assumed that trade credit is evenly split between households and non-financial corporations, reflecting the trend observed for the period 2004–2009 and ignoring marginal amounts for general government.

With respect to the categorisation of debt by holder, in the case of Spain and Portugal, the data provided by the national Financial Accounts for externally-held debt are not broken down by issuing sector. This information was obtained from an alternative source, the International Investor Position of the Balance of Payments, which gives information, broken down by domestic sector and by type of foreign capital flow: direct investment, portfolio investment

---

95 General government; financial corporations; non-financial corporations; households.

(equity and debt securities) and 'other investment' (primarily bank lending). The total volume of external debt was thus obtained by summing the liabilities of domestic sectors to direct investors and affiliated enterprises, portfolio investment debt and "other investment" liabilities. In the case of Greece, more detailed information about external debt was given in the Financial Accounts, however this did not match the equivalent figures in the International Investor Position – see the subsequent section for more detail.

As the two sources adopt different classification criteria, some assumptions needed to be made in order to make the balance of payments' data compatible with the financial accounts:

1. Once again, monetary authorities' liabilities were not considered; and
2. Liabilities to direct investors, classified as 'other capital' in direct investment rubric were classified as 'other sectors' debt', which includes non-financial corporations and households.

A final remark is in order regarding the data on the holders of debt securities, and in particular the split between domestic and foreign holdings. As debt securities are easily exchanged in capital markets it is particularly difficult to know where they are held if we do not use data about holders at clearing houses. This classification frequently refers to the data provided by the issuer based on the original placement in the market. Therefore any data about the location of debt holders needs to be treated with some caution.

GREECE

This section provides more detail on the methods used to calculate the debt profile of Greece. This is provided for two main reasons: first, the ECB liquidity provision operations were largest in Greece and this is illustrated by showing the changes in the balance sheet of the bank of Greece; second, there were discrepancies between different data sources, particularly with respect to external debt. This is discussed in more detail below.

As in the other cases, the primary source for the data on Greek indebtedness was the set of "Financial Accounts", published by the Bank of Greece.[96]

---

96 http://www.bankofgreece.gr/Pages/en/Statistics/accounts.aspx

FIG. 2B1 Bank of Greece liabilities (euro bn)

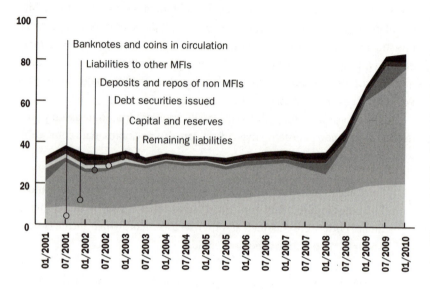

Source: *Bank of Greece*

This data set provides a detailed breakdown of the stocks of financial assets and liabilities of each sector of the Greek economy.

It is notable that both the assets and liabilities of the Bank of Greece have ballooned in recent years. This was cross-checked against the balance sheet of the Bank of Greece.[97] What was found was that liabilities to "other euro-area MFIs" accounted for this increase, while on the asset side, corresponding claims were held against domestic MFIs. This is illustrated in figures 2B1 and 2B2.

It can be seen that "Liabilities to other MFIs" (which is dominated by "other euro-area MFIs") and "Claims on other MFIs" (dominated by domestic MFIs) jump sharply following the onset of the financial crisis. This expansion of the balance sheet is accounted for by operations by the ECB for the purposes of liquidity provision: repo operations take place via the home country central bank, resulting in the expansion of both sides of the balance

---

97 http://www.bankofgreece.gr/BogDocumentEn/Balance_sheet_BoG.xls

FIG. B2 Bank of Greece assets (euro, bn)

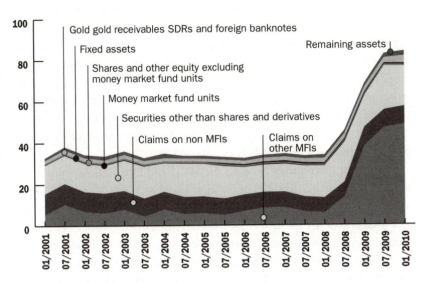

Source: *Bank of Greece*

sheet, giving the appearance of increasing indebtedness at the country level. However, as these operations are essentially domestic liquidity provision by the central bank, they do not in fact constitute an expansion of debt. For this reason the external liabilities of the Bank of Greece were excluded from the total debt figures.[98]

A further issue that arose was a significant discrepancy in the external debt figures between the Financial Accounts, and the equivalent figures in the "Gross External Debt Position"[99] that is published by the Bank of Greece as part of the "Special Data Dissemination Service" – an IMF initiative aimed

---

98 This is clearly an aspect of the expansion of TARGET accounts within the Eurosystem which is discussed more fully in Part 3.

99 http://www.bankofgreece.gr/BogDocumentEn/Gross_External_Debt_Position-Data.xls

at providing standardised external debt statistics. The SDDS figures[100] for the private sector are significantly lower than those in the Financial Accounts with the most significant difference occurring in the "Financial Corporations" sector. It was found that by subtracting the volume of central bank liquidity-providing operations from the reported external liabilities of the Financial Corporations, a figure almost exactly matching that reported in the SDDS figures was obtained. The assumption was therefore made that the Financial Account figures include the liabilities arising from these liquidity operations in the accounts of the financial corporations. The data used to generate the figures in Chapter 2 thus had these liabilities removed from them.

Finally, the discrepancy between the SDDS and Financial Account statements of the external liabilities of the Household and Non-Financial Corporation sectors remains unresolved. In both cases, the higher of the two values were used to generate the figures, i.e. those reported in the Financial Accounts. By way of an illustration, the level of private sector debt, excluding financial corporations, as reported in the SDDS figures for the final quarter of 2009 was almost EUR 25 bn. When calculated using the Financial Account figures, the volume of externally held private sector debt was more than double this amount at around EUR 67.5 bn. Although the difference is large, it is still relatively small when put in the context of total private sector debt (both domestically and externally held) reported in the Financial Account, which is almost EUR 290 bn.

---

100 The SDDS figures match those on the IMF sponsored "Quarterly External Debt Statistics" website: http://web.worldbank.org/WBSITE/EXTERNAL/DATASTATIS-TICS/EXTDECQEDS/0,,menuPK:1805431~pagePK:64168427~piPK:64168435~theSit ePK:1805415,00.html

APPENDIX 2C

DECOMPOSITION OF AGGREGATE DEMAND

The decomposed aggregate demand graphics for GDP Growth were built using the European Commission's AMECO database, deploying absolute values for each category at constant prices. Rates of growth for each category were then calculated as:

$r = (X_t - X_{t-1})/X_t$

The contribution of each category to growth was measured by weighing each rate of growth with its relative weight in GDP:

$r*(X/GDP)$

In order to simplify the graph, a single category for net external demand was created of (Exports–Imports).

GDP growth figures were calculated from final GDP provided by AMECO. Small discrepancies between the two methods for calculating GDP (adding each demand category contribution and using the absolute values for GDP at constant prices) were identified in certain years for particular countries. However, such differences were insignificant and few.

Part 3 BREAKING UP? A RADICAL ROUTE OUT OF THE EUROZONE CRISIS

C. Lapavitsas, A. Kaltenbrunner, D. Lindo, J. Meadway,
J. Michell, J.P. Painceira, E. Pires, J. Powell, A. Stenfors,
N. Teles, L. Vatikiotis
October 2011

13. HITTING THE BUFFERS

A global upheaval

The fundamental features of the global upheaval that commenced in August 2007 are well understood by now.[101] A vast real estate bubble occurred in the USA in 2001–6, spurred by low interest rates due to the policy of the Federal Reserve in 2001–3. The bubble was subsequently sustained by capital inflows from developing countries forced by the operations of the world market to hold huge dollar reserves. Availability of cheap funds together with relentless

---

101 The brief account given here derives from Lapavitsas C. (2009), 'Financialised Capitalism: Crisis and Financial Expropriation', *Historical Materialism*, 17.2, pp. 114–148. Further arguments can be found in several discussion papers by Research on Money and Finance, www.researchonmoneyandfinance.org. Broadly speaking, the global crisis reflects the financialisation of contemporary capitalism, a complex and multifaceted phenomenon that has concerned political economists for well over a decade, see, for instance, Epstein G., (ed.) (2005), 'Financialization and the World Economy', Cheltenham: Edward Elgar. The view of financialisation that underpins the analysis in this report stresses three features of contemporary, mature economies: first, the ability of large corporations to finance investment out of retained profits as well as to participate in financial markets on their own account; second, the turn of banks toward making profits out of trading in financial markets and lending to individuals; third, the increasing involvement of workers and households in financial markets to borrow and to place savings.

financial engineering allowed US financial institutions to generate mortgage debt among subprime borrowers on the assumption that it would subsequently be securitised and sold in the open markets.

In 2004 US interest rates began to rise, signalling the end of the period of very cheap credit. Rising rates eventually led to large debt delinquencies among the indebted poor, thus bursting the bubble and resulting in enormous volumes of bad securitised debt in the possession of financial institutions across the world. The ensuing banking crisis in 2008–9 brought credit contraction and caused a collapse of aggregate demand, partly through investment and partly through exports. Among EMU countries, Germany was hit especially hard, as its exports collapsed and its banks found themselves exposed to bad securitised debt.

Falling aggregate demand induced a sharp global recession that led to state intervention with the aim of: first, rescuing banks; and second, ameliorating the effects of the crisis. Given that tax revenue declined as economies went into recession, the result was ballooning budget deficits in the USA, the UK and elsewhere. The negative impact on public finances was particularly severe in the periphery of the eurozone, eventually leading to loss of control in Greece, Ireland and Portugal, while Spain struggled to avoid the same fate. The persistence of the crisis in 2010–11 eventually raised the spectre of contagion for countries of the core, primarily Italy which has stagnated throughout its period of eurozone membership and which can be considered to occupy an intermediate place between the periphery and the core. Once the sovereign debt crisis had acquired major dimensions in the eurozone, it became clear that European and other banks were at risk, threatening to re-ignite the banking crisis across the world.

The euro: A novel form of international reserve currency

The tendencies of global crisis were mediated in Europe by the institutional mechanisms of the eurozone. The euro is not simply a common currency devised to facilitate trade and financial flows among member countries. More important than that, it is an international reserve currency, or in more precise political economy terms, a form of world money.[102] This is ultimately the reason

---

102 The significance of the euro as world money is more fully analysed in Lapavitsas, C. (2012), 'The eurozone crisis through the prism of world money', forthcoming in Epstein, G., Kregel J., and Wolfson, M. (2012). A discussion of the role of the euro as world money

why it has impacted with such ferocity on peripheral economies, and why the EU has pursued relentless austerity to protect the euro.

The world market lacks a corresponding world state to give it homogeneity of accounting and trading practices, law, norms, and even weights and measures. It also lacks an integrated credit system that could provide credit and liquidity facilities under the supervision of a world central bank. Consequently, its functioning relies heavily on an international currency that is expected to act as trusted means of reserve (hoarding) and means of payment for international operations, on the assumption that it already functions as a reliable unit of account. In addition, the international reserve currency must also act as reliable means of payment and reserve among states in the world market. Command over the reserve currency is a means of establishing a hierarchy among states and ultimately a weapon of imperial power.

Historically the reserve currency has taken the form of a commodity, gold or silver, but for most of the twentieth century gold has been reduced to a hoard-of-last-resort. The functioning of reserve currency money is currently undertaken by national currencies, above all, the US dollar. This development has transformed the reserve currency into a partly managed economic entity that affords extraordinary power to the issuing state.[103] For this reason, the dollar has been subject to continuous competition from other forms of money. This is the perspective from which the European Monetary Union has been analysed throughout this book, establishing its contradictory and discriminatory character.

The euro is the main competitor to the dollar as reserve currency, aiming to meet the paying and reserve requirements of large European enterprises

---

can also be found in Lapavitsas, C. (2011), 'Default and Exit from the Eurozone: A Radical Left Strategy', forthcoming in *Socialist Register*. Throughout this report the term 'international reserve currency' will be used to avoid unnecessary problems for those unfamiliar with the terminology of political economy.

103 The USA has drawn many and varied benefits, including several degrees of freedom in undertaking domestic monetary policy. Perhaps the most egregious benefit, however, has been a form of rent extracted from developing countries forced to keep extraordinary dollar reserves, see Painceira, J.P. (2009), 'Developing Countries in the Era of Financialisation: From Deficit Accumulation to Reserve Accumulation', *RMF Discussion Papers*, no. 4, February, www.researchonmoneyandfinance.org

and facilitating the global operations of European states. Yet, the euro is a very unusual form of international reserve currency. Unlike the dollar it is not a pre-existing national money that has been catapulted into its world role because of the intrinsic power of its economy and state. Nor has it arisen organically out of the commercial and financial operations of large capitals in Europe and elsewhere. Instead, it has been created *ex nihilo* by an alliance of European states. The peculiar construction of the euro is a source of considerable strength but also weakness for its role as international reserve currency.

The institutional framework of the eurozone has been determined by the large European banks and enterprises that primarily deploy the euro. Thus, the ECB took it upon itself to keep inflation below 2 percent, while creating a homogeneous market for bank liquidity across Europe. Fiscal discipline was shaped by the Stability and Growth Pact, but responsibility for compliance was left to each sovereign state. Finally, the eurozone has directed the pressures of economic adjustment to the labour market: competitiveness in the internal market would depend on productivity growth and labour costs in each country, while labour mobility would be in practice relatively limited. As a result, a 'race to the bottom' for wages and conditions has emerged in the eurozone benefiting large industrial capital.[104]

In addition, the institutional mechanisms of the EMU have reflected hierarchical relations among member states. Extending the membership of the eurozone to include smaller and weaker states was a rational step to create a substantial internal market that would allow the new currency to function as global means of reserve and payment. Core countries – particularly Germany – then exercised partial control over lesser states.[105] The euro has provided German financial and industrial capital with competitive advantages in the European and the world market. For industrial capital it has meant lower transaction costs within the common market and improved capital allocation, facilitating the outsourcing of parts of productive capacity. The euro

---

104 The fundamental economic mechanisms underpinning these processes were discussed in depth in Parts 1 and 2 of this book.

105 It matters not at all whether Germany or France played the main role in setting up the eurozone in the 1990s. The point is that Germany has emerged as the dominant country of the core of the eurozone, fully conscious of its place.

has also eliminated one of the major instruments European countries have traditionally deployed in the face of German exporting prowess: currency depreciation.

But the most attractive aspect of the euro for German capital has been its role as reserve currency, potentially creating a much stronger substitute for the old Deutschmark. Advancing financialisation in Germany and other core countries has turned the euro into a decisive instrument for obtaining finance in international financial markets, for lending across the world, and for engaging in financial transactions to earn trading profits. A strong euro, accepted globally as a reserve currency, has been sought by both banks and industrial capital in Germany. It has turned Germany into an important international financial center, while allowing its industrial capital to gain further access to capital markets as well as relocate across Europe.[106]

A final requirement for a managed global reserve currency is to possess an ideological shroud. In the case of domestic money this shroud is provided by nationalism which treats money as part of the 'national identity'. Since nationalism could not be used within the EMU, the euro has had to rely on the presumed solidarity and unity among European peoples. The euro is the very essence of the neoliberal Europeanism that presently dominates the EU. Its actual deployment has in turn strengthened Europeanist ideology, particularly among the smaller states of the union.

But the core has never been prepared to accept fiscal costs on behalf of its lesser partners. For Germany, in particular, the eurozone was not to be allowed to become a field of systematic 'fiscal transfers'. The Europeanist ideology of the monetary union has always had a hard edge reflecting the underlying character of the common currency. This feature has been of vital importance in the unfolding of the crisis.

The euro mediates the global crisis in Europe

The euro has mediated the world crisis in Europe and determined its characteristic form. Fundamental to it has been the sharp internal division of the

---

106 See Macartney, H., (2009), 'Variegated neo-liberalism: Transnationally oriented fractions of capital in EU financial market integration', *Review of International Studies*, 35: 451–480.

FIG. 1 Evolution of nominal unit labour costs (1995 = 100)

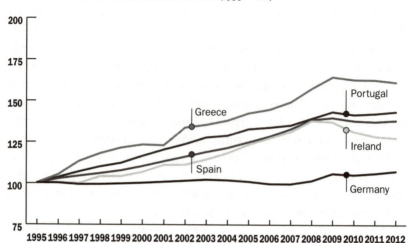

Source: *AMECO (2011 and 2012 are forecasts)*

eurozone between core and periphery, the latter including Spain, Portugal, Ireland and Greece. The 'race to the bottom' fostered by the monetary union was won by Germany in the 2000s by keeping wages down since the early 1990s, while weakening trade union organisation. Figure 1 shows the path of nominal unit labour costs – a standard measure of competitiveness – in Germany and peripheral countries since the mid-1990s.

Germany has had significant competitive advantages from the beginning but the divergence of nominal unit labour costs – reflecting higher rates of inflation in the periphery countries – has exacerbated its lead. The roots of the division of the eurozone into core and periphery lie in the systematic gains of competitiveness by Germany. [107] It is worth stressing that German gains have resulted entirely from keeping the nominal cost of labour low, i.e., from applying severe wage restraint on German workers. The structures of the EMU might have been

---

107 As was already mentioned, the eurozone also has an external periphery in Eastern Europe which has presented similar tendencies to the internal periphery but does not concern us here.

FIG. 2 Evolution of productivity growth (1995 = 100)

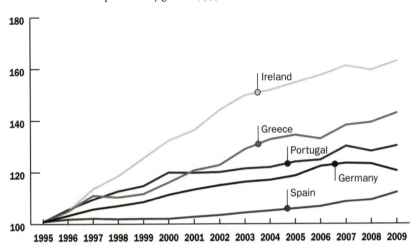

Source: *OECD*

beneficial for German capital, but they have been inimical to German workers.

It seems that since 2009 unit labour costs have begun to converge. German costs have risen gently as the country recovered rapidly from the recession of 2008–9, mostly on the back of strong export performance. Greek and Irish costs, on the other hand, have collapsed as severe austerity plans were imposed following the eruption of the eurozone crisis, while Spanish and Portuguese costs have probably declined more gently. The preferred adjustment policy of the EU in the face of the crisis is apparent: reduce unit labour costs drastically in the periphery through austerity. This policy has had severe social costs and class implications, and would take several years to reduce the gap of competitiveness significantly, particularly in view of persistent German wage restraint.

Note, finally, that the gains in German competitiveness during the preceding period have had nothing to do with advances in productivity, which has been considerably worse in Germany than Greece and Ireland. The weakness of German productivity growth, moreover, has not been ameliorated in the course of the crisis, as figure 2 shows.

Loss of competitiveness led to persistent current account deficits for the periphery, mirrored by equally persistent surpluses for the core, above all, Ger-

FIG. 3 Current account balances as percent of GDP

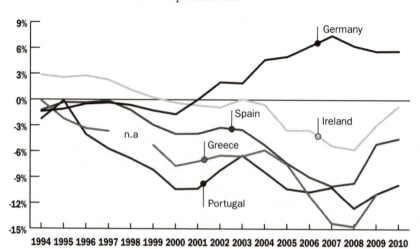

Source: *IMF BOPS Yearbook (BPM5)*

many, as is shown in figure 3. There is variation among peripheral countries in this respect. Greece, for instance, has recorded enormous current account deficits driven by equally large trade deficits, while Ireland has had much smaller current account deficits and its trade balance has typically been in surplus.[108] Note, finally, that the divergence has narrowed in the course of the crisis as austerity has narrowed the competitiveness gap. It would be a long time before the scissors closed simply on the basis of austerity measures.

Rising current account deficits in the periphery were financed by foreign lending, both private and public, which was easy for much of the 2000s as the ECB kept interest rates low. Figure 4 shows the exposure of core banks – mostly French and German – to the periphery, which peaked in early 2008. But note that there was also a second, lower, peak in 2009. Following the collapse of Lehman Brothers in late 2008, core banks increased their lending to peripheral countries, including Greece. Much of this lending was to sovereigns on

---

108 Nonetheless, the bulk of German surpluses have not derived only – or even mostly – from the periphery, but from across the eurozone.

FIG. 4 Core bank exposure to eurozone periphery ($ million)

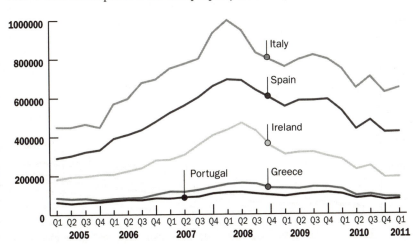

Source: *BIS consolidated banking statistics*

the assumption that they would not default: there was plain market failure.[109]

At the same time, peripheral banks had access to cheap funds available in the interbank euro market. They were, therefore, able to expand their assets rapidly particularly after 2005, as is shown in Figure 5. Note that Irish banks operated on a hugely greater scale than the rest, partly reflecting the development path adopted by Ireland privileging foreign capital inflows.

For a brief period cheap credit made peripheral membership of the eurozone seem successful as rates of GDP growth were generally higher than in the core, with the exception of Portugal. When the crisis of 2007 broke out, however, it became apparent that peripheral success lacked foundations, shown by the divergence in competitiveness. The periphery found itself enormously indebted, domestically and abroad, privately and publicly, though the particular mix of debt varied in each country according to its social and political features.[110]

---

109 These points were established in detail in Parts 1 and 2.

110 The macroeconomic processes of peripheral indebtedness and the profile of peripheral debt were shown in Part 2.

FIG. 5 Total bank assets (percent of GDP)

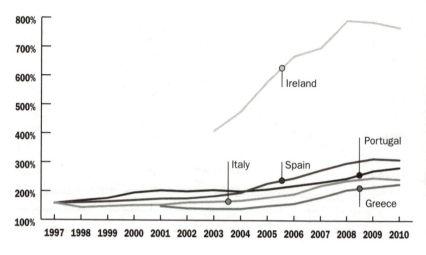

Source: *National Central Banks*

By 2009 Greece carried a large public debt, although private debt had increased much faster during the preceding period. Even more strikingly, the composition of Greek public debt had changed and by the end of the decade two thirds were owed to foreign lenders. Ireland and Spain, on the other hand, carried lower public debt, but much greater private debts generated by banks that financed real estate bubbles in the 2000s. Portugal also had a relatively modest public debt, while facing increased debts of households and banks. Similarly to Greece though, public debt was owed heavily to foreign lenders. The process through which the debt crisis broke out in the periphery is not in doubt. The collapse of Lehman Brothers in 2008 led to recession in both the core and the periphery of the eurozone as exports and investment fell. Eurozone states faced falling tax revenues, while attempting to support aggregate demand and to rescue banks. Rising budget deficits followed, the direct result of the crisis and not of state profligacy, even in Greece, as figure 6 shows.

Escalating budget deficits and unfolding recession led to rapid growth of sovereign debt in the periphery. Bond markets began to have doubts about the creditworthiness of the debt of peripheral sovereigns. It gradually became clear that the core would not accept responsibility for the public debt of the periphery.

FIG. 6 Government primary balances (percent of GDP)

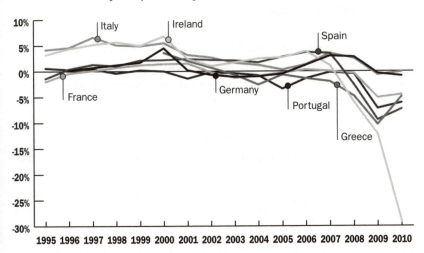

Source: *Eurostat*

Consequently, Greece, Ireland and Portugal were successively shut out of bond markets in 2010–11. The attitude of the core has been entirely consistent with the nature of the euro as a *sui generis* reserve currency. Core countries, above all Germany, have never accepted fiscal responsibility for the periphery since they have lacked effective means of monitoring and sanctioning fiscal performance.

The real problem for the core, however, has been the likely impact of peripheral default on core banks. Indebted peripheral states have posed a threat to the banks of both core and periphery - which had grown enormously by taking advantage of the common currency. The countries of the core have been forced to respond to protect their own banks as well as the euro. As contagion began to spread beyond the periphery in 2011, threatening Spain and Italy, the danger to banks and to the monetary union as a whole loomed large. The response of core countries has reflected the contradictory and discriminatory nature of the monetary union, and has also indicated that the euro is probably not sustainable in its existing form, if at all. The political economy of the threatened rupture is examined in the following chapter.

14. MONETARY DISUNION: INSTITUTIONAL MALFUNCTIONING AND POWER RELATIONS

Several economists have argued that the EMU is inherently unstable and could lead to crisis. A cursory list would include Flassbeck, who has claimed consistently that the monetary union would prove untenable in view of the entrenched differences in competitiveness that favour Germany.[111] It would also include Arestis and Sawyer who have examined the institutional defects of the eurozone.[112] Others, such as Feldstein and Friedman, have noted the contradiction between the homogeneity of monetary policy and the fragmentation of fiscal policy across the eurozone.[113]

When the crisis burst out, several economists claimed that its resolution would require radical change of the monetary union. Thus, Goodhart and Tsomocos have proposed the creation of a dual-currency system for peripheral countries;[114] Aliber has argued that devaluation and exiting the eurozone would prove inevitable for Greece; [115] and Rogoff has insisted that peripheral countries, above all, Greece and Portugal, would probably default and exit the eurozone.[116]

---

111 For a succinct summary, see Flassbeck, H. and Spiecker, F. (2009), 'Cracks in euroland and no way out', *Intereconomics* 44: 1, pp. 2–3.

112 See, for instance, Arestis, P., Brown, A., and Sawyer, M., (eds), (2001), *The Euro: Evolution and Prospects*, Cheltenham, UK and Northampton, USA: Edward Elgar.

113 See Feldstein, M. (1997), 'The political economy of the European Economic and Monetary Union: Political sources of an economic liability', *National Bureau of Economic Research Working Paper Series*, no. 6150. See also 'An interview with Milton Friedman. Interviewed by John B. Taylor, May 2000', in Samuelson, P. and Barnett, W., (eds), (2007), *Inside the Economist's Mind: Conversations with Eminent Economists*, Blackwell: Oxford.

114 See Goodhart, C. and Tsomocos, D. (2010), 'The Californian solution for Club Med', *Financial Times*, January 25.

115 See Aliber, R. (2010), 'The Devaluation of the Greek euro', *International Political Economy*, Marvin Zonis & Associates, February 17.

116 See for instance, Pressley, J. (2010), 'Harvard's Rogoff Says EU's Bazooka Won't Prevent Defaults', *Bloomberg*, May 19.

As the crisis deepened in 2010–11 it became conventional wisdom that the eurozone suffered from major institutional weaknesses. Above all, the union was thought to possess a unitary monetary policy backed by a single central bank and a homogeneous money market, but not to have made equivalent provision for fiscal policy. During the 2000s the eurozone has relied on the Stability and Growth Pact which stipulated limits for budget deficits and the aggregate national debt (3 percent and 60 percent of GDP, respectively), an approach that has worked badly since responsibility was left to individual sovereign states.

However, the institutional malfunctioning of the eurozone was not merely the result of poor design, and nor of bad economic theory. It was, rather, the outcome of political and social relations that have underpinned the creation of a new international reserve currency. At the root of the turmoil in the eurozone lie class and imperial interests, not the 'technical' errors of monetary union. Both the crisis and the subsequent response of the EU have been shaped by these interests, leading to contradictory and problematic outcomes, as is shown in subsequent sections.

The ECB and the limits of liquidity provision

The main agent of EU intervention has been the ECB for two reasons. First, the true threat posed by the crisis has been to the financial system of Europe, which is the natural province of a central bank. Second, in the absence of a unitary state to support the EMU, the ECB has been forced to substitute itself in part for a fiscal authority. The result has been to complicate, instead of resolving, the crisis. To establish this claim consider the following points about central banking.

A central bank is the dominant bank of the interbank (or money) market overseeing the supply of liquidity among private banks. It can play this role because its own liabilities are typically the most acceptable form of credit money. The specific ways of liquidity provision depend on the institutional composition of the financial system. For much of the post-war period, central banks provided liquidity directly, for instance, through the discount window. Financialisation brought rapid growth of financial markets and increased trading of financial assets, encouraging central banks to provide liquidity through market transactions, including the outright purchase of securities, or more often the use of repos.

Nonetheless, the principle has remained that central banks can act as last line of defence in terms of liquidity because their liabilities are the most acceptable form of credit money. The ultimate guarantor of this function, however, is the state whose power – fiat – turns the liabilities of the central bank into legal tender for commercial and other obligations. The state is also the ultimate guarantor of the solvency of the central bank which remains, after all, a bank. By lending freely at times of crisis the central bank acquires substantial credit risk, and hence relies on the state to replenish its capital out of tax and other revenues, should there be major losses. In short, the unencumbered delivery of central banking functions ultimately depends on the fiscal authority.

In this light, the ECB is a peculiar central bank, as befits the principal institution supporting a novel and peculiar form of reserve currency. It is by far the dominant bank in the EMU interbank market determining benchmark interest rates and normalising the supply of liquidity. It formulates and conducts monetary policy through the medium of the National Central Banks, as is described in Box 1. Yet, it cannot rely on the backing of a unitary state, and has to draw its legitimacy from social trust mobilised across the eurozone as well as from shifting relations among member states. This is a major weakness for the ECB.

It is important to note in this respect that ECB capital has been provided by member states in carefully calibrated proportions, each carrying individual responsibility for its share, as is shown in Box 2. These proportions – as well as locating the ECB in Frankfurt – reflect the inherently hierarchical nature of the EMU, with Germany at the top. It is no accident that these proportions have been used as the benchmark for the rescue loans to member states in 2010-11.

It is equally important to note that the ECB was set up as an 'independent' central bank, in part following the theoretical fashion of the 1990s. From its inception it has been an exclusionary agglomeration of public servants, bureaucrats and technocrats operating under the explicit mandate of controlling inflation. Under no circumstances was the 'independent' ECB to finance the borrowing of member states since that could potentially breach the fundamental principle of EMU construction, i.e., that weaker states should not impose fiscal obligations on stronger ones.

In the wake of the Lehman Brothers' collapse in 2008, the ECB has provided liquidity to banks on a large scale, at very low rates, through a variety of methods summed up in Box 3. Much of this funding has been through longer-term financing operations typically on the basis of accepting illiquid private securities and problematic sovereign bonds as collateral.

As the crisis has deepened, however, the ECB has come under increasing pressure to play an implicit fiscal role by acquiring sovereign paper from banks in the secondary markets. Indeed, in 2011, it faced demands to assume an explicit fiscal role by acquiring sovereign paper directly from weaker countries, possibly running in the trillions of euro. In effect, the ECB has been asked to homogenise public borrowing in the EMU and substitute itself for the missing unitary or federal state. And yet, the ECB would itself require the presence of a unitary or federal state, if it was to act as a fiscal agent for the entire EMU. This absurdity reflects the contradictory and unsustainable nature of the monetary union.

Much of the trouble for the ECB has arisen because sovereign debt and banking difficulties are inextricably intertwined within the EMU, as was discussed in Parts 1 and 2, and have become even more closely related in the course of the crisis. European banks indeed face liquidity shortages, but their deeper problem is weak solvency as a result of exposure to sovereign debt, particularly in the periphery. Dealing with solvency requires either shutting down the insolvent agent, or making injections of fresh capital. Liquidity provision is of no use and it can even make the problem worse by sending good money after bad.

The proper agent to deal with insolvent banks would be an arm of the Ministry of Finance able to shut down insolvent banks as well as provide fresh capital by mobilising the state's capacity to tax. A central bank is not equipped for this task, either by nature or by design. In the absence of a Ministry of Finance, however, the ECB has been forced to take problematic sovereign and private paper from banks, allowing the latter to shift credit risk onto the balance sheet of the central bank. Pressure on the ECB to play an even more active fiscal role has meant that it could find itself providing gigantic loans to states, which would be partly used to bolster the solvency of the European banking system. For a central bank that lacks a state to lean on, the complexities of this policy could become serious, particularly regarding the acceptability of its own liabilities. In sum, the ECB has been under pressure to play a role that it cannot deliver well and which creates risks both for the central bank and for the common currency.

BOX 1 CENTRAL BANKING IN THE EMU

The ECB was established on 1 June 1998 as the central bank in charge of the single European Currency. The ECB manages the European System of Central Banks (ESCB), which comprises the ECB and the National Central Banks (NCBs) of all members of the EU, including those that have not adopted the euro. The Eurosystem refers to the ECB and the NCBs of the 17 countries that have adopted the euro.

On 1 January 1998, the third and final stage of monetary union (EMU) was launched, with the irrevocable fixing of the conversion rates of the 11 member states that initially chose to adopt the euro, the surrendering of monetary policy control to the ESCB, and the introduction of the single currency.

The objectives of the ESCB are defined as follows: 'The primary objective of the ESCB shall be to maintain price stability. Without prejudice to the objective of price stability, the ESCB shall support the general economic policies in the Community with a view to contributing to the achievement of the objectives of the Community as laid down in Article 2' (Article 105.1 of the Treaty Establishing the European Community). Article 2 of the Treaty specifies that the objectives of the economic policy of the European Community include a high level of employment and sustainable, non-inflationary growth.

The independence of the ESCB is legally encoded in the Treaty establishing the European Community and in the Statutes of the ESCB and the ECB. This serves to preclude the possibility of the national government of any member state exerting influence on either the ECB or the NCBs of member states.

The ESCB formulates and implements monetary policy, with the primary objective of maintaining price stability. Although monetary policy is decided by the ECB, policy implementation is undertaken by the NCBs on the behalf of the ECB.

Monetary policy implementation is carried out by using three main instruments: standing facilities, open market operations and reserve requirements. The technical details of monetary policy implementation are briefly discussed below with reference to a consolidated Eurosystem balance sheet.[117]

---

117   Adapted from Bindseil, U. (2004), *Monetary Policy Implementation, Theory, Past, Present,* Oxford: Oxford University Press.

Under normal circumstances, the ECB does not hold securities outright for the purposes of monetary policy implementation. Instead, repurchase agreement operations (repos) are used as the primary tool for liquidity management of the eurozone banking system. These operations are shown on the balance sheet as 'OMO short term' and 'OMO long term'. However since the start of the Securities Market Programme (SMP) in 2010, aimed at easing conditions in government bond markets, the ECB has been making outright purchases of government securities in the secondary markets. These are recorded under the category 'Domestic securities incl. government debt and SMP', which has expanded significantly in recent months. Purchases made through the SMP reached around EUR 160 bn by the end of September 2011. The ECB aims to 'sterilise' liquidity released through these operations by using offsetting operations. The item 'fixed term deposits' on the liabilities side of the balance sheet represents one of the mechanisms by which the ECB attempts to withdraw liquidity, auctioning fixed-term deposits at above-market-rates of interest.

The ECB provides both a borrowing and a lending facility with unlimited access. Under normal market conditions, recourse to both is very limited and tends to be symmetrical. This reflects the fact that the ECB is able to control money market interest rates such that they stay close to the target level by using open market operations as the primary policy instrument. However, as can be seen from the balance sheet shown in the figure below, while recourse to the marginal lending facility was negligible at around EUR 0.5 bn, recourse to the deposit facility was significant at EUR 150 bn. This reflects increasing tension in the money markets as banks have become more wary of lending, and have instead chosen to keep liquidity safe at a low rate of interest (currently 0.75 percent) at the ECB.

Note that NCBs remain crucial to the eurozone. In the course of the crisis NCBs have become even more important, signalling a reassertion of national interest across the eurozone, as is shown in chapter 16. NCBs retain the ability to act separately from each other, while the financial system of each country gains access to the ESCB through its own NCB. Transactions between NCBs, or between NCBs and the ECB, give rise to reciprocal (gross and net) NCB claims within the eurozone.

The Eurosystem can thus be considered as a kind of European interbank market for NCBs in which central banks with surplus reserves lend to others that are short of reserves. At the same time, NCBs are also linked to domestic money markets, allowing domestic banks to have access to a continental pool of liquidity through the Eurosystem.

Consolidated financial statement of the Eurosystem as at 23 September 2011 (bn euro)

ASSETS		LIABILITIES	
Gold and net foreign assets	541.1	Banknotes in circulation	852.5
Domestic securities incl. government debt and SMP	586.1	Capital, reserves, incl. revaluation accounts	398.1
Other domestic assets	70.8	Other autonomous factors	125.3
OMO Short term	201.1		
OMO Longer term	369.6		
Borrowing facility	0.5	Deposits of credit institutions	154.0
		Reserves of credit institutions	223.5
		Fixed-term deposits	152.5
Other Assets	344.1	Other liabilities	207.4
TOTAL	**2113.3**	**TOTAL**	**2113.3**

Source: *ECB, Monetary Policy Statistics, figures rounded to the nearest million.*

BOX 2 NATIONAL CENTRAL BANK (NCB) CONTRIBUTIONS TO ECB CAPITAL

The data refers to the amounts paid up by NCBs on 01/01/2011, which reflect:

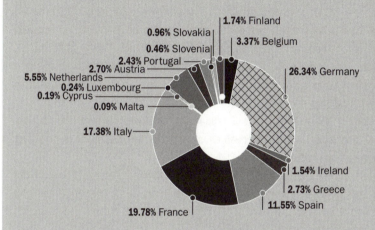

Source: *ECB, available at http://www.ecb.int/ecb/orga/capital/html/index.en.html*

NCB shares in ECB capital – calculated using the respective country's share in the total population and gross domestic product of the EU, with equal weights. They are adjusted every five years and whenever a new country joins the EU.

The EU non-euro area NCB contributions – reflecting the operational costs incurred by the NCBs due to their participation in the European System of Central Banks (ESCB) which is equivalent to 3.75 percent of their subscribed capital. The non-euro area NCBs are not entitled to receive any share of the profits of the ECB, nor are they liable to fund losses of the ECB.

The recent increase in ECB subscribed capital of €5 billion, from €5.76 billion to €10.76 billion, with effect from 29 December 2010. In order to smooth the transfer of capital to the ECB, additional capital contributions by NCBs have been subscribed in three equal annual instalments, starting on 29 December 2010.

BOX 3 MAIN ECB OPERATIONS FROM AUGUST 2007 TO LATE 2011

August 2007: (1) temporary supply of additional liquidity; (2) supplementary longer-term refinancing operations – more than €600 billion of refinancing to the banking sector.

December 2007: To meet the dollar funding problems of banks the ECB provided US$ liquidity, against collateral eligible for Eurosystem credit operation, in connection with the Federal Reserve System's US$ Term Auction Facility (TAF). The US dollars were provided by the Federal Reserve System to the ECB by means of a temporary swap line and the Eurosystem passed them on to its counterparties in repo operations.

September 2008: (1) special-term refinancing operations; (2) fixed rate full allotment procedure; (3) narrowing of spreads formed by the rates on the two standing facilities around the MRO rate.

October 2008: (1) expansion of the securities eligible as collateral, to enhance the provision of longer-term refinancing, with effect from 30 October 2008 and until the end of the first quarter of 2009; (2) provision of US dollar liquidity through foreign exchange swaps.

May 2009: (1) enhanced credit support; refinancing operations with a maturity of 12 months; (2) purchase of euro-denominated covered bonds.

May 2010: The Governing Council of the ECB decided on several measures to address severe tensions in financial markets. In particular, it decided to conduct interventions in the public and private debt securities markets (Securities Markets Programme) and to adopt a fixed rate tender procedure with full allotment in the regular three-month longer-term refinancing operations in May and June 2010.

August 2011: (1) Provision of liquidity to banks by means of full allotment at fixed rates extended until at least early 2012; (2) Eurosystem will conduct a liquidity-providing supplementary longer-term refinancing operation with maturity of approximately six months as a fixed rate tender procedure with full allotment; (3) active implementation of the SMP.

September 2011: ECB announces additional US dollar liquidity-providing operations. To sum up, ECB interventions have amounted to:

A. Non-standard monetary measures:
Securities Markets Programme (SMP), i.e. provision of unlimited liquidity at various maturities (up to 1 year) with fixed interest rates in exchange for eligible securities the criteria for which have become more flexible in the course of the financial crisis

B. Main liquidity provision measures:
On the ECB's asset side:
Main refinancing operations
Longer-term refinancing operations
SMP
Covered bond purchase programme
US dollar repo and swap operations
On the ECB's liability side:
Banknotes
Liquidity absorbing fine-tuning operations
Overnight deposit facilities as main counterparty to the refinancing operations and more recently the SMP

C. Features of SMP Operations
Collateral accepted after a haircut
Only in secondary markets, not directly from governments
Fully sterilised by means of specific liquidity absorbing operations, mainly through term-deposit facilities

EFSF and ESM fumbling

The knotty problem of bank solvency ultimately reflects the contradictory and hierarchical relations at the heart of the eurozone. The monetary union possesses both a homogeneous monetary sphere and a homogeneous interbank market, but there is no such thing as a 'European' bank. Banks are international when it comes to liquidity, but national when it comes to solvency. If credit losses put solvency at risk, the last recourse of a bank in Europe would be to its nation state.

This contradiction has had a vicious aspect in the context of the eurozone crisis since the major threat to bank solvency has arisen precisely because of the debt of nation states. How could a nation state be the rescuer of its banks when it is also the pre-eminent threat to them? Given the close interconnection among European banks, the insolvency of some banks could thus pose a major threat to the stability of the system as a whole. By implication, the monetary union would be at risk of collapse.

In principle the problem could be solved through private takeover of weak banks, or through capital injections by another state, or states. The former option remains valid and might well materialise in the long term thus leading to wholesale restructuring of European banking. The latter option, however, has proven exceedingly difficult to materialise because the eurozone lacks an over-arching state. The sovereign states of the core have had neither the disposition, nor the legitimacy, to rescue troubled banks in the periphery, or indeed in other countries of the core. If they did provide the required capital injections, they would also require a hardnosed *quid pro quo*.

The EMU has consistently skirted around this difficulty, mostly because of the inherent complexity of the problem. Its preferred response has been to advance rescue loans to peripheral states, thus enabling states to support banks and to continue financing public expenditure. This had the further advantage of concealing the banking problem under the cloak of a putative fiscal crisis caused by profligate and dissolute peripheral countries. The mechanism chosen for the purpose was the European Financial Stability Facility (EFSF), an essentially temporary mechanism that would presumably be replaced by the permanent mechanism of the European Stability Mechanism (ESM) in 2013, or even earlier. Both are briefly discussed in Box 4.

These mechanisms were the product of social and political relations constitutive of the EMU. The EFSF was set up essentially as a Special Purpose Vehicle (or Collateralised Debt Obligation) issuing its own bonds to lend to states in distress. Its own borrowing has nonetheless stuck rigidly to the fundamental EMU principle of individual responsibility for the debt of each guarantor state.

The support that peripheral countries have received from the EFSF (and the support Greece initially received through its special programme of May 2010) has comprised loans guaranteed on an intergovernmental basis, pro rata to each state's contribution to the capital of the ECB. Even toward the end of 2011, and as the crisis became acute, the core of the union showed no disposition to setting up a system of jointly honouring the debts of the periphery. Rescue loans have remained temporary, crisis-driven measures forced upon core countries. Hierarchical relations, enshrined in capital provision to the ECB, have been strictly maintained with the result that Germany has had the final word on all rescues.

Furthermore, rescue loans were initially designed to be punitively expensive presumably to teach a moral lesson to delinquent sovereign borrowers. The contrast with the exceptionally cheap liquidity that the ECB provided to equally troubled banks could not be sharper. Perhaps private banks were not in need of additional moral fortitude. Last, but far from least, support for the periphery came on condition of tough austerity policies, designed and supervised by the IMF, which also contributed to the bailouts.

The inadequacy of this response has become vividly apparent in late 2011 as austerity led to a worsening of the crisis thus making sovereign default more likely. The risks to banks increased correspondingly. If the EFSF was to confront the problem, it would have to command greater resources but, more significantly, it would also have to rescue the banks of failing sovereigns. For this, it would need either to operate on the basis of joint and several liability for its debts, or it would have to draw directly on the guarantees of the leading states of the EMU to rescue the banks of other states. In both cases it would come into direct conflict with the fundamental fiscal principle of the EMU regarding fiscal responsibility of member states. Try as it might, the EMU cannot get away from the underlying absence of a unitary or federal state. The implications for both the ECB and the EFSF are considered in more detail in chapter 15 after briefly examining the results of the rescue programmes and austerity in the periphery.

BOX 4 THE EFSF AND THE ESM

The EFSF resembles the Special Purpose Vehicles (SPVs) that allowed banks to remove risky assets from their balance sheets during the sub-prime bubble, and which played a central role in the early stages of the crisis. It is an independent company, headquartered in Luxembourg, with the remit of issuing bonds in capital markets to raise funds to assist eurozone countries facing serious fiscal difficulties. It was established in May 2010 with an initial lending capacity of around EUR 250 bn, but has subsequently been expanded to raise the lending capacity to EUR 440 bn.

The bonds issued by the EFSF have been guaranteed by eurozone member states according to the share of the latter in the capital contributions to the ECB. The initial design of the EFSF made provision for EUR 440 bn of guarantees, which allowed for a total lending capacity of around 250 bn at an over-guarantee rate of 120 percent. The facility was subsequently expanded to allow for up to 440 bn of lending against guarantees of 780 bn, an over-guarantee rate of 165 percent. Of that 780 bn in guarantees, around 450 bn was AAA-rated, with the rest AA and below. The largest guarantee contributions came from Germany and France, at 210 bn and 160 bn respectively. The structure of the vehicle has implied that lenders would be fully covered on the principal as long as defaults by sovereign guarantors would not exceed 165 percent of the total amount borrowed.

In late 2011 the Facility could use the funds raised to provide assistance to distressed sovereigns in one of three ways:

Sovereigns that were not in an IMF programme could borrow directly from the EFSF on the basis of strict conditionality on the debtor government. Conditionality would inevitably entail austerity packages aiming to reduce fiscal deficits through deflationary policies.

Countries could also borrow from the EFSF for the purposes of domestic bank recapitalisation. This borrowing would not be provided directly to the banks that required the funds, but would be undertaken by the government of the country in which the bank to be recapitalised would be resident.

The EFSF could intervene directly in the secondary bond markets, buying up the debt of distressed countries with the aim of stabilising yields. In exceptional circumstances the EFSF would be allowed to make purchases directly in the primary bond markets.

The EFSF was conceived initially as a temporary 'holding measure' to calm markets and to allow for short-term emergency lending. At the same time, a permanent entity, the European Stabilisation Mechanism (ESM), was due to come into existence in June 2013 in a phased takeover from the EFSF.

The proposed ESM would act as a permanent lending facility, with powers similar to that of the EFSF, and was to be capitalised with EUR 700 bn, allowing for a total lending capacity of EUR 500 bn. Of the EUR 700 bn capitalisation, EUR 80 bn would take the form of paid-in capital, with the remainder taking the form of guarantees, as in the EFSF. This capital was to be paid in instalments of EUR 16 bn on an annual basis starting from 2013.

15. FAILING AUSTERITY: CLASS INTERESTS AND INSTITUTIONAL FIXES

Virtuous austerity: Hurting without working

The rescue packages for the periphery have been driven by neoliberal ideology convinced of the virtues of 'fiscal responsibility' as both cure and preventative of crises. Austerity has been imposed, coupled with liberalisation and privatisation: public spending has been cut, taxes increased, wages reduced, markets have been further deregulated, and public enterprises have been lined up for privatisation. A summary of the most recent measures is given in Box 5 below.

BOX 5 THE HOLY TRINITY: AUSTERITY, LIBERALISATION, PRIVATISATION

Since the end of 2010 cuts in public expenditure, increased taxes, privatisations and further labour market deregulation have been adopted, more or less, across Europe. But the degree and incidence have varied considerably among countries of the periphery, or those close to it.

Spain and Italy, confronted with increasing difficulties in accessing international bond markets, have adopted austerity programs voluntarily, though almost certainly under pressure from the EU. Spain, in particular, has endured an adjustment programme that was initiated in 2010 bringing spending cuts, tax increases and labour market liberalisation. In 2011 Spain also accepted the introduction of formal public deficit limits in its constitution. Italy has approved an austerity package of EUR 45.5 bn that would entail spending cuts and increased taxes, affecting in particular local council services.

Portugal, Ireland and Greece have signed memoranda with the "troika" institutions (IMF, ECB and EU). Provision has been made for spending cuts and higher taxes, but the memoranda have been far more than fiscal road maps to lower public deficits and debt. They entail profound change in the historic organisation of these societies, including liberalising reforms in health, education, social security, the judicial system and so on.

In a little more detail:

Greece

After more than a year of unrelenting austerity, and under pressure from the troika,

---

Greece announced in September/October 2011 a new round of measures, despite the severity of recession in 2010–11. Key points were the dismissal of 30,000 public sector workers and further cuts of 20 percent on pensions above 1200 euro (or 40 percent for retired people under 55 years old). The Greek government has also proposed an extremely ambitious – and widely perceived as unattainable – privatisation programme that would ostensibly raise EUR 50 bn.

Portugal

The new right-wing Portuguese government has announced its intention to go beyond the troika memorandum signed by the previous government. Following a cut of 5 percent of public sector workers wages and pensions in 2011, further cuts of 14 percent were planned for 2012–13. New taxes have been announced: income tax equivalent to 3.5 percent of annual income, VAT on essential goods and utilities (gas and electricity have risen to 18 percent), property taxes, and so on. Further cuts in unemployment and other social benefits and labour market liberalisation were scheduled for 2011–2. The privatisation programme was also accelerated forecasting revenues of EUR 5 bn.

Ireland

In Ireland, the troika has forced reform of income tax by widening the tax base, lowering tax bands and reducing various tax benefits. New taxes were to be imposed on property and capital gains. The pension system was to be reformed by raising the average age of retirement, while new entrants would suffer a 10 percent cut in their expected pension. An average cut of pensions of 4 percent was expected for 2011. Social protection and the number of public sector workers were to be reduced in coming years.

These policies have aimed at protecting the interests of banks and bondholders by preventing default as well as protecting the interests of industrial capital by changing the balance of power against labour. Pressure has been so severe that the conditions of life of the middle class have also been disrupted in terms of income and employment, including the operations of small business.

Predictably, austerity has failed to resolve the crisis and indeed made things worse, since the crisis has not been caused by fiscal profligacy, as was established in Part 1. Rather, its roots lie in the loss of competitiveness by the periph-

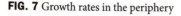

FIG. 7 Growth rates in the periphery

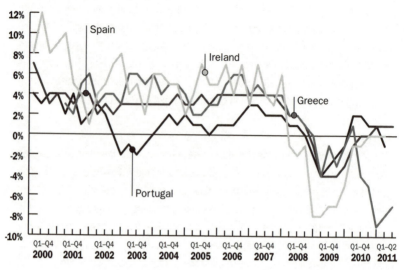

Source: *Eurostat*

ery coupled with the enormous expansion of the financial system in the 2000s. Therefore, austerity and additional pressure on labour in the periphery would be unlikely to prove effective in the short run, if at all. The competitiveness gap and the current account imbalances between core and periphery would probably persist. At the same time, public expenditure cuts and tax increases, together with credit shortages due to problems of banks, have exacerbated recession in the periphery. Conditions in Greece in particular have become extremely severe.

Figure 7 indicates that recovery from the recession of 2008-9 in the periphery is at considerable risk following the application of austerity. Greek GDP has collapsed as the country has entered one of the most severe contractions in its recent history. It is likely that the other peripheral countries will also re-enter recession in the coming period.

The counterpart to recession has been a rise in unemployment, a true reflection of the social cost of austerity. Emigration, especially among the young, also appears to be increasing in the periphery. Figure 8 shows the rapid growth in unemployment, particularly in Spain and Greece where conditions have begun to resemble the Great Depression of the 1930s.

FIG. 8 Unemployment rates in the periphery

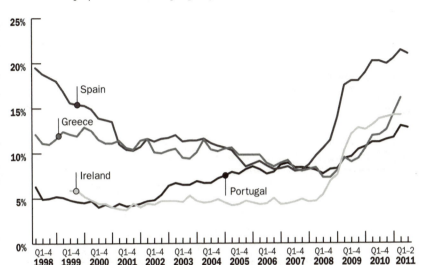

Source: *Eurostat*

The failure of austerity, however, is even more apparent in the ratio of public debt to GDP. Far from declining, or even coming under control, the ratio has been rising across the periphery, especially in Greece and Ireland, as is shown in Figure 9. This is hardly surprising, considering the contraction of GDP in Greece, but also the gigantic shift of private debt onto the public books in Ireland because the state offered a foolish guarantee for private bank debt, partly under pressure from the EU.

The failure of austerity has been in large part due to the inability of the periphery to devalue, thus regaining competitiveness decisively. The contraction of aggregate demand has been barely offset by the narrowing of the current account deficits. In effect, peripheral countries have found themselves trapped within the eurozone, facing austerity and high unemployment for the foreseeable future. The rising burden of sovereign debt, meanwhile, has exacerbated the prospect of insolvency and default for peripheral states.

The EU response to the crisis offers an example of policies that aim to protect the interests of large financial and industrial capital, only to undermine them. As recession in the periphery deepened and insolvency became worse,

FIG. 9 Ratio of public debt to GDP in the periphery

Source: *Eurostat*

the banks of both core and periphery have faced greater risks. The creditworthiness of Italy and other large countries in the eurozone was affected since they carry sizeable volumes of debt and their economies have performed weakly for years. Financial capital and neoliberal ideology in the eurozone appeared to burying themselves in a hole of their own making.

Desperately searching for alternatives

In response to perceived failure of austerity, various alternative proposals have been mooted, most prominently the suggestion of issuing eurobonds.[118] Despite

---

118 See, most notably, Delpla, J. and von Weizsäcker (2010), 'The Blue Bond Proposal', *Bruegel Policy Brief 2010/13*, May; Delpla, J. and von Weizsäcker (2011), 'Eurobonds: The Blue Bond Concept and its Implications', *Bruegel Policy Contribution 2011/02*, March; Juncker, J.C. and Tremonti, G. (2010), 'E-bonds would end the crisis', *Financial Times*, December 5; Amato, G. and Verhofstadt, G. (2011), 'A plan to save the euro and curb speculators', *Financial Times*, July 3.

variations, the basic notion is the same: a single authority, such as the EFSF or the ECB, would take it upon itself to borrow on behalf of the union, subsequently allowing individual states to meet shortfalls in funding. Debts issued in this way would be guaranteed jointly and severally, thus breaking with the underlying principle of individual sovereign responsibility.

The idea of eurobonds has been held in abeyance by the determined opposition of the governments of Germany and other core countries. German political opposition has owed to petty electoral calculation and to the dominance of conservative neoliberal ideas within the political establishment. But it also bespeaks powerful interests that are keenly aware of the risks of making tactical fiscal innovations such as eurobonds.

For one thing, eurobonds would entail higher borrowing rates for core countries, above all, for Germany. The higher creditworthiness of the core would act as a subsidy for the periphery. For another, the issuing of eurobonds would be a great stride in the direction of creating an aggregate fiscal authority in the EU. If there is no backing from a federal budget, eurobond liability would ultimately rest on the public purse of core economies. However, creating a substantial federal budget for an over-arching fiscal authority is a very thorny problem for the EU, as was discussed in previous chapters. A tactical move that anticipated the creation of unitary fiscal authority, such as issuing eurobonds, would generate major political problems in both core and periphery, if there were no parallel strategic steps to bring about fiscal union.

Finally, eurobond proposals frequently fail to address the structural problems of competitiveness between core and periphery. If the monetary union is to become viable, core countries must willingly reduce their current account surpluses. Not only would transfers have to be made to peripheral countries, but national labour markets, social policy and tax systems would need to be harmonised among all participants. Resolving the crisis is not just a matter of devising ingenious methods of borrowing and effecting fiscal transfers, but one of radical political and social change across Europe.

Note that left-minded eurobond supporters have generally been in favour of using the borrowing powers of the union to engage in large-scale investment programmes. The intention would be to raise productivity and competitiveness across the periphery, for instance through the European Investment Bank. Under such an outcome, neoliberalism could at last be overcome and the EMU would acquire a more Keynesian character. Yet, given the social and political interests characteristic of the eurozone, this is a remote prospect.

The search for alternatives, even when it has been fruitless, as per eurobonds, has helped to clarify the range of alternative options available to policy makers at present. These vary from full European fiscal federalism at one extreme, to allowing the ECB to purchase large volumes of the debt of member states, thus also cleansing the balance sheets of insolvent banks, at the other.[119] All options would involve some sort of redistributive transfer mechanism between the core and the periphery of Europe, from straightforward taxation and expenditure by a European federal state, to using the seigniorage 'revenues' of the ECB to transfer value from euro holders to the creditors of insolvent institutions, or to states and peripheral taxpayers. In this light, three broad strategic directions for policy stand out.

The first strategy would be full fiscal federalism that could also give full vent to eurobonds. A European federal state, with an autonomous budget financed by levying its own taxes, would issue federal bonds in order to calm debt markets and undertake bank recapitalisations. In theory, it could also allow for European investment policies that might serve to lessen the chronic problems of competitiveness between core and periphery. It is clear from the preceding discussion of the eurozone, however, that this possibility is unlikely to materialise in the near future.

The second strategy would be to rely more heavily on the ECB. The central bank has considerable latent powers of credit and could act as lender of last resort to states in difficulties. ECB credit could be mobilised directly, for instance, by intervening heavily in both the secondary and the primary markets for sovereign bonds.[120] To this purpose the ECB could also fund itself by

---

119 See Buiter, W. (2011), 'The future of the euro area: fiscal union or blundering towards a "you own it you break it europe"', *Citi Economics, Global Economics View*, September 9, for a more detailed analysis of these proposals.

120 Buiter has been advocating widened ECB intervention from the start of the crisis, see Buiter, W. (2011), 'Europe: fear and panic make poor counsellors', *Citi Economics, Global Economics View*, 12 August; Buiter, W. and Rahbari, E. (2011), 'The future of the euro area: fiscal union, break-up or blundering towards a "you break it you own it Europe"', *Citi Economics, Global Economics View*, 9 September. See also De Grauwe, P.

issuing a variant of eurobonds. The costs of bad sovereign debt would thus be transferred to the ECB, avoiding the normal processes of democratic scrutiny applying to fiscal transfers. Unfortunately, there are major problems with assigning this convenient role to the ECB, even without taking into account that its statutes would have to be changed, and that in Germany there is strong public awareness of how it manages its balance sheet.

The fundamental difficulty, already discussed in chapter 15, is that the strategy would delegate a major fiscal role to the ECB, when the latter is no more than a central bank. Even worse, the unitary or federal state on which the ECB would have to rely if it was to assume this role does not exist. The result would be highly precarious: the ECB would expand its balance sheet enormously in the absence of a fiscal authority that would guarantee such an expansion.

If, for instance, the ECB proceeded to lend another EUR2 tr, its balance sheet would roughly double from the current level of EUR2.1 tr, shown in Box 1. Its ability to absorb credit shocks would remain substantial (standing at about EUR 465 bn of revaluation accounts plus capital and reserves, as is shown in the table of Box 1) though extensive recapitalisation would probably be necessary. At the same time, the quality of its assets would decline precipitously since it would be acquiring credit risk while its monetary liabilities would balloon. In the absence of a unitary or federal state to act as ultimate back up for the ECB in confronting these problems, the international acceptability of the euro would be immediately in doubt.

The third strategy would be to make heavier fiscal transfers from the core in exchange for loss of sovereignty by peripheral countries. Fiscally sound countries would endure continued and open-ended bailout guarantees to the periphery with the aim of helping the latter to overcome solvency and competitiveness; the price would be surrender of control over fiscal policy. This would essentially represent a development of the current *status quo*, with discretionary bailout loans replaced by uncapped fiscal transfers.

The instrument could be the EFSF, deployed to buy sovereign debt and recapitalise banks on a large scale. To this purpose, its lending capacity of EUR 440 bn would have to be increased by a factor of at least five and possibly more.

(2011), 'Only a more active ECB can solve the euro crisis', *Economic Policy, CEPS Policy Briefs*, 4 August.

The problem with this tidy suggestion, however, is that it would require core countries to commit substantial further public funds. Given the social and political relations of the eurozone, this would not be very likely.

With the reluctance of core countries to commit further public funds in mind, various proposals have been made to leverage the lending power of the EFSF. Thus, one far-fetched suggestion has been to turn the EFSF into a Collateralised Debt Obligation by tranching its bonds into an 'equity' and a 'junior' layer thus expanding its lending capacity up to two or more trillion.[121] Since the EFSF is already a CDO (its EUR 440 bn lending capacity rests on state guarantees of up to EUR 780 bn) the suggestion would turn it into a CDO squared. The risks would be enormous and, unlike the subprime crisis in the USA, there would be no state to pick up the pieces should a collapse ensue.[122]

Another and more plausible suggestion has been to turn the EFSF into a bank that would then raise its capacity to lend up to EUR2tr by borrowing from the ECB.[123] The new bank would be able to rescue other private banks and buy sovereign paper. In effect this scheme would amount to mobilising ECB credit indirectly and thus by-passing the limitations posed by ECB statutes.

Proposals to deploy the EFSF as fiscal transfer mechanism, whether by committing further public funds or by leveraging it, would run up against two underlying structural weaknesses already mentioned above. First, if the expanded lending capacity of the EFSF relied on the ECB, the question would reappear: who would back up the expanded ECB? Second, if the EFSF undertook a Europe-wide programme of recapitalising banks, the implication would

---

121 See Brunnermeier, M., Garicano, L., Lane, P., van Nieuwerburgh, S., Pagano, M., Reis, R., Santos, T., Vayanos, D. (2011), 'European Safe Bonds (ESBies)', The Euronomics Group, 26 September, http://euro-nomics.com/wp-content/uploads/2011/09/ESBiesWEBsept262011.pdf

122 See Munchau, W., 'Eurozone fix a con trick for the desperate', *Financial Times*, 2 October 2011.

123 See Gros, D. and Mayer, T. (2010), 'How to deal with sovereign default in Europe: Toward a euro(pean) Monetary Fund', *CEPS Policy Brief No 2*, CEPS, Brussels, February/updated May; Gros, D. and Mayer, T. (2011), August 2011: 'What to do when the euro crisis reaches the core', *Economic Policy, CEPS Commentaries*, 18 August.

be that, in effect, the German state would be guaranteeing the rescue of, say, French banks. There is no evidence that the alliance of social and political interests required for such action could emerge in Europe.

And yet, despite the problems inherent to all policy options, there remained overwhelming pressure on core states, especially Germany, to take further steps to confront the deepening crisis by both rescuing banks and relieving lesser sovereigns. The most plausible outcome would be for core powers to continue muddling through by mixing bits of several options. Needless to say, austerity in the periphery and elsewhere would continue as well as privatisation, and deregulation. There could perhaps be further rescue loans to states in trouble. If the debt burden of the periphery became unsustainable, as would be likely, the core would even tolerate default, provided that the process would be managed by the leading powers and creditors of the union. Finally, there would be heavier reliance on the ECB and EFSF along lines discussed above, though the precise form would remain unclear.

Thus, in an important step, the ECB launched on 6 October 2011 two new long-term refinancing operations with maturity, respectively, of 12 and 13 months, to take place in November and December 2011. They would be conducted as fixed rate tender procedures with full allotment on top of regular ECB liquidity operations. In addition, the ECB announced a new covered bond purchase programme with the intended amount of EUR 40 bn. Purchases were due to begin in November 2011 and were expected to be completed by the end of October 2012.

In Box 3 it can be seen that the original long-term refinancing operations and the covered bond purchases by the ECB began in May 2009 and lasted for about a year. The operations bought time for EMU authorities; when they expired in the middle of 2010, the authorities launched the Securities Market Programme (SMP) and the EFSF. Both of the latter were radical measures to support peripheral states and thus the banks of Europe. The announcement of fresh liquidity provision by the ECB similarly intended to buy time and to prepare the ground for more radical measures to support banks, perhaps through heavier purchases of bonds by the ECB.[124]

---

124 Indeed in December 2011, two months after these lines were written, the ECB intervened on a huge scale in the inter-bank market providing liquidity and ameliorating immediate pressures on European banks.

Even more important was the EU summit in Brussels on 26 October which took a number of strategic decisions but without immediately providing requisite detail. Thus, European banks would be asked to reach a higher – 9 percent – capital adequacy threshold after revaluing sovereign bond holdings at market prices. The shortfall was estimated at more than EUR 100 bn, and it was supposed to come from reserves, issuing equity, or state support. For states that were in a weak fiscal position, the funds would presumably come from the EFSF.

The summit also openly contemplated peripheral default with significant haircuts for banks. The contours of default had already been sketched in a deal offered to Greece in July 2011. On that occasion, private lenders to Greece (banks and other bondholders) were to take modest losses (presumably 21 percent of the exposure on average) in exchange for new bonds with better creditworthiness. The deal unravelled quickly as financial agents calculated that, if default was officially possible for Greece and private lenders were forced to take a modest haircut, then default would also be possible for other countries, including Spain and Italy. Given the fraught state of the financial system, the possibility of such losses caused flight from the sovereign debt of these countries.

The summit of 26 October proposed, under intense German pressure, to apply an even deeper haircut to private holders of Greek sovereign paper, perhaps of 50 percent, or even higher. Greece would effectively default, but pressure would be placed on private banks to accept the haircut 'voluntarily' in order to avoid formal default that would trigger CDS payments. The expectation was that Greek debt would be reduced to 120 percent of GDP by 2020. It remains to be seen whether banks would agree to such a prospect and, if not, how they could be coerced into it by states that are not counterparties to the rescheduled obligations.[125] The implications of a 50 percent haircut are examined in more detail in chapter 6.

There would naturally be a price to pay for Greece for the debt reduction. In the first instance, it seemed probable that the country would have to accept direct supervision and monitoring of its fiscal affairs by the EU.

---

125 Negotiations between Greece and its private creditors, but led by the EU and the IMF, were continuing in February 2012, as this book was prepared for publication.

Irrespective of the precise details, there was little doubt that national sovereignty would be severely compromised. Furthermore, there would probably be an extensive programme of privatising public assets. If the press was to be believed, the German government has considered plans of widespread privatisation in Greece along the lines of the Treuhand Model in East Germany. Privatisations would be executed by German officials in the hope of netting EUR125 bn that could be used to pay off remaining lenders to Greece.[126]

To prevent the 26 October agreement from unravelling similarly to that of 21 July, EU leaders attempted to make stronger provision for the EFSF enabling it to purchase sovereign debt as well as supporting banks. But the structural weaknesses of the EFSF could hardly be wished away. The summit did not announce a precise way of boosting the lending capacity of the EFSF, although it appeared that some version of turning the EFSF into even more of an SPV was contemplated. In addition, there were suggestions that the EFSF should be turned effectively into an insurance company, using its capital to guarantee the first 20 percent of sovereign paper issues. In this way, presumably, the EUR 440 bn of the EFSF would be levered into trillions of euro.

It is hard to believe that these policies would decisively resolve the crisis. The increased lending capacity of the EFSF remains largely a mirage since the levered EUR 440 bn has in part been already committed to existing rescue programmes for Greece, Ireland and Portugal. In late 2011 there was barely EUR 250 bn left in practice and even that, as was discussed above, was already levered on a far smaller amount of actual cash. Twice-levered EFSF funds might be enough to support a short period of sovereign borrowing by Spain and Italy, should the need arise, but no more than that.

More fundamentally, though, the entrenched policies of austerity remained likely to continue fomenting the crisis. For Greece to reach a sustainable level of debt it would have to register strong growth. Even to attain the level of 120 percent of GDP, which would be far from low, the country would require sustained growth. If growth did not materialise, there would be a risk of severe social unrest. As recession began to take shape in Spain and Italy in 2012, fur-

---

126 See Roland Berger Strategy Consultants, http://www.rolandberger.com/media/press/releases/Recovery_plan_for_the_Greek_economy.html

thermore, the ability of these countries to access bond markets would be continually tested. In these circumstances, the prospect of a break up of the EMU would continue to arise. To consider the content and the implications of a possible rupture, however, it is first necessary to have a closer look at European banks in chapter 16.

16. CENTRIFUGAL FINANCE: RE-STRENGTHENED LINKS BETWEEN BANKS AND NATION STATES

The proudest achievement of the EMU has been the creation of a homogeneous money market for European banks, presided over by the ECB. Nevertheless, the banking space of Europe has never been homogenised, banks continuing to retain a national outlook. One of the more striking aspects of the eurozone crisis has been that it has re-strengthened the importance of national compared to supranational relations in the field of banking. Interdependence between sovereign states and their domestic banking systems has increased, revealing centrifugal tendencies within the EMU.

The ECB has acted as bank of banks within the EMU, also putting in place mechanisms for trading, holding and funding sovereign debt, thus creating elements of a supranational financial system. Yet, sovereign debt is a claim on future taxes; debt markets are a device to allow individual holders of bonds access to money before the claim falls due. When the credibility of the claim is in doubt, the liquidity of the market evaporates. That moment arrived in the eurozone in 2010. It then transpired that there were constraints to ECB intervention because of the absence of a unitary or federal state. Consequently, the underlying relation between, on the one hand, the sovereign state as collector of taxes and, on the other, domestic banks as lenders to the state and hence claimants to future taxes, came forcibly to the fore.

As the eurozone crisis has deepened, each member country has become increasingly concerned about its own predicament, and thus more tightly bound up with its own banking system. Extraordinary measures, sidelining the mechanisms of the Eurosystem, have been used to support national banks. At the same time, relentless pressure by eurozone authorities has gradually given shape to a harsh dilemma for some peripheral countries: either complete the tight embrace with domestic banks by nationalising them, or forcibly sell them. This choice will be important to deciding whether peripheral countries remain within the EMU.

The re-strengthening of national financial relations

Huge holdings of sovereign debt by banks coupled with abundant and cheap liquidity from the ECB have had the paradoxical result of loosening the links between member states and the supranational financial mechanisms of the

FIG. 10 Government securities as a percent of total MFI assets for Spain, Greece, Ireland, Italy and Portugal

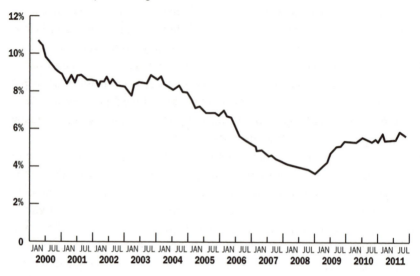

Source: *National Central Banks*

eurozone. Bank holdings of sovereign bonds have begun to switch toward domestic issues as banks have become imperilled by the sovereign debt of the eurozone periphery. Remarkably, peripheral banks have also switched to domestic issues.

Figure 10 shows that holdings of government bonds as a proportion of total Monetary Financial Institution assets fell during the 2000s, but began to rise in the periphery after October 2008.

In Greece and Italy, holdings of non-domestic government bonds started to fall from 2006, as is shown in Figures 11 and 12, respectively. Holdings of domestic government bonds, meanwhile, have been on the rise since late 2008.

Three reasons stand out for this development. First, government bonds (particularly those of own jurisdiction) have traditionally been regarded by banks as low-risk, and even riskless. A bank's risk profile is typically skewed in favour of the debt of its own sovereign, since the latter is perceived as the collector of taxes and the ultimate guarantor of means of payment within the bank's original territory. The eurozone crisis has exacerbated

FIG. 11 Government securities as a percent of total MFI assets for Greece – domestic and non-domestic

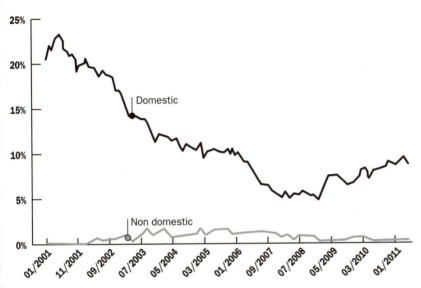

Source: *Bank of Greece*

this preference even though banks have discovered that the debt of sovereigns is generally far from being risk-free. Second, domestic banking systems may be subject to a variety of subtle – or not so subtle – pressures from the government to acquire bonds thus funding public expenditure. Third, member states of the eurozone have been forced to rely more heavily on their domestic banking systems as a reaction to eurozone policies after the outbreak of the crisis.

From the middle of 2010 the switch from the supranational to the national has become ever more pronounced. Sovereigns and their domestic banking systems have pulled closer together with the result that in late 2011 several eurozone states and their banking systems are so intertwined that they face joint default.

Fundamental to this trend has been the decision of the ECB to start buying sovereign bonds in the secondary markets in 2010 through the SMP. It has thus offered the opportunity to private banks – particularly those of the core – to

FIG. 12 Government securities as a percent of total MFI assets for Italy – domestic and non-domestic

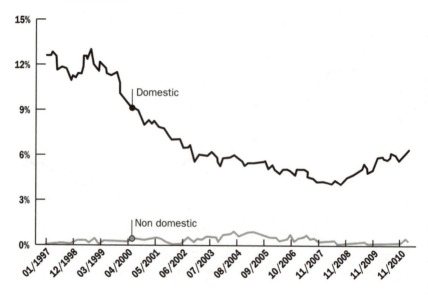

Source: *Banca d'Italia*

divest from the sovereign bonds of the weakest eurozone states. At the same time, banks in both core and periphery have reduced funding to other banks, enterprises, and foreign sovereigns. They have began to accumulate liquidity newly available from the ECB with their own NCBs. Figure 13 shows this trend as an accumulation of fixed-term deposits by banks within the Eurosystem in the course of the crisis.[127]

At the same time, persistent shortage of liquidity in the money markets has forced banks to continue borrowing from official lenders, which means the Eurosystem, as is shown in Figure 14. However, national financial systems can only access the Eurosystem via their own NCBs, as was discussed

---

127 The effects of the vast provision of liquidity by the ECB in December 2011 remain to be seen. But they are likely to be in the same direction as long as the underlying imbalances of the eurozone are not removed and the threat to state solvency remains.

FIG. 13 Deposits in the Eurosystem balance sheet (euro million)

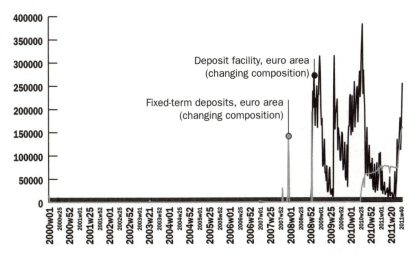

Source: *ECB*

FIG. 14 Bank borrowing from the Eurosystem: Selected items from the Eurosystem balance sheet (euro million)

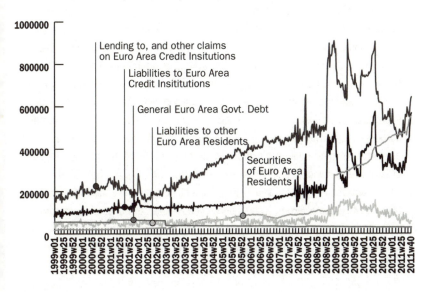

Source: *ECB*

in chapter 14. The result has been to increase intra-ESCB obligations among NCBs which appear as the so-called Target2 accounts, briefly described in Box 6 below.

To sum up, as the eurozone crisis has deepened, core banks have reduced their exposure to peripheral sovereigns and to other banks in response to declining creditworthiness. Spare funds from ECB liquidity provision were posted at the NCBs of the core. Meanwhile banks and sovereigns of the periphery resorted increasingly to borrowing from the ESCB, which could only be accessed via their NCBs. The result was an accumulation of liabilities among NCBs within the Eurosystem.

BOX 6 TARGET

Normally, a country's current account deficit is financed with inflows of foreign private capital. In a currency union, however, central banking credit may play this role, if private capital flows are insufficient. This is what has happened in the eurozone when the interbank market first broke down in mid-2007.

The ECB operates the system of so-called Target claims and liabilities in the National Central Banks' balance sheets. Target is the acronym of Trans-European Automated Real-time Gross Settlement Express Transfer System. It appears as a mere technicality, nothing more than a settlement system for inter-bank transactions within the eurozone. However, the system is not merely a mechanism of book-keeping entries but can also act as a means of financing/funding across the member countries of the eurozone, thus supporting domestic financial systems.

In practice, Target balances are interest-bearing public loans used to finance current-account deficits. The balances resemble short-term eurobonds since they function as short-term finance for deficit countries. By the end of 2010, the aggregate stock of central-bank money in the euro area was around EUR 1.1 tr, and EUR 380 bn was already absorbed by ECB credit to Greece, Ireland, Portugal and Spain together. This figure is close to the current-account deficit needs of these countries. Furthermore, between the end of 2008 and the end of 2010 central bank facilities increased from EUR 120 billion to EUR 380 billion. At the same time, the accumulated current account deficit of the four countries amounted to around EUR235 billion.

The amount of the ECB's "replacement lending" is shown by the so-called Target2 account, which measures the deficit or surplus of a country's financial transactions with other countries. As the account includes international payments for both trade in goods and financial claims, a deficit in a country's Target account indicates foreign borrowing via the ECB's system, whereas a surplus denotes foreign lending via the ECB. It is clear from the figure below that the Bundesbank has been financing the NCBs of the periphery.[128] The Bundesbank has been able to do that in part because German banks have chosen to store liquidity with the Bundesbank rather than lending it out to enterprises and others.

Surpluses and deficits

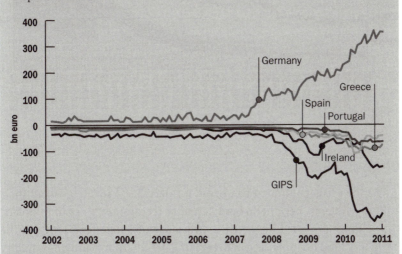

Notes: Germany: Other Assets of the Bundesbank. Spain: Banco de Espana. Liabilities: Other euro area countries: MFIs: of which: euro. Greece: Bank of Greece: Liabilities: Liabilities to Other MFIs: Other Euro Area Countries. Portugal: Central Bank Balance Sheet Liabilities: Non-Residents: Deposits & Related Instruments. Ireland: Central Bank Liabilities: Other Liabilities. GIPS is the sum of Greece, Portugal, Ireland and Spain.
Source: *Haver, Bundesbank, Central Bank of Ireland, Bank of Greece, Banco de Espana, Banco de Portugal, Citi Investment Research and Analysis.*

---

128 See Whittaker, J. (2011), 'Intra-Eurosystem debts', Monetary Research, Lancaster University Management School, 30 March, http://www.lancs.ac.uk/staff/whittaj1/Eurosystem.pdf

FIG. 15 Eurosystem 'other assets' plus 'total securities' holdings as proportion of total assets

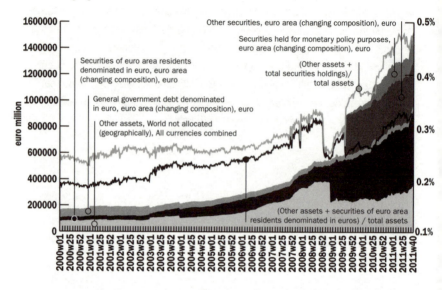

Source: *ECB*

As the crisis continued to worsen for peripheral sovereigns and their banking systems, peripheral bank liquidity requirements began to exceed the volumes provided by the ECB. Consequently, states and NCBs of the periphery (and not only) began to take unilateral action to provide liquidity to their stricken banking systems. The clearest evidence for this trend is Emergency Liquidity Assistance (ELA) afforded by NCBs to their banking systems.

ELA is provided temporarily to commercial banks by NCBs to support domestic financial institutions over and above the assistance provided by the ECB. It is supplied under the rules of the EMU but independently of the ECB and, as a result, possible gains or losses are not shared with other members of the eurozone. The ECB does not have legal authorisation to approve the activation of ELA but it does have the right to stop it, if two thirds of the Governing Council vote against it. It appears that ELA has been activated at least in Ireland, Germany, Belgium, Portugal, Spain and Greece, though little is known about either the amounts, or the terms, including interest rates, maturity and collateral requirements. The ways in which NCBs have financed the provision of ELA also remain opaque.

It is clear, nonetheless, that ELA represents the shifting of credit risk from private banks to their nation state within the eurozone. It is also clear that it reveals a re-strengthening of national at the expense of supranational financial mechanisms. Figure 15 below depicts these decentralised actions as part of the Eurosystem balance sheet under 'other assets' plus 'securities'. They have increased substantially accounting for 45 percent of the total assets of the ESCB, and also rising as a share of the total balance sheet of the Eurosystem, which is itself expanding rapidly.

In addition, governments and/or NCBs have aided their national banking systems in a variety of other ways. The Greek government, for instance, has extended guarantees to national banks when securitisations of loans that were held on balance sheet no longer qualified for ECB funding. This allowed Greek banks to unbundle these securitisations, use the guarantee of the sovereign, and thus receive ECB funding on the enhanced assets. In Ireland, under the Eligible Liabilities Guarantee scheme, the sovereign has guaranteed parts of the banks' liability structure.[129] In some cases Irish banks appear to have issued claims to themselves, subsequently posting those at the ECB and at the NCB to secure liquidity under ELA.[130]

These national mechanisms of support have often amounted to a subsidy for stricken banks. As funding dried up, banks were forced to increase the rates offered on deposits in the hope of sustaining the inflow of private liquidity. Banks that could not attract enough deposits had to turn to the ECB and to national ELA mechanisms for funding. Fortunately for them this often represented a saving compared to deposits – ECB rates hovered at 1.5 percent and Greek ELA funds cost 3.5 percent. The result was to boost net interest income for banks, even as they teetered on bankruptcy.[131]

---

129 See http://www.finance.gov.ie/viewdoc.asp?DocID=6522
130 See http://ftalphaville.ft.com/blog/2011/02/22/495041/irelands-stylised-sovereign-bank-loop/
131 See http://ftalphaville.ft.com/blog/2011/09/02/667561/hooray-for-erm-greek-ela/

FIG. 16 Greek bank aggregate liabilities

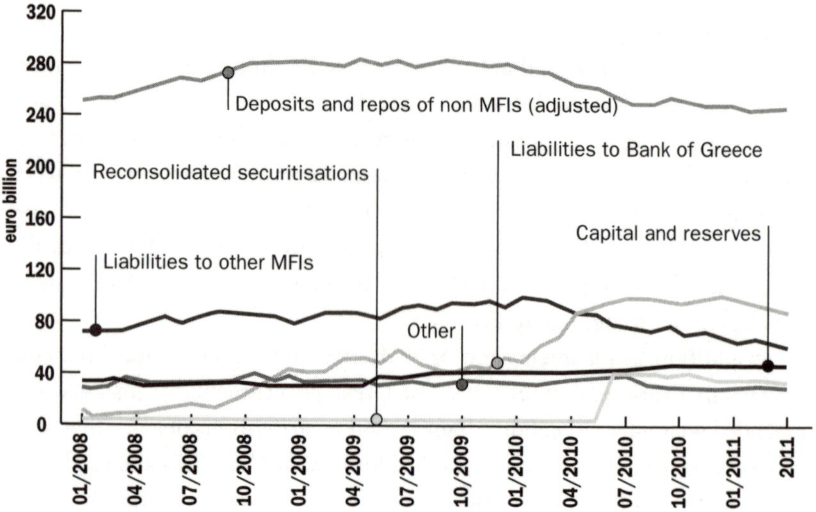

Source: *Bank of Greece*

Greek banks draw closer to the Greek state

A closer look at the banks of Greece would bring out further aspects of the broader trend of re-strengthening national links within finance. Consider first the liability side of the balance sheet of Greek financial institutions, shown in figure 16 above.

The following points stand out:

1. Non-financial sector deposits and repos stopped rising around the onset of the global financial crisis and started to fall from the beginning of 2010. Note that, in the figure, 'deposits and repos of non MFIs' has been adjusted by adding back 'liabilities associated with assets disposed of in a securitisation but still recognised on the statistical balance sheet'.

2. Funding from other Monetary Financial Institutions also started to fall from the beginning of 2010. Figure 17 below gives more detail and shows that MFI lending to Greek banks from outside the eurozone fell from the onset of the financial crisis. Lending from within the eurozone took up the slack but declined dramatically from early 2010. Domestic interbank lending was by far the smaller part of bank funding and also began to decline as eurozone bank lending fell.

FIG. 17 Greek bank borrowing

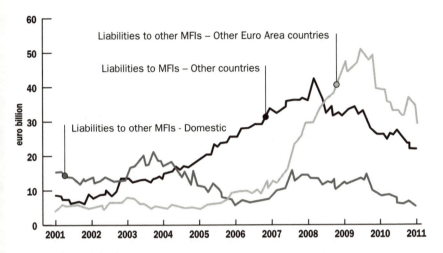

Source: *Bank of Greece*

3. Funding losses from these sources were mostly compensated by increasing liabilities from the Bank of Greece. However, with the rising intensity of the Greek sovereign crisis in June 2010, funding from the Bank of Greece ceased to rise while other funding sources continued to fall. At that point the aggregate balance sheet of Greek banks started to shrink.

4. In June 2010 Greek banks appear to have unbundled securitisations previously used for funding at the ECB, which were subsequently brought on the balance sheet. Consequently, banks incurred gross liabilities of roughly EUR 40 bn. This marked a substantial unilateral action by the sovereign guaranteeing the resulting assets to enable banks to receive continued ECB funding against them.

On the asset side, shown in figures 18 and 19, Greek banks appear to have deleveraged with regard to private and foreign borrowers, while increasing their lending to the Greek state:

1. There has been a significant drop in lending abroad both in the eurozone and to areas outside.

2. Government securities holdings rose significantly after the outbreak of the eurozone crisis in late 2009.

FIG. 18 Greek bank aggregate assets (excluding domestic non-MFI, non-government lending) millions of euros

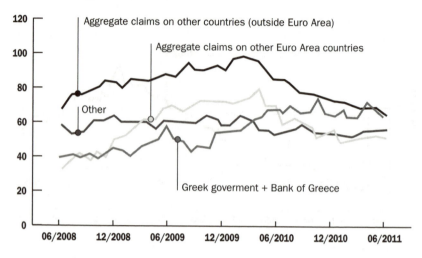

Source: *Bank of Greece*

3. Lending to the domestic economy has been flat or declining throughout this period, as is shown in figure 19, thus contributing to the worsening of the recession. Until the middle of 2010 Greek banks appear to have removed loans from their balance sheets via securitisations which were partly held on balance sheet. In mid-2010, due to ratings downgrades, these securitisations were unwound and the underlying loans were taken back on balance sheet. Figure 19 shows clearly the sudden jump in lending, some of which was already held by the banks themselves as securities, as can be seen from the accompanying fall in securities holdings. From mid-2010 domestic lending has shown a slow contraction as banks' balance sheets have shrunk.

To recap, banks and their sovereign states have come closer together in the course of the crisis. The fundamental problem has remained the insolvency of several sovereigns. Increasing reliance of banks on essentially insolvent sovereigns in the periphery has multiplied the risks for the financial system as a whole, exacerbating the prospect of a break up in the eurozone.

In September 2011 the European Banking Authority declared that 16 banks from across the eurozone had to boost their capital ratios by April 2012. The

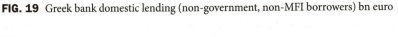

FIG. 19 Greek bank domestic lending (non-government, non-MFI borrowers) bn euro

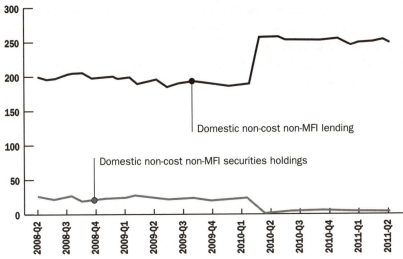

Source: *Bank of Greece*

internal markets commissioner stated: "We want the recapitalisation for these banks to be by private means. The era of bailing out banks must end. But I cannot of course exclude the possibility that some of the above banks will require state aid."[132] These were fine sentiments but, in practice, policy makers in the periphery had already begun to face a tough dilemma: either full nationalisation, or selling banks to foreigners, for instance, to sovereign wealth funds of the emerging east or of the oil producers.[133]

---

132 See http://www.ft.com/cms/s/0/49d6240e-e527-11e0-bdb8-00144feabdco.html# axzz1YNIbQpro

133 The merger of Eurobank and Alpha Bank in Greece was indeed announced with an equity injection of EUR 500 mn from Qatar. It has also been rumoured that Greek government preference shares could be bought for roughly EUR 2 bn. This could be a first indication of what lies in wait for Greek banks were default to materialise in the eurozone in the near future, though Qatar is unlikely to be a major source of funds.

Selling the banks abroad echoed the continuous calls for privatisation made by lenders to peripheral nations: repay at all costs, even if it means a firesale of future revenue streams. Nationalisation, on the other hand, would only be a first step in resolving the crisis. It would simply create a more propitious context to deal with the problem of state insolvency but also to confront the profound economic dislocations created by the eurozone, as is shown in the next chapter for Greece.

17. THE SOCIAL AND POLITICAL SIGNIFICANCE OF BREAKING UP

The context of rupture

It was shown in previous chapters that the eurozone has been deeply problematic from its inception, in large part due to the social and political interests on which it rests. The world crisis of 2007 has exacerbated the contradictions of monetary union and the response by eurozone authorities has worsened the problem. In late 2011 and early 2012 the euro has faced a decisive challenge which could lead to a break up emerging within the eurozone.

The form of the break up would be impossible to predict. One or two peripheral countries could exit; there could emerge a group of 'hard' euro countries and a satellite group of 'soft' euro countries, with variable exchange rates between the two; there could even be complete collapse of the monetary union. Core countries appeared reluctant to push peripheral countries out of EMU, since there are major risks for the banks of both core and periphery. Yet, the institutions of the eurozone have exacerbated the crisis by forcing austerity on the periphery causing enormous social and economic strain without the prospect of growth.

Breaking up could occur from a range of events, including spontaneous departure by a peripheral state, or the core gradually forcing out a peripheral state. In all instances the catalyst is likely to be the inability to service public debt, or what amounts to the same thing, the inability to meet the conditions imposed by official lenders to continue to disburse rescue funds. The country that is closest to this eventuality is Greece.

The rest of this chapter focuses on the likely implications of default and exit for Greece, and to a lesser extent for the rest of the eurozone. To keep the analysis manageable, it is assumed that only Greece defaults and exits, abstracting from Portugal, or another country, following suit. For the same reason, only the first order effects on European banks, the ECB and other institutions are considered. Effects of a further order, for instance, through the interbank market, are left out of account because the degree of complexity would be simply forbidding.

The exercise below deploys quantitative data and makes specific quantitative assumptions, but keeps well away from quantitative estimates of the impact on GDP, personal income, the balance of payments, and so on. The reason is clear: given the complex and fluid nature of the problem, the value of such quantitative estimates would be pretty close to zero. Quantitative data and assumptions are important to establishing the economic content of Greek default and exit, but no more.

There is, however, a further and deeper purpose to the analysis. Exit from the eurozone could have highly variable implications for working people and society as a whole. It could, for instance, be chaotic, undertaken at the last moment, under extreme pressure from the untenable policies of austerity, and with minimal preparation. The costs to Greek economy and society, already weakened by austerity, would be substantial. It is far from inconceivable that chaotic exit could create phenomena similar to Argentina in 2002–3, where the economic shock combined with popular anger caused phenomena of social disintegration.[134]

Exit could also be 'conservative', that is, led by private interests keen to protect the existing balance of social forces, and persevering with the austerity. The result might be an authoritarian polity atop an economy characterised by successive devaluations, poor growth outcomes, and worsening income distribution. As the prospect of Greek default and exit has gradually entered the mainstream in recent months, several studies have attempted to assess the likely implications, typically within the parameters of 'conservative exit'.[135]

Yet, there could also be 'progressive exit' favouring labour against capital. This is the type of exit considered in this chapter, and it is arguably the most radical course of action available to the Greek people, and possibly to others in the eurozone. Progressive exit could open the way to social and economic change transforming Greek society in the interests of labour. However, to this purpose progressive exit would also have to adopt a broad programme including, at the very least, public ownership and control over financial institutions, control over capital flows, income and wealth redistribution, sustained industrial policy to protect employment and ensure growth, and total restructuring

---

134 For a fuller discussion, see Appendix 2A.

135 See Buiter, W. and Rahbari, E. (2011), 'The future of the euro area: fiscal union, break-up or blundering towards a "you break it you own it Europe"', *Economics, Global Economics* View, 9 September. For a completely alarmist and poorly substantiated offering, see UBS, (2011), 'Euro break-up – the consequences', UBS Investment Research, *Global Economic Perspectives*, 6 September.

of the state in a democratic direction. In essence it would be a transitional programme for the Greek economy – and potentially others – in the direction of labour ascendancy.

The particulars of such a programme cannot be discussed in this book. Analysis in the rest of this section rather concentrates on 'the next day' of default and exit, ascertaining the likely impact on both the private and the public sector. But important elements of the transitional programme inevitably come into focus when considering the storm that would follow default and exit. In this light, analysis below is fully compatible with the notion that default and exit could trigger a deep and progressive transformation of the Greek economy in the longer term.

More broadly, rupture in the eurozone could put profound social change on the agenda in Europe for the first time in decades. The preceding period of financial ascendancy has resulted in a precarious balance of economic, social and political forces in Europe and elsewhere. The relentlessly conservative response to the crisis has exacerbated discontent, tensions, and the search for alternatives. Greek default and exit could catalyse broader change, loosening the hold of financial and industrial interests on the life of the continent.

An important factor in this respect would be the ideological impact of a break-up of the EMU. Money is far more than a simple means of exchange, or a means of payment and reserve. In a capitalist society it functions as a social organiser providing signals of scarcity or surplus and facilitating the shifting of resources. In a society driven by the self-interested pursuit of profit, it provides the glue that holds together disparate areas of economic and social activity. Money is the '*nexus rerum*' of capitalist society, the thing that condenses impersonal social power, social distinction, and social value. It is at once the purpose, the means, and the measure of social achievement.

For this reason domestic money becomes an element of national identity, a thing that purports to capture national virtues and vices. In the world market where national capitals compete, the relative value of domestic money becomes a reflection of the worth of a nation. Possessors of 'hard' currencies are far more than mere holders of a reliable store of value. They bestride the field of global interaction looking down on the holders of 'soft' currencies. It might be fetishism, but it reflects an underlying reality: powerful nations are expected to have strong currencies.

For an international reserve currency (world money) the ideological impact is incomparably magnified. Not only is the issuing nation perceived to be dominant, but the institutional and political mechanisms supporting a reserve currency ensure the issuer's paramount position. A managed reserve currency is by construction a mechanism of global power economically, politically, ideologically, even militarily.

It is no surprise, therefore, that the euro has come to be identified with the notion of Europeanism and the idea of a united Europe. Indeed, it is entirely appropriate that a united Europe driven by big banks and big business would find its true reflection in a form of money. And yet, precisely because of the contradictory construction of the EMU, even the ideological role of the euro is contradictory.

For core countries – the main beneficiaries of the EMU – the euro is tainted by association with the weak periphery. The holy anger of EU leaders with Greece at the beginning of the crisis is partly due to having their money sullied by Greek unreliability. The suspicion constantly resurfaces that perhaps a return to a 'hard' national currency would provide greater global standing; or that the expulsion of the problematic periphery, if it could be achieved without disaster, would restore the euro to its rightful place in the global pecking order.

For peripheral countries that have suffered most from the crisis the opposite holds true. A return to a 'soft' national currency is perceived as a loss of prestige, a failure to join 'first class economies'. Among the leading social strata there is palpable fear that quitting the euro would mean a loss of identity as true Europeans. Hence the most profound paradox of the current crisis: the harder the periphery is buffeted by EMU policies, the more desperately its leadership clings on to EMU membership.

Economic reality has, of course, the ability to impose itself, irrespective of the ideology of politicians and others. The contradictory and untenable nature of the EMU cannot be overcome by imagining a united Europe. But the ideological role of the euro would be of paramount importance in shaping alternatives. It is one thing for a country to be forced willy-nilly into exit by ruthless reality, quite another to choose the moment of exit itself. The latter would allow for the marshalling of the required strength, and it could become the path to progressive exit.

For that, however, it would also be necessary to possess a different ideological narrative of European identity with a correspondingly different perception of national worth. There is nothing preordained about the form that ideology would take as Europeanism lost its shine alongside the euro. It could indeed lead to a revival of competing nationalisms with all the terrible echoes from European history. But it could also bring a genuine internationalism that respected national independence and aspired to a united Europe based on the interests of working people rather than banks and big business. The final outcome would be entirely dependent on the actions of the main social players.

Modalities of default

In light of the above, it is necessary to spell out key issues regarding default on public debt. Default is a catch-all term indicating several ways in which a debtor would fail to meet contractual obligations, thus imposing losses on the creditor. The legal aspects of default are not relevant to the analysis, for instance, the period of grace during which non-payment of interest would not be considered default, or agreed changes in repayment that would prevent the debtor from being officially declared in default. What matters is the economic impact irrespective of the debtor's precise legal status.

In general, default entails rescheduling debt, that is, changing (one or more of) the term, the rate of interest and the face value of debt; all these changes naturally affect the Net Present Value of debt. From the perspective of the creditor, however, changing the face value of debt is a critically important element because it implies failure to receive return of the principal, which creates losses and denies the fundamental logic of the lending of money. The trickiest part of default is always the cancellation of part of the debt.

Broadly speaking, default can be divided into creditor-led and debtor-led.[136] This distinction does not admit of great theoretical precision and should be deployed heuristically. But it captures the policy dilemma better than the distinction between orderly and disorderly default that has been extensively used by the mainstream in recent months. For, 'orderly' in this context means largely in the interests of the lender. Versions of creditor-led, orderly default have been discussed for Greece since July 2011 and, as was mentioned in chapter 15, they have tended to be to the benefit of the creditors rather than the country.

Given the parlous state of the Greek economy, mild rescheduling of the term and rate of interest, and even some reduction of the face value of the

---

136 The difference between creditor-led and debtor-led default was discussed in some detail in Part 1.

debt, would not decisively deal with the country's debt problem. Greece needs a deep reduction of the face value of its debt, i.e. cancellation on both officially and privately held debt, which would restore the debt/GDP ratio to manageable levels once the country entered a sustainable growth path. The terms of remaining debt must also be reset in favour of its people and its economy.

This is unlikely to occur under creditor-led default, and even if significant debt cancellation took place, the price that the creditors would extract would be correspondingly high, including possession over key national assets and direct control over the country's fiscal policy. At the limit, creditor-led default would pose issues of national independence and sovereign rule in Greece. In this light, debtor-led default is probably the only effective way for the country to free itself from the shackles of debt. For that, two political and social conditions would be paramount.

First, default would have to occur in a sovereign way, i.e., the borrower would have to coerce banks. This would certainly mean cessation of payments of interest and principal on public debt, in the first instance. Negotiations with the lenders would then follow seeking final settlement that would involve the cancellation of a large part of the debt. Greece is not without advantages in this connection. It appears that 90 percent of Greek bond debt has been issued under Greek law without Collective Action Clauses. A unilateral act of Greek parliament could alter the terms of settlement, benefiting the debtor and coercing private banks into accepting an offer.

Second, default would have to take place in a democratic way by breaking the hold of technocrats and politicians over the management of public debt and directly involving civil society and organised labour. Public debt is a complex and obscure entity, with many claimants and several types of indebtedness. Society has a democratic right to know the constitution of the debt and to be directly involved in its management.

From the long experience of developing countries in dealing with sovereign debt problems, it appears that the best way of ensuring democratic participation is to form an Audit Commission. The Audit Commission should be independent of the political system of both Greece and the EU. It should be international in composition, comprising specialists (lawyers, economists, fiscal auditors, and others) but also representatives of civil society and the organised labour movement. Its task would be to audit public debt with a view to ascertaining its legality, legitimacy, odiousness, and sustainability from a social standpoint. To do its work it should have access to information regarding all forms of public debt as well as being able to call witnesses and even to examine private bank accounts.

After auditing the debt, the Commission would make appropriate recommendations regarding cancellation as well as the general management of public debt. It is conceivable, for instance, that the rescue loans advanced to Greece since 2010 would be declared illegitimate on account of the extraordinary political pressure applied on Greece, even by-passing the normal constitutional and parliamentary process. It is even conceivable that the entire burden of Greek debt in excess of 60 percent of GDP would be declared illegitimate since it directly contravenes the Maastricht Treaty. The latter was a deeply flawed agreement from the outset, but nonetheless the lenders to Greece were fully aware of its existence.

It is not surprising in this light that debtor-led default would appear disorderly to the entrenched interests in the eurozone and more generally. Yet, what is perceived as lack of order could actually be an injection of democracy and the reassertion of national independence. Debtor-led default could hold the promise of deep social transformation in favour of labour in Europe and elsewhere. By this token, it would probably prove impossible within the confines of the eurozone, and it would cause Greece to exit.

The likely implications of default and exit are considered in the next section, but two general points are important before engaging with the analysis. First, default and exit would immediately raise the prospect of banking, monetary, and foreign exchange crisis for Greece. These aspects of crisis would be closely interconnected, but not identical. Policy ought to focus on keeping them separate, for if they coalesced the outcome would be deeply problematic. Of the three, the banking crisis would be by far the most serious as it would directly impede the capacity of the economy to sustain the core of production, and therefore employment.

In this regard, analysis in chapter 18 shows that the main danger to banks is posed by default, rather than exit. Exit would add banking problems of its own, but it could also make it easier to deal with the banking problems caused by default. Exit would certainly generate the risk of monetary and foreign exchange crises, but it would also bring advantages that could allow the country to recover. In sum, if Greece were to default, it would also make sense to exit.

Second, confronting default and exit would require the marshalling of economic, social and political resources across the country. In this respect, the adjustment programme imposed by the troika has been a disaster since it has considerably weakened the Greek economy. The cumulative loss of output for 2010–11 would probably exceed 10 percent of GDP; official unemployment was in the region of 19 percent at the end of 2011. Time has, therefore, been of the essence: the longer Greece has delayed defaulting and exiting, the weaker has become its economy and the greater the difficulty of recovering.

18. DEFAULT AND EXIT: CUTTING THE GORDIAN KNOT

Analysis below is conducted in two distinct steps: it is assumed initially that default would take place within the EMU; it is then assumed that default would be followed by exit. The extent of debt cancellation will be taken at 50 percent, though the figure is purely for analytical purposes and too much should not be read into it. The proper way to ascertain the extent of cancellation as well as the terms and conditions of repayment would be to form an Audit Commission, along the lines that were discussed earlier. Finally, analysis proceeds on the assumption that the composition of Greek public debt is as shown in Box 7 below. A summary of the key results is given in Box 8.

BOX 7 HOLDINGS OF GREEK PUBLIC DEBT, BY CATEGORY (€M)

DOMESTIC	Greek banks	55,740
	Greek central bank	7,087
	Social security and other public entities	30,000
	Non-financial corporations	3,679
	Insurance companies	3,230
	Mutual funds	41
	Households and non-profit organisations serving households	12,133
FOREIGN	European banks	52,258
	Non-European banks	1,938
	ECB	50,000
	National European central banks	6,013
	IMF	15,000
	EU	38,000
	Rest of the world official institutions	25,000
UNALLOCATED		60,000
TOTAL		360,120

Sources: *Bank of Greece Financial Accounts; BIS Quarterly Review, July 2011; Barclays Capital*

Three main sources were used to construct this table: the Bank of Greece's Financial Accounts and aggregated balance sheets, updated to July 2011; the Bank of International Settlements' Quarterly Review, published July 2011; and Barclays Capital's own calculations of Greek debt holdings by individual institutions, reproduced in the Financial Times Alphaville blog of June 19.

Holdings by Greek banks are taken from Bank of Greece, 'Aggregated balance sheet of monetary financial institutions', and tally with Barclays Capital's total. Greek central bank holdings are from Bank of Greece, 'Balance sheet of the Bank of Greece'. Social security and other public entity holdings are taken directly from Barclays Capital reported holdings, and match other figures reported (eg JP Morgan reported 'social security and other public entity holdings', FT Alphaville 9 May 2011). The figure for non-financial corporations is taken from the Bank of Greece, 'Financial Accounts: non-financial corporations quarterly'. Insurance companies and mutual funds figures are from the aggregated balance sheet of both categories produced by the Bank of Greece under their Financial Accounts. Households and non-profit institutions serving households are likewise taken from Bank of Greece, 'Financial accounts: households quarterly'.

European bank holdings are given in the BIS Quarterly Review, July 2011, Table 9E. This tallies with the total derived from the Barclays Capital reported holdings of individual institutions. Non-European bank holdings are from the BIS Quarterly Review, July 2011, Table 9E. Holdings for the ECB are taken from JP Morgan, reported in FT Alphaville 9 May 2011, which matches Barclays Capital's figures. The figure for the national central banks of Europe is from Barclays Capital, removing the Bank of Greece from the original figure. IMF, EU, and Rest of the World public institutions are from Barclays Capital. Holdings unallocated are a residual from the headline Greek debt of €360 bn, and can be assumed to consist largely of private sector holdings largely outside of Greece not reported elsewhere.

BOX 8 PATHS OF DEFAULT AND EXIT

Modalities of default	Implications for debt holders	Impact on total debt and broader repercussions
1. Creditor-led default on privately held debt	No losses for ECB and NCBs on bonds held Significant losses for terminal bondholders including: Domestic social security and pension institutions Domestic households and non-profit organisations Other domestic investors Non-resident terminal bondholders Major losses for domestic banks Modest losses for international banks	The final reduction of debt is limited by the exclusion of ECB, NCBs, EU and IMF. Recapitalisation of domestic banks takes place through state borrowing, hence increases Greek public debt. Recapitalisation of international banks takes place through private equity or EFSF. Greek banks are reluctantly nationalised and could end up under foreign ownership in the medium term.
2. Debtor-led default with redenomination into drachma of domestically held debt only	ECB and NCBs also face losses on bonds held. Official lenders (IMF and EU) could potentially face losses despite superseniority Significant losses for terminal bondholders including: Domestic social security and pension institutions Domestic households and non-profit organizations Other domestic investors Non-resident terminal bondholders Major losses for domestic banks Modest losses for international banks	The final reduction of debt is greater as the haircut also applies to bonds held by ECB and NCBs. The impact could be even greater if official loans by the EU and IMF took a haircut Greek banks swap existing bonds for long-term, low yielding paper of the same face value. Recapitalisation of European banks via private equity or EFSF. Domestic terminal bondholders could be protected through swapping bonds for long-term paper and through guarantees by the state. Maintaining external debt in EUR imposes some foreign exchange risk on the sovereign. ECB, NCBs and Greek NCB face modest losses. Access to liquidity is lost for Greek banks which now need domestically-generated liquidity. Purposeful nationalisation of Greek banks, shrinkage of balance sheet, redirection to domestic economy. Banks carry significant foreign exchange risk for a period.

Modalities of default	Implications for debt holders	Impact on total debt and broader repercussions
3. Debtor-led default with complete redenomination of debt	As for 2	The final impact on debt is as for the previous case but the haircut could also operate through the fall in the exchange rate Redenomination of the total debt into drachma imposes foreign exchange risk on non-resident bondholders, but not on the sovereign. Domestic terminal bondholders can be protected through swapping bonds for long-term paper and through guarantees by the state. Purposeful nationalisation of Greek banks, shrinkage of balance sheet, redirection to domestic economy. Banks carry foreign exchange risk for a period as some assets and liabilities cannot be redenominated. Recapitalisation of international banks via private equity or EFSF.

Greece defaults but stays in the EMU

Assume that creditor-led default amounting to a 50 percent write-off of Greek public debt was agreed upon while Greece remained within the EMU, taking the form of a swap of new for old bonds.[137] Assume further that the write-off referred exclusively to privately held sovereign bonds. This chapter considers the impact of the write-off mainly on domestic and foreign banks, and the concomitant risk of a banking crisis.

Needless to say, the EU would face major difficulties in persuading private banks voluntarily to accept – or indeed in coercing banks into accepting – a 50 percent write-off of the value of Greek debt. Note further that by leaving untouched the debt held by official lenders – including EUR56 bn by the ECB and other NCBs, EUR38 bn by the EU and EUR15 bn by the IMF – the overall reduction of Greek debt would be modest. Furthermore, roughly half of the privately held debt that would be subjected to the writeoff would belong to Greek bondholders, be they banks, social security institutions, or even individuals. The impact of a creditor-led default, consequently, would be felt primarily by Greek rather than foreign lenders.

Thus, Greek households and non-profit organisations run the risk of severe losses on the EUR 12 bn they hold. Significant numbers among them are likely to be small savers who had opted for what they probably imagined to be a conservative option when they purchased sovereign bonds. Even more serious is the risk to social security and pension institutions which would face losses of up to EUR 15 bn on bonds held. In the absence of fresh funding from the state and given the low level of reserves and weak balance sheets – due to long-term mismanagement – the implications could be disastrous for pensions, health insurance and other forms of welfare in the medium term.

The banks and the primary deficit

The immediate impact on Greek banks would be losses in the region of EUR25–30 bn, wiping out the bulk of their capital. The required recapitalisation within the structures of the EMU could only be undertaken by official institutions. It would be in the interests of the EU to recapitalise Greek banks to forestall a

---

137 To keep things simple disregard the composition of the write-off in terms of face value, term, coupon and discount rate for the remaining and the original debt.

knock-on effect on European and other banks. But the manner in which recapitalisation would take place would be a matter of negotiation.

The most probable method would be increased borrowing by the Greek state as part of a new rescue package for the country. The new loan would immediately annul some of the reduction of the national debt brought by the write-off. The new loan, furthermore, is likely to mean even harsher conditionality than previous loans, perhaps including direct supervision of public finances by EU bureaucrats. Since the funds would be provided to the banks via a loan by the Greek state, the outcome would mean effective nationalisation of Greek banks.

However, it is highly unlikely that nationalisation would be purposeful, with the aim of deploying banks to restructure the economy as a whole. It is even possible that recapitalisation loans would not be managed by the Greek state, although they would be officially incurred by it. Effective control over Greek banks could pass to the official lenders of the eurozone, primarily Germany. That could prove the first step in transferring ownership over Greek banks to international hands once balance sheets would have been cleansed under public control.

If Greeks banks were indeed to pass under foreign control, the long-term implications for investment, growth, and employment in the Greek economy would become extremely uncertain, and probably negative. In broad terms, the Greek ruling class – the original bourgeois class of the Eastern Mediterranean – would find itself without direct ownership and control over its banks for the first time in its history. There would also be implications for national independence as the Greek state would be dominated by the EU in dealing with Greek banks.

A 50 percent write off of Greek debt would also entail losses for international (mostly German and French) banks, probably of the order of EUR25 bn. This would be a significant blow, but European banks could probably replenish their capital through private equity issue or EFSF funds without undue difficulty, on the assumption that only Greece defaulted. Nonetheless, they would be likely to resist strongly the imposition of losses since they would be accountable to shareholders and not to states. From the perspective of banks, it would be far better if taxpayers carried the losses of a Greek default. The possibility of persistent hold-outs who would resort to litigation cannot be dismissed.

Note that the prospect of lender resistance and litigation would be even greater for the EUR 60 bn of Greek debt whose ownership was not possible to attribute in Box 7. It is likely that significant parts of the EUR 60 bn would be held by hedge funds and similar investors who would not easily accept a 50 percent loss on a voluntary basis. The feasibility of creditor-led default for Greece, therefore, remains to be seen in practice.

The real risk to international banks, however, would arise from contagion in financial markets, including the secondary markets for European sovereign debt, once sovereign default became a reality. Writing off Greek public debt could potentially act as the trigger of a major crisis, even if it the process was creditor-led. For one thing, there could well be debtor hold-outs. For another, there would be no a priori guarantees that losses of the order of 50 percent would be accepted by all banks as voluntary reductions without leading to formal default. If holder resistance led to activation of CDS, it is conceivable that interbank markets would freeze, leading to global banking crisis. If, on the other hand, CDS were not activated despite losses of 50 percent, the CDS market would be completely discredited.

Creditor-led default for Greece, consequently, would be a protracted and risky process. It would also have to rely on the readiness of the ECB to intervene decisively should the worst materialise. Important as these risks would be, for the perspective of Greece they would nonetheless be only of marginal concern. It is not incumbent on the Greek state to rescue the European and the international financial system. If the EU was truly concerned about contagion and the possibility of a global banking crisis, the troika ought to adopt a different approach to Greek debt.

Banks aside, a 50 percent write-off of Greek public debt would also bring to the fore the problem of the primary budget deficit of Greece. The presumption must be that, if the EU provided funding to prevent Greek banks from collapsing, it would also provide sufficient fresh loans to allow the Greek state to continue meeting its current expenditures, above all, on public sector salaries and pensions. But it must equally be presumed that the price extracted by the EU would be more severe than for the previous rescue in May 2010. At the very least, it can be expected that there would be a measure of direct control over Greek public finances by EU officials. In addition there would probably be pressure to privatise public assets on an extensive scale to repay official debts. The implications for national independence would be negative.

To recap, Greek creditor-led default of, say, 50 percent occurring within the EMU would be a significant shock for European banks. To avoid a generalised banking crisis it would be necessary to have concerted intervention to recapitalise at least Greek banks and to make liquidity generally available; but there would still be no guarantees of success. Meanwhile, Greek banks would probably end up under state control that might eventually lead to foreign ownership.

The implications for the Greek economy would probably be negative since austerity would continue and the inability to compete within the eurozone would not be lifted. Greece would face many years of stagnation and high unemployment, while its banks and public assets would be auctioned off. At the same time, it would probably have to submit to direct external control over its public finances, thus abrogating parts of its national sovereignty.

Greece defaults and exits the EMU

In contrast to creditor-led default, if Greece opted for debtor-led default it would probably also exit the EMU, for reasons discussed in earlier chapters and in Part 2. It is apparent that this would be a difficult option for Greece, or for any other country of the periphery. But it is important at the outset to establish the benchmark against which to judge its consequences. Clearly, that would not be the pre-crisis state of affairs. The appropriate comparison would be with the likely state of the country if it continued with austerity policies within the EMU, even after a measure of creditor-led default. It has been argued throughout this book that the outcome would probably be a deep contraction of GDP followed by low growth, persistent high unemployment, and low incomes. Not least, there would be loss of national independence and erosion of domestic democracy.

Support for this assessment has come from unexpected quarters. In late October 2011 there was a leak of an official document detailing a Debt Sustainability Exercise for Greece performed at the highest levels of decision-making within the EU and the IMF. Recognising that the Greek economy had taken a turn for the worse since the summer of 2011, the document expected 5.5 percent and 3 percent GDP contraction in 2011 and 2012 respectively. This would be followed by growth slightly higher than 2 percent until 2020, only to subside to about 1.7 percent in the decade to 2030. Greece would effectively stagnate for twenty years. The study did not state it openly, but it was clear that high unemployment would become permanent.

The authors were more concerned about the implications for national debt which was expected to peak at 186 percent of GDP in 2013, fall to only 152 percent of GDP by end-2010, and remain at 130 percent of GDP by end-2030. Greece would be profoundly insolvent even in 2030 and would require continuous official assistance running in the hundreds of billions of euro throughout this period. The study concluded that Greece would therefore need cancellation of its debt, possibly by up to 60 percent, with much of the cost to be borne by private banks.

Numerical accuracy aside, there can be no quibbling with the drift of these conclusions. It is logical to expect poor growth outcomes when severe austerity is imposed on an economy already hollowed out by a decade of credit-driven consumption. Even more fundamentally, poor growth would result from the inability to devalue the exchange rate, and the attempt to recover competitiveness via the brutal method of driving down unit labour costs. These constraints would not be removed if Greece was offered a measure of creditor-led default. The likely outcome would still remain long-term economic and social decline with deeply problematic implications for national independence and democratic practice.

There can be little doubt that debtor-led default and exit could have better long-term results for both growth and employment. At the very least the country would be freed from the grip of austerity as well as a fixed and overvalued exchange rate. More broadly, a path could be opened towards dynamic improvements in productivity away from the tired shibboleths of liberalisation and privatisation. If debtor-led default and exit were accompanied by an appropriate programme, they could deliver better growth outcomes with greater equality, while also strengthening the position of labour in society.

The real analytical difficulty lies not in working out the likely long-term results for Greece but in ascertaining the adjustment path, especially during the initial period. Real incomes, in particular, would be likely to fluctuate in unpredictable directions as relative prices would change following exit. It is likely, for instance, that food prices would decline as Greek agriculture would reoccupy the domestic market. But the prices of cars, foreign travel, clothing and other consumer goods would be likely to rise. Once growth returned to a higher path, access to several of those goods would also improve since real incomes would rise. However, adjustment in the short term would remain difficult.

Consequently, several factors militate in favour of progressive exit led by forces that would actively shape the adjustment path. A progressive government that drew strength from popular support – particularly from organised labour – would recapture control over the instruments of economic policy. It would be able to offer effective protection of employment, loss of which is the single most important cause of poverty for working people. It would also be able to support small and medium businesses – the backbone of the Greek economy – by deploying credit and tax policy. Stability of employment and a stable framework for small and medium businesses would create better living conditions for working people, irrespective of how real income might fluctuate in the short term.

A progressive government in command of policy instruments would also be able to intervene in income allocation in the short term. The weaker sections of society could be supported through selected wage and salary increases as well as through subsidies for public transport, heating oil, and other key commodities. Equally important, redistribution of income and wealth could be effected by restructuring the tax system in favour of direct taxes, including the better off strata of society that have systematically evaded tax for decades.

Several key issues of the adjustment path are examined in the rest of this chapter. It is, however, important to make one final point at the outset. If Greece defaulted and quit the EMU it would probably come into conflict with the EU since the required interventions would be at odds with the neoliberal core of the Maastricht Treaty and a raft of other treaties and agreements. The path of the adjustment would therefore depend on social and political struggle that would involve both Greece and the EU.

Default and exit occurring on a progressive basis with grassroots support would re-strengthen democracy in Greece allowing the country better to confront the challenge. If the Greek people decided that the necessary policies were incompatible with remaining in the EU, it would be up to them to exercise their choice. But it is also likely that progressive Greek default and exit would lead to rapid change in the EU, in view especially of the unsustainable nature of the monetary union. The EU would probably look very different after the turmoil of Greek default and exit.

Once again, the debt, the banks, and the primary deficit
Assume that the Greek state declared a unilateral cessation of payments on its debt, also announcing that it would stop recognising further accrual of interest. There would be immediate problems of recapitalisation and liquidity for banks,

but no ready access to the mechanisms of the EU and the EMU. It would thus become imperative for Greece to re-acquire direct command over monetary policy. It is likely that exit would follow in short order, also altering the terms on which default would be handled.

Following cessation of payments, the state would engage in negotiations seeking substantial cancellation of debt. It is intuitive that, were Greece to enter this path, it would not necessarily accept a mere 50 percent reduction, or indeed any rate that the creditors wished to impose. After subjecting the debt to independent examination by an Audit Commission, the country could opt for significantly deeper cancellation. Since the process would be debtor-led, it would also apply to debt held by official institutions, including the ECB, the EU, and the IMF. To keep things broadly comparable with the case above, however, assume that the cancellation was still 50 percent; assume further that it affected only private holders of sovereign paper and the ECB, but left untouched the loans advanced by the EU and the IMF.

Even with the assumption that the write-off would still be at 50 percent, exit would significantly alter the problem of public debt. For one thing, it would be possible for domestically held public debt to be redenominated in the new currency – the new drachma. It is conceivable, though, that the state would retain the denomination of internationally held debt in euro. Since the new drachma would depreciate rapidly, the ratio of euro-denominated debt to GDP would rise. This possibility often leads to a misconception among those who oppose Greece quitting the euro. If, for the sake of argument, the new drachma was depreciated by 50 percent, the ratio of externally-held euro-denominated debt to drachma-denominated GDP would still remain very high even after a 50 percent default. The country would seem to lose much of the benefit of default.

This is plain confusion of arithmetic with economics. If default took place, the economic burden of the public debt on the Greek economy would be lessened by the equivalent of the loss taken by the creditors, i.e., by 50 percent. The real resources required to service the remaining euro-denominated debt would be substantially reduced, irrespective of its higher value in new drachma. The real difference for both the Greek state and its creditors would be that some foreign exchange risk would now be attached to remaining euro-denominated debt. But this predicament would be no worse for Greece than for a host of developing and other countries that currently borrow in foreign currency.

Exit, however, would give to the Greek state further options with respect to debt, since even its internationally-held obligations could also be re-denominated in new drachma. After all, Greece borrowed in its national currency when it accumulated euro debt, and it would be paying back in its national currency if it used new drachma for settlement. The state could at a stroke transform the entire stock of euro debt into domestic new drachma debt. The inevitable depreciation of the new drachma would shift the burden onto the lender – the haircut would occur through the fall of the exchange rate. Greece would gain the further advantage of encouraging core countries to support the new drachma, though the effectiveness of any such support would be very limited during the initial period as the new currency would be aggressively sold.

Note, finally, that the reputation costs of debtor-led default and exit would not necessarily be greater than those from imposing a severe haircut on euro-denominated debt following creditor-led default within the EMU. As far as the international bond markets are concerned, Greece would be a delinquent whether default occurred within the EMU or outside it, in euro or in drachma. The sensible thing to do for Greece would be to default in the most beneficial way to itself.

For Greek banks a write-off of 50 percent would again bring losses of EUR25–30 bn. In the absence of bailout funds by the EU there would be no option other than nationalisation without compensation for private equity holders. The difference with the previous case would be that nationalisation would be purposeful, aiming to rescue banks subsequently to deploy them to restructure the economy. Under public ownership, sovereign debt held by banks could be swapped for very long term, low interest bonds of the same face value. The new bonds could be backed by state property, including real estate and public enterprises. The debt-servicing burden of the state would be reduced, in effect creating the equivalent of a haircut.

If nationalised banks were reorganised in this way, they would face a drop in income and profitability since assets would become low-yielding. A plausible response would be to create effectively a 'bad bank' under public ownership which would hold the bulk of the new very-long-term bonds against fresh corresponding liabilities issued under very deep discount with state guarantees. These could be made available domestically under conditions of national emergency. The balance sheet of the remaining banks would be cleansed, leaving them free to concentrate on rebuilding capital and reorganising their lending.

A necessary step in this regard would be to scale back the international presence of Greek banks, probably selling subsidiaries in Turkey, the Balkans and elsewhere. Under public ownership and control, banks would then rebalance the supply of credit to the economy, including to Small and Medium Enterprises. Nationalisation of banks would give to a progressive government the tools to apply credit policy thus reviving output and protecting employment.

Exit, however, would bring further complications for banks since they would acquire foreign exchange risk due to both assets and liabilities incurred under foreign law and thus remaining in euro. Moreover, banks would not be able to roll over euro liabilities since they would be shut out of interbank markets and they would lose access to liquidity from the ECB. The loss of euro-denominated liquidity for banks would impact on funding for bank assets, whether denominated in euro or new drachmas.

To deal with this aspect of the shock to banks, the state would have to reconstitute the central bank immediately, detaching it from the Eurosystem and enabling it to provide drachma-denominated liquidity to banks. Command would have to be re-established over monetary policy, thereby allowing banks to support drachma-denominated assets. Nonetheless, banks would still have to off-load euro-denominated assets in line with the inevitable shrinkage of their euro-denominated liabilities. This process is likely to take time, leading to bankruptcies of private enterprises and litigation. At the end of it, once again, Greek banks are likely to be smaller and more focused on the productive sector, thus acting as a lever for the restructuring of the Greek economy.

As for the EUR 30 bn held by pension and social security institutions, it would be important again to swap their sovereign paper for very long-term new bonds backed by real estate and other public property. The aim would be to prevent losses that would threaten the viability of the institutions. Regular payment of pensions would, meanwhile, be guaranteed out of the government budget. It should be stressed in this connection that pensions are a part of annual GDP accruing to various claimants. The best guarantee for pensions would be to restart the process of growth, which can be expected following default and exit. Finally, small savers could also be helped through swapping their holdings of sovereign paper, always on the basis of an independent audit of the debt.

A write-off of 50 percent would also imply losses for the ECB and other NCBs in the Eurosystem, in the first instance on bonds held outright. These bonds were acquired mostly through the SMP, operated by the ECB on the basis of shared responsibility for losses. But they were also acquired through covered bond purchases, operated by the Greek NCB which has sole responsibility for losses. The magnitude of losses would depend on the haircut applied at the time of purchase, which is not public information.

On the assumption that Greek bonds were acquired at a haircut of 20 percent, and given that total holdings are in the region of EUR56 bn (50 bn, ECB and 6 bn, NCB), a 50 percent default would probably lead to losses of less than EUR20 bn. This is not a significant sum for the ECB, and nor is the Greek NCB likely to suffer much from its own share of losses. However, the blow to the reputation of the ECB would be substantial.

Of greater complexity would be the impact of the write-off on the collateral held by the ECB against liquidity provided to Greek banks as part of its long-term refinancing operations. According to the ECB, the average amount of eligible collateral in 2010 stood at EUR14 tr, of which 41 percent was general government debt and the balance comprised a variety of private debt instruments, including uncovered bank bonds, covered bank bonds, corporate bonds, asset-backed securities and other bonds. However, the actual collateral placed with the ECB was in the region of EUR2 tr and comprised mostly private securities, including a rising volume of non-marketable assets (bank loans). Less than 20 percent was government paper, though the proportion had increased in the course of the crisis.[138]

The haircut already applied to collateral is not known. The difference in the composition between eligible and actually deposited securities, and the heavy preponderance of private securities, would indicate that the ECB has imposed a significantly lower haircut on private compared to public securities. As far as Greek collateral is concerned, there is no information on its composition, and nor on the haircut imposed on private and public paper. However, it is reasonable to assume that the total liquidity borrowed by Greek banks in October 2011 was at least EUR100 bn and that collateral composition was 80 percent private to 20 percent public paper.

On this basis, a 50 percent default on public bonds would immediately lead to substantial losses forcing the ECB to issue a fresh call for more collateral.

---

138 See ECB Annual Report 2010, pp. 97–98, http://www.ecb.eu/pub/pdf/annrep/ar2010en.pdf

Note also that the value of private paper would decline, leading to further losses in effective collateral, if the ECB attempted to dispose of it in the open markets. Faced with fresh calls for collateral, Greek banks would default on liquidity borrowed. Total losses for the ECB are impossible to estimate given the paucity of public information, but it would not be surprising if they proved higher than losses on bonds held under the SMP and the covered bonds programmes. Again, the most significant effect would be on the reputation of the ECB.

It is also worth noting that the Greek NCB would find itself in trouble since it has acted as a channel for ECB liquidity throughout this crisis. To be more specific, if Greek banks defaulted on their liquidity obligations to the ECB, they would be effectively defaulting on the Greek CB, which would then be forced to default on the ECB. Losses on collateral would be incurred first by the Greek CB, subsequently to be passed to the ECB. As for the impact of default on ELA obligations by Greek banks, it is impossible to surmise given the lack of information. Reconstituting the central bank would be a vital task for these reasons too.

As far as the primary deficit is concerned, finally, default and exit would offer further options to Greece in the short term. Note first that the official budget for 2011 (drafted on the assumption of higher expenditures and lower revenues than those currently prevailing) estimates that tax income (excluding net receipts from EU) suffices to cover the most pressing social and national security needs in Greece. Specifically, total expenditures on salaries and pensions, funding for social security, for the Ministry of Health, for the Ministry of Education and for the Ministry of National Defence were projected at EUR51.6 bn. Total revenue from direct and indirect taxes, on the other hand, was projected at EUR52.9 bn. The first step in confronting the problem of the primary deficit should thus be to re-order public expenditure on the basis of social priorities.

Beyond re-ordering expenditures, the state would be able to monetise the deficit for a short period of time since it would have re-acquired command over monetary policy. The immediate impact of monetisation would be beneficial to the economy by lifting the austerity that is currently strangling it. There would be no need to impose the additional cuts in public expenditure, nor the increases in indirect and other taxes that are planned for 2012 and beyond. Indeed, the troika strategy of imposing extreme fiscal tightness to achieve a primary surplus in the shortest possible time to placate bond markets and allow

Greece to return to international borrowing would be abandoned altogether. Greece would be able to adopt a sensible strategy of reducing fiscal deficits through growth over a period of time.

There would, of course, be a risk of inflation, if monetisation continued for a long time, especially in view of the rise in import prices following depreciation. But note that the size of the primary deficit is likely to be modest for the rest of 2011 and probably for 2012, possibly of the order of 2-3 percent of GDP, or even less. Even if the planned austerity was abandoned and the primary deficit turned out to be 5–6 percent of GDP in 2012, that would still not be a huge gap to monetise for a short period. In the current heavily depressed conditions of the Greek economy, monetisation would allow for a boost to aggregate demand. The risk of inflation should not be exaggerated.

If, nonetheless, significant inflation did materialise for a period of time, wages and salaries could be indexed to protect the income of working people. Furthermore, significant inflation would have the beneficial effect of eating away at the value of the remaining public and private debt and thus lowering the burden on the Greek economy. All in all, given the current predicament of its economy, Greece should not be excessively concerned about inflation.

The longer-term response to the problem of the government deficit, on the other hand, would have to be structural. The answer to deficits must be provided through growth rather than austerity. Moreover, there must be wholesale restructuring of the tax system to reduce tax avoidance and to force the well-off to pay taxes regularly. The Greek tax system is one of the most unfair systems in Europe. Implicit tax rates on capital in Greece would have to rise from 15.8 percent in 2006 (the last year for which data is available) to at least the average for the EU, at 25.4 percent, or to the average for the eurozone, at 26.9 percent.[139] Restructuring the tax system would also eliminate institutionalised tax evasion of ship-owners, the Orthodox Church, and the banks.

Finally, the government would be able to finance modest deficits by rebalancing the domestic credit system through public ownership. Domestic borrowing was the standard means of financing primary deficits in Greece to

---

139 Eurostat, 2010, 'Taxation trends in the European Union'. Main results, p. 34, http://epp.eurostat.ec.europa.eu/cache/ITY_OFFPUB/KS-EU-10-001/EN/KS-EU-10-001-EN.PDF

the end of the 1990s. The adoption of the euro has had two profoundly negative results that eventually led to disaster. First, it encouraged the growth of domestic expenditure financed by cheap credit, which resulted in aggregate consumption of the order of 70 percent of GDP. Saving became correspondingly small, even negative in the second half of the 2000s, thus removing domestic sources of public finance.[140] Second, the Greek state was able to access international markets because it could borrow in euro. Consequently, it changed the composition of its debt, turning two thirds of it into foreign debt, as is shown in Box 7.

No state can avoid major problems for long if there are no domestic savings on which to draw and if it has to rely on international bond markets to finance current expenditure. The only partial exception is the US state, and that is because the USA issues the dominant reserve currency. Adopting the euro turned the Greek sovereign into a hostage of international bond markets, the IMF and the EU. A country such as Greece ought to sustain its public sector by restarting the process of growth as well as by re-strengthening domestic borrowing. It needs no more than sporadic access to international bond markets.

The monetary problem

The monetary problem of switching to the new drachma is conceptually trivial, although it presents several technical complexities. A bank holiday would have to be declared for a limited period of time, perhaps a week, to lessen the scope for a bank run. The conversion would have to occur as suddenly as possible, probably on a Friday evening. The state would immediately declare the new drachma to be legal tender, and would make all public obligations payable in it. Banks would be instructed to convert their balance sheets accordingly, including loans and deposits. The legal basis for converting assets and liabilities issued under Greek law is clear. However, since banks also hold assets and liabilities issued to non-residents, or under foreign law, the banking system would retain significant euro-denominated assets and liabilities, as was discussed above.

It would thus be necessary to impose capital controls with immediate effect, including on currency that could be physically taken out of the country. With-

---

140 See Part 1.

drawals from remaining euro accounts would have to be frozen until some normality returned to transactions. By far the most decisive step to stabilising monetary circulation, however, would be the nationalisation of banks that would allow the state to offer a blanket guarantee for drachma-denominated deposits.

The printing press would have to be set immediately to work to produce the new currency for circulation; resetting the ATMs would also have to start straight away. It would, of course, prove physically impossible to effect the physical change in a single week, particularly as new drachmas can hardly be printed prior to announcing the change. Thus, some euro already in possession of banks and the state could be stamped and called new drachmas, though it would be desirable to keep this to a minimum to economise on what would now effectively become foreign exchange.

Given the physical difficulties of replacing the currency, the state could also resort to issuing short-term promissory notes and bonds denominated in new drachmas to make its own payments. This would be a crude fiat money with limited acceptability outside the circuits of personal consumption. The sooner it would be eliminated, the better for the stability of monetary circulation. However, it could facilitate transition to the new drachma for several months.

Once the new drachma found itself in circulation it would take time to gain public confidence. There would be parallel circulation of the euro and the new drachma for a period, and a system of dual prices reflecting the fluctuating exchange rate between the two. Dual prices would entail transactions costs for businesses and households, also offering opportunities for speculation. However, these phenomena would be unlikely to persist as long as the state continued to make payments and purchases in new drachma.

A more costly problem would be the redenomination of existing contracts. The legal basis would be provided by the adoption of a new legal tender by the state, but there would be transaction costs as well as scope for arbitrary alterations of relative prices particularly as existing contracts would have some time to run. Furthermore, the adjustment of the banking system to the new accounting unit would also be costly. There would have to be adjustment of computer programming, clearing techniques, accounts keeping, and so on. It would take several months before banks learnt to operate smoothly with the new drachma.

None of these technical problems would be insuperable, and none would justify remaining within the EMU.[141] The price system and the domestic functioning of the new drachma would probably settle down within a few months. Note, finally, that switching to a new drachma has the advantage of creating scope for redistributive policies. The simplest conversion rate for banks' liabilities and assets could be 1:1 EUR/GRD, but a range of other rates could also be used to effect wealth redistribution. Thus, deposits of, say, less than 10000 euro could be converted at 0.5:1 EUR/GRD, those between 10,000 and 30,000 could be converted at 0.8:1, and those above 30,000 at 1:1. Redistribution could also make it easier to accept the new currency in a country as unequal as Greece.

The foreign exchange problem

The new drachma would immediately fall in value in the foreign exchange markets, though it is impossible to assess the extent of depreciation. It seems likely that the rate would at first overshoot downwards, then subsequently rise but with continuous fluctuations. During the first period it would be impossible to adopt conventional exchange rate policy because the new drachma would be aggressively sold off, but also because Greece runs a current account deficit and lacks foreign exchange reserves.

Still, it might be possible to exercise some controlling influence on the exchange rate through administrative controls on particular foreign exchange transactions, and through controls over capital flows. In the medium term, and if the current account deficit began to shrink and reserves to accumulate, it would be possible for the state to adopt a policy of stabilising the exchange rate.

Depreciation is likely to be beneficial to the Greek economy. The alarmist assertions – emanating mostly from bank research departments – that depreciation would be ineffective and that it would bring accelerated inflation, cannot be

---

141 It is interesting to note that as the crisis has deepened, it has become clearer that the main problems of exit lie with foreign exchange and banking. Even mainstream commentators who are against Greece exiting the EMU acknowledge that the purely monetary side of things is not particularly important. See Buiter, W. and Rahbari, E. (2011), 'The future of the euro area: fiscal union, break-up or blundering towards a "you break it you own it Europe"', *Citi Economics, Global Economics View*, 9 September.

taken seriously.[142] One of the few careful studies of the issue estimates that a 50 percent depreciation of the new drachma would lead to inflation of 5–9 percent in the first year, while raising competitiveness by 37–42 percent.[143] Depreciation would immediately deliver a large positive boost to the Greek economy by recapturing lost competitiveness without the socially destructive method of directly lowering unit labour costs. The current account would benefit directly.

Depreciation would, however, raise the price of imports and thus impact negatively on the income of workers and others. Note that the problem in this connection is not inflation as such, even though imported inflation would probably rise. In the depressed state of the Greek economy a modest measure of inflation is unlikely to cause major difficulties, as was already mentioned above. The real problem would be that depreciation would change the relative prices of imports, thus affecting the consumption basket of workers and others. The following three points are vital in this respect.

First, contrary to the policy of directly reducing unit labour costs (or internal depreciation, as it is sometimes called) currency depreciation does not work by reducing workers' income. This is a misconception that is often purposely cultivated in the mass media and elsewhere. Rather, depreciation works by changing the relative price of exports and imports, therefore influencing demand. In effect, depreciation releases abroad some of the pressure on the domestic economy by allowing it to recapture lost competitiveness.

Second, by raising the relative price of imports, depreciation would certainly reduce the income of workers and others. However, the pass-through to import prices would not be full in the short run – the rise would be unlikely to reflect the full effect of depreciation. Furthermore, workers would be able to exercise some choice over which commodities to include in the consumption basket. The fall in real income, therefore, would not be externally determined and across the board, as it is with the present policy.

---

142   See, for instance, Buiter, W. and Rahbari, E. (2011), 'The future of the euro area: fiscal union, break-up or blundering towards a "you break it you own it Europe"', *Economics, Global Economics View*, 9 September.

143   See Mariolis, T. and Katsinos, A. (2011), 'Return to a depreciated drachma, cost inflation, and international competitiveness: an input-output study', (in Greek), paper presented to the 'Study Group on Sraffian Economics', mimeo.

Third, workers are likely to benefit from the increased production and therefore from the boost to employment that would result from depreciation. Once again, the benchmark is given by the current policies of stagnation and high unemployment. Workers might also draw benefits from further changes in relative prices as the economy picks up. The introduction of the euro led to substantial increases in the prices of several food staples in the early 2000s, including vegetables and dairy produce. It is plausible that the relative price of food would decline following the return to the drachma and the recovery of Greek agriculture.

In the very short run, however, the sudden rise in the relative prices of energy, food and medicine, on all of which Greece has significant import dependence, would be problematic. Note that the country is practically self-sufficient in electricity, generated through domestically produced lignite, which would have to be intensified for a period. Nonetheless, up to two thirds of its energy is supplied by imported oil that is used mostly for transport, and national reserves are unlikely to last for longer than three months.

The priority for the authorities in the very short run, therefore, would be, first, to secure access to foreign exchange and, second, to secure emergency access to energy supplies. Bilateral deals with oil producers, such as Russia, would probably be very important. The same holds for medicine and food. Still, it is likely that there will have to be rationing and other administrative measures for oil and other key commodities during the first months following exit from the EMU.

The pressure would be felt by households since they have the heaviest dependence on imported oil and other commodities. It would thus be necessary to use tax and subsidy policy to lighten the burden for the poorest in terms of transport and heating. In effect, the country would find itself in a state of emergency for several months during the initial period and until the economy began to recover. This would be part of the cost of escaping long-term decline within the EMU.

Short-term problems aside, depreciation would still be insufficient to produce longer-lasting benefits for the Greek economy by itself. After a period, its beneficial impact would be eliminated as the rise in the price of imports would eventually pass through to domestic prices and to the price of exports. However, the aim of exiting the EMU is not to restore the health of the Greek economy through depreciation. Rather, the aim is to rescue the Greek economy from the destructive grip of the EMU – depreciation would be an inevitable by-product of exit.

Default and exit, therefore, should be the preamble to a broad programme that would restructure Greek economy and society. By removing austerity and allowing competitiveness to be quickly recaptured, they would create propitious conditions for measures that could raise productivity, improve technology, streamline commerce by removing privileges and market-fixing practices, break the monopoly position of corporations in key markets, such as medicine and food, and so on. It is worth noting that productivity growth in Greece has been considerably faster than Germany in recent years, as was shown in figure 2, indicating latent strength in the productive sector.

Exit from the EMU would thus make it possible to reshape the Greek economy in the interests of working people, while also creating conditions for sustainable growth. The aim of the programme would be to sustain high employment and to raise the share of labour in the national product. A vital element would be the expansion of public investment, particularly in view of the complete collapse of private and public investment since 2008. Resources could be generated in part through default on public debt: interest and principal payments are expected to fluctuate between EUR15 bn and EUR20 bn in the immediate future. Resources could be further generated through the nationalised banking system and as national saving recovers.

The requisite policy should also aim to rebalance the Greek economy in terms of industry, services and agriculture, but also tradables and non-tradables. Greece has had visible trade deficits for years, typically offset by surpluses of invisibles (tourism, shipping). The decline in competitiveness since joining the EMU has enlarged the visible deficit, while the invisible surplus has declined. The current account has gone even further into the red because interest payments on the debt have increased, as have profit outflows. The capital account has covered the current account deficit via borrowing from the banks of the core, as was discussed in Part 1.

The shift away from industry and toward services in the Greek economy in recent years has been accompanied by a shift away from tradables and toward non-tradables, while productivity growth in the tradables sector has been insufficient. The Greek service sector has failed to generate rapid growth of exports, probably due to low productivity but perhaps also because it has lacked strategic direction and organisation. Services, in any case, are notoriously weak in generating exports. Thus, even from this perspective, Greek entry into the EMU (and the EU) has been a failure.

Exit from the EMU would offer the opportunity to rebalance the service and industrial sectors as well as tradables and non-tradables, but the rebalancing should not be left to the free market. Rebalancing should certainly not involve the decimation of the public sector on the assumption that this is where the inefficiencies of the Greek economy lie. This is pure neoliberal ideology that is currently causing economic destruction in Greece, and which has had poor growth outcomes across the world during the last three decades.

A thorny issue in this respect would be the euro-denominated liabilities of Greek enterprises and households. One estimate of their size is in the region of EUR68 bn, which is large enough to cause significant disruption due to foreign exchange risk and difficulty in renewing credit lines.[144] Both enterprises and households would need state guarantees of their private debt as well as of their ability to obtain international credit, if mass bankruptcies are to be avoided. On the other hand, on the assumption that most of these enterprises would be export-oriented, their capacity to generate euro-receipts would probably increase, thus improving their ability to renegotiate terms with their creditors.

To sum up, Greece requires a sophisticated industrial policy capable of protecting and furthering the interests of labour and thus of society as a whole. The policy must place both the public and the private sector on a different footing by drawing on the strengths of each. A strategic plan would be necessary to rebalance tradables and non-tradables. Room should also be created for Greek industry to re-establish itself in the domestic market, shifting the economy toward more productive activities and tradables.

To support such a strategy it would be necessary to rely on a nationalised banking system and capital controls, but also on a thoroughly restructured state. Above all, it would be necessary to rely on the leadership of organised labour and civil society. The aim would be to shift the social balance strategically in favour of labour and against capital. If, finally, the strategy came into conflict with the EU, it would be up to the Greek people to re-consider their relations with the latter.

---

144 See Part 2.

In lieu of a conclusion

Debtor-led default and exit from the EMU would be far from easy options for Greece, or any other country of the periphery. But what alternative is on offer for peripheral countries? Trapped within the eurozone, they are threatened with continued austerity, low competitiveness, high unemployment, growing social tensions, and loss of national independence. Not least, their democratic polity is likely to suffer as decision making would be transferred to the ECB, the EFSF and other unelected bodies of the EU. The prospect for the periphery is economic, social and political decline for the foreseeable future. This is the price that weaker economies would have to pay to remain within the confines of a new international reserve currency designed to serve the interests of big banks and big business.

Debtor-led default and exit offer a way for Greece and other peripheral countries to escape the trap of the eurozone. Indeed, continuing membership of the eurozone is creating impossible conditions that are already pushing the periphery in the direction of exit. But if Greece was forced to default and exit while its political system faced collapse and its society unravelled, the result could be chaotic.

If, on the other hand, default and exit were managed carefully by a decisive government that drew on grassroots support, they could lay the foundations for recovery. At the very least they would free Greece from the vice of austerity imposed by the EMU. They would also offer relief from the burden of debt as well as allowing the country immediately to regain competitiveness. They would, finally, allow Greece to reclaim national independence which has been battered in the course of the crisis.

Moreover, if the forces leading the country had a clear vision of social change and adopted an appropriate transitional programme for economy and society, the opportunity would arise of decisively altering the balance of forces in favour of labour. Greek society could rejuvenate itself by entering a path of sustainable growth with greater equality while cleansing its state. The shockwaves would be felt across Europe already reeling under the impact of the global crisis.

Greece thus faces a historic choice: surrender to the dominant powers of the eurozone and face a bleak economic, social and political future, or find the courage to act, changing itself and even Europe. We will soon know the answer.

INDEX

Key pages are marked **in bold**